CHRISTIAN FORMATION

CHRISTIAN FORMATION

INTEGRATING THEOLOGY & HUMAN DEVELOPMENT

James R. Estep & Jonathan H. Kim

EDITORS

ACADEMIC

Nashville, Tennessee

Christian Formation:
Integrating Theology and Human Development

Copyright © 2010 by James R. Estep and Jonathan H. Kim

ISBN: 978-0-8054-4838-2

Published by B&H Publishing Group
Nashville, Tennessee

Dewey Decimal Classification: 230
Subject Heading: THEOLOGY\CHRISTIAN
EDUCATION\HUMAN BEINGS (THEOLOGY)

Scripture quotations are from the *Holman Christian Standard
Bible* ® Copyright © 1999, 2000, 2002, 2003, 2009 by
Holman Bible Publishers. Used by permission.

Printed in the United States of America

3 4 5 6 7 8 9 10 11 12 • 17 16 15 14 13

R

TABLE OF CONTENTS

<u>ACKNOWLEDGMENTS</u>

This book is dedicated to my wife Christie and my daughters Ashlynne and Kaitlynne for their unfailing love and support throughout my career as a teacher-pastor.

Jonathan Kim

This book is dedicated to my parents, James and Sue Estep, for their living example of love and faithfulness, and unwavering support for my ministry.

James Estep

Introduction

Robert Frost's poem "The Road Not Taken" (1949) poses the dilemma of a traveler confronted with two paths—one frequently traveled and the other less but more "longing for wear." He pens, "Two roads diverged in a yellow wood: And sorry I could not travel both: And be one traveler, long I stood." The only resolution Frost provides is: "I took the one less traveled by, And that has made all the difference."[1] Christian educators, as well as many others in the practical ministries field, face the same dilemma.

The *social sciences* are those sciences in which humans are the subject of study. Most relevant to the Christian educator are those that address human development—the growth and maturing of humans over their lifespan—and learning theories, which are frequently tied to the development of cognition or intellect in humans.

The Christian educator is caught between two roads: the theological and the theoretical. The theology road is traveled frequently by theologians and by all those professing Christian faith, while the theory road is congested with those participating in the scientific community—in this instance, those who engage in the social sciences. But must we choose? Is there not a new path—a third way—to travel through the woods?

Christian Formation: Integrating Theology and Human Development deals with the interrelationship of theology and psychology by making available an integrated framework of spiritual formation to be used in both academic and church contexts. It explores how the interpretation of development theories intersects with the theology of anthropology and sanctification. The purpose of the book is threefold: first, to survey pertinent biblical data and theological perspectives of the Christian doctrine of humanity as they relate to Christian formation; second, to explore the major theories of human development and learning from a biblical perspective; and third, to offer a comprehensive overview of Christian spiritual formation and development. Like the authors of Scripture, we too ask the question, "What is man?"[2] and we respond as did the psalmist:

I praise You,

because I have been remarkably and wonderfully made.

Your works are wonderful,

and I know [this] very well.

My bones were not hidden from You

when I was made in secret,

when I was formed in the depths of the earth.

Your eyes saw me when I was formless;

all [my] days were written in Your book and planned

before a single one of them began.

(Psalm 139:14-16)

Christian formation is the central tenet of Christian education. As Paul wrote to the church in Colossae, "We proclaim Him, warning and teaching everyone with all wisdom, so that we may present everyone mature in Christ. I labor for this, striving with His strength that works powerfully works in me" (Colossians 1:28-29). Facilitating the process of Christian formation within the believer is the ultimate aim to which Christian educators likewise commit themselves. The Christian educator must travel both roads simultaneously. The integration of theology of the church with the findings of the social sciences into a distinctively Christian perspective on human development theories—as it relates to Christian formation—is the task of this book.

Assumptions

Having already affirmed the purpose of the text, the reader should be aware of three fundamental assumptions that guide the direction of this book. These assumptions are somewhat self-evident as one reads the book and, on occasion, will be explained or even defended as a necessary and legitimate approach toward Christian formation. *First*, Christian formation is, in part, human. This is, by no means, diminishing the place and involvement of the Holy Spirit in the life of the believer but acknowledging that humanity was created to have a relationship with God. A part of that creation is the human development process. For example, spirituality is not a disembodied experience—as with the many Eastern religions or New Age groups—but an embodied experience, affirming the reality of human existence.

Second, our understanding of Christian formation is informed by both theology and the social sciences—with primary voice typically going to theology. For spiritual formation to be distinctively Christian, theology is an indispensable and irreplaceable element. However, the social sciences can provide equally valuable insights into the process of Christian formation over the lifespan. For example, when one acknowledges that children, adolescents, and adults (younger through older)—throughout the decades of life—change, grow, and mature, then explaining and facilitating Christian formation must take into account the developmental level of the individual, necessitating the inclusion of social science insights.

Third, Christian formation can be influenced by the ministry of the church and glean valuable insights from the social sciences. Christian education is a very broad and diverse ministry. For example, ministering to children not only requires a theology of childhood but also an appreciation for how children think, socialize, learn, etc. The social sciences enable us to do ministry more effectively since we better understand those to whom we are ministering.

About This Book

Comprised of nine chapters, *Christian Formation: Integrating Theology and Human Development* essentially has three sections. Chapters 1-2 provide insights on a Christian rationale for the integration of theology and the social sciences. They remind the Christian educator of the essential nature of humanity as the *imago Dei* and theoretical framework for integrating the insights of the social sciences. Chapters 3-6 address the classical dimensions of human development. The development of intellect, personality, morality, and faith are addressed in these chapters. Each one identifies chief voices and theories in their respective fields as well as provides biblical-theological insights and an integration of ideas into a distinctively Christian perspective on the developmental dimension. Likewise, each one concludes with practical insights for ministry. Chapters 7-9 address development from three additional specialized dimensions: adult, spiritual, and cultural. These are more specialized and of interest to the Christian educator.

The contributors are all evangelicals and represent the rich diversity of those comprising modern-day evangelicalism. The two contributing editors of this book are Jonathan Kim, Associate Professor of Christian Education at Talbot School of Theology (LaMirada, California), and James Estep, Professor of Christian Education in the Seminary at Lincoln Christian University (Lincoln, Illinois). They were, in fact, classmates in the Ph.D. in Educational Studies at Trinity Evangelical Divinity School (Deerfield, Illinois), both graduating in the class of 1999.

The chapter on faith development and Christian formation was penned by Timothy Jones and Michael Wilder—both of whom serve at the Southern Baptist Theological Seminary (Louisville, Kentucky). Timothy is Associate Professor of Leadership and Church Ministry, and Michael is the Director of the Doctor of Educational Ministry Program and Assistant Professor of Leadership and Church Ministry. With offices down the hall from one another, the task of jointly penning a chapter was most amenable.

Greg Carlson serves as Chair and Professor of Christian Ministries at Trinity International University (Deerfield, Illinois) and wrote the chapter on adult development and Christian formation. Mark Maddix, Dean of the School of Theology at Northwest Nazarene University (Nampa, Idaho), provided the chapter on spiritual formation and Christian formation. He likewise was a Trinity classmate of James Estep and Jonathan Kim.

Perhaps the hidden agenda of this book is that Christian educators and other Christian leaders would no longer regard the theologies of the Church and the theories of the social sciences as independent from one another—or even adversaries—but as interdependent in regard to Christian formation, mutually endeavoring to understand the process and product of growth in Christ.

James Riley Estep, Jr., Ph.D.
Professor of Christian Education
Seminary at Lincoln Christian University
Lincoln, Illinois

Jonathan H. Kim, Ph.D.
Associate Professor of Christian Education
Talbot School of Theology, Biola University
LaMirada, California

September 2009

ENDNOTES

[1] www.internal.org.
[2] *On several occasions, Scripture poses the question, "What is man... ?" Sometimes it is raised in relation to divine awe (Job 7:17, Psalm 144:3), expressing amazement at the attention God bestows upon them. In other contexts, it is a phrase used to introduce criticism (Job 15:14) or in Messianic-Christological contexts (Psalm 8:4-5, Hebrews 2:6-8).*

CHAPTER 1

CHRISTIAN ANTHROPOLOGY:

HUMANITY AS THE *IMAGO DEI*

By James R. Estep Jr.

When I observe Your heavens,

the work of Your fingers,

the moon and the stars,

which You set in place,

what is man that You remember him,

the son of man that You look after him?

You made him little less than God

and crowned him with glory and honor.

You made him LORD over the works of Your hands;

You put everything under his feet.

Psalm 8:3-6

What does it mean to be *human*? What is it that makes us human? In the televised documentary "Ape to Man," the theory of evolution's history is unveiled over the last two centuries. It chronicles the scientific "quest to find the origins of the human race."[1] It surveys the search for the proverbial *missing link*, begging the question, "How much ape and how much man would he be?" While modern evolutionary theory no longer regards human evolution as a single line of progression over millions of years but rather a line with multiple deviations and dead ends, it still continues the search for the common "root of the human family tree," which marks the origin of humanity. *But what makes us human?* What could they look for? What is the definitive mark that makes us human? Is our humanity a matter of brain size, cranial capacity? Was it signaled by the development and use of tools, "stone technology," or the use of fire? Did the development of language or our ability to walk upright on two legs signal the birth of humanity?[2] Evolution is a theory in search of the elusive quintessential question in life: *What makes us human?*

For the Christian, the question is not as elusive. For us, the answer is not found in evolutionary theories but in Scripture. We are human because we are made in the image of God. We are the bearers of God's image, the *imago Dei*. This is the quintessential distinction of humanity within God's creation. It is perhaps best illustrated by the difference between humanity as portrayed in an evolutionary chart versus the ceiling of the Sistine Chapel. The *imago Dei* is the divinitive mark of our Maker.

The Christian educator must remember that, while social science theories about learning, development, and lifespan changes describe the processes of growth in all of their dimensions, our humanity is more than the social sciences can discover; it is the *imago Dei*. While the biblical teaching on humanity includes more than the *imago Dei*, humanity, as God's image-bearers, remains central to the Christian understanding of anthropology. This chapter is not intended to be an exhaustive treatment of the doctrine of humanity. Rather, it is a reminder to the Christian educator that our understanding of humanity is not only based on the social sciences but more so on theology—what Scripture teaches about humanity. It will first describe the biblical sketch of humanity as the *imago Dei*, identifying passages and providing a summation of Scripture's teaching. It will then turn to the portrait provided by theology as to the meaning and nature of the *imago Dei*. From this, an assessment of the human condition will be rendered, evaluating the impact of sin (Adam's and our own) on humanity. The chapter will conclude not only with integrative observations about the *imago Dei* but also with developmental theories in Christian education.

Biblical Sketch of Humanity as the *Imago Dei*

We are introduced to humanity's unique and special distinction "in the beginning." Genesis 1:26-28 reads (emphasis added):

> Then God said, "Let Us make man in *Our image [tselem], according to Our likeness [demūth]*. They will rule the fish of the sea, the birds of the sky, the animals, all the earth, and the creatures that crawl on the earth."

So God created man in His *own image [tselem]*;

in the image [tselem] of God he created him; male and female he created them.

God blessed them and said to them, "Be fruitful and increase in number; fill the earth and subdue it. Rule over the fish of the sea and the birds of the air and over every living creature that moves on the ground."

Much has been made over the choice of these two interactive terms, *image* and *likeness*. *Tselem*, most often translated *image*, signifies something cut or carved, a physical representation; whereas *demūth, likeness*, conveys the idea of being similar, bearing a similarity to the original.[3] It is generally agreed that the first term is typically related to the physical representation of something, in this instance, its Creator; while the second is in reference to representations that are not necessarily physical in nature. However, the specific relationship of image/likeness is widely debated.[4] For example, the Western Christian tradition has historically viewed these two terms as synonymous or interchangeable; whereas the Eastern Christian tradition (beginning with Irenaeus c. AD 180) has viewed the terms as parallel—not merely synonymous—with each one designating a particular dimension to the image of God in humanity. Regardless, it is obvious that "the two words together tell us that man is a representation of God who is like god in certain aspects."[5]

By using these two words, Moses indicates we are wholly God's representation; we are His image-bearers. This would be consistent with similar phrases used in the ancient Near East. For example, in Egypt, Pharaoh was regarded as being the image-bearer of Ra (chief deity of the Egyptian pantheon), meaning he was Ra's representative on earth[6]—a status typically reserved for royalty in ancient Egypt. The Old Testament openly ascribes to every human, male and female, that we are all God's image-bearers—tasked with being His representatives in His creation. We are the Creator's temporal representation within His creation.

The language and sentiments of Genesis 1 are echoed throughout the Old Testament in regard to the uniqueness of humanity. The next occurrence of image/likeness language in the Old Testament is Genesis 5:1-2, which reaffirms the uniqueness of the creation of humanity and their special place in creation. This is further expressed in Genesis 9:6, "Whoever sheds man's blood, his blood will be shed by man, for God made man in His image." We cannot treat human life as of relative importance—on the same level—as that of animals. That we are made in God's image "explains why human life is specially protected, but animal life is not."[7] Human life is sacred, requiring a capital penalty for a capital offense. Ethical implications accompany the *imago Dei*.

While the psalmist did not use the phrase "image of God," he certainly echoed it in Psalm 8's affirmation of the uniqueness, significance, and place of humanity in creation. While the psalm starts and concludes with the affirmation "O LORD, our LORD, how majestic is Your name in all the earth!" (vv. 1a, 9), its contents focus on the place of humanity within the Lord's creation:

> "what is man that You remember him, the son of man that You look after him? You made him little less than God and crowned him with glory and honor. You made him LORD over the works of Your hands; You put everything under his feet."
> (Psalm 8:4-6).

Once again, Scripture affirms the uniqueness of humanity and its distinctive place in the creation. The psalmist continues with the theme of "everything under his feet" by listing those pieces of creation over which humans have dominion: "all the sheep and oxen, as well as animals in the wild, birds of the sky, and fish of the sea passing through the currents of the seas" (8:7-8). In comparison with the opinions of ancient Mesopotamia, such as those reflected in the Babylonian creation epic, "the status of the human race in Israelite thinking was very high"—wherein humanity was created in the image of God, rather than regarded as mere servants of deities tired of work, and wherein human dignity was achieved through service rather than innate within humanity as the *imago Dei*.[8] The Old Testament affirms the value and innate worth of every human as being God's image-bearer.

Imago Dei in the New Testament

The *imago Dei* concept and language are not limited to the Old Testament. Many of the references to humanity as God's image-bearer in the New Testament are parallel to those made in the Old Testament. As in the Old Testament, the New Testament authors seem to use two terms that are almost synonymous. They favor *eikōn*, which is the Greek term parallel to Hebrew *tselem,* translated *image*, and *homoiōsin* to parallel the Hebrew *demūth*, translated *likeness.* For example, 1 Corinthians 11:7 describes man, specifically the male gender,[9] as being "God's image *[eikōn]* and glory . . . ." Likewise, James warns his readers of the inconsistency of using the tongue to "bless our LORD and Father, and with it we curse men who are made in God's likeness *[homoiōsin]*" (3:9). Notice that, in this last passage, the image of God is identified as the grounds for moral implications—as did Genesis 9. Because we are God's image-bearers, our relationship with our fellow image-bearer must be consistent with our relationship with God.

However, unique to the New Testament is the Christological element ascribed to the *imago Dei*. As a part of its introduction, Paul incorporates what is perhaps a familiar hymn or early creedal statement into his letter to the Colossian congregation.[10] In it, he affirms of Christ, "He is the image of the invisible God, the firstborn over all creation" (Colossians 1:15). Paul returns the image-bearer idea with a more soteriological focus in 3:9b-10, "since you have put off the old man with his practices and have put on the new *[neos]* man, who is being renewed *[anakainoumen]* in knowledge according to the image of his Creator." This is clearly a reference back to the Genesis creation narrative but with a new context. The basic thrust of the passage is that, as Christians, we are in a new *[neos]* state; we are new creations; and we are in the process *[anakainoumen]* of reimaging ourselves, according to the Creator's image. Paul uses the perfect participle, signifying a completed action with ongoing implications, i.e., we are new and continue to become new. This is consistent with what Paul writes in 2 Corinthians 5:17: "Therefore if anyone is in Christ, there is a new creation; old things have passed away, and look, new things have come." In the New Testament, the image of

God is not only anthropological but adds a new dimension to the concept with one's identity in Christ.

General Biblical Observations

Humanity's existence and identity are dependent on God. Scripture depicts our creation as the direct intent of the Triune God who determined, "Let Us make man in Our image, according to Our likeness . . . " (Genesis 1:26). Our origins are dependent on God, and we would not exist without Him. Additionally, our identity as humans—and individuals—is tied to our being created in His image.

Humanity was created unique and distinctive from the rest of creation. While humanity is a part of God's creation, it cannot be considered just another part of it. Genesis 1-2 affirm that the creation of humanity was indeed different than any other part of creation. Nothing else in creation can claim to bear the distinctive mark of the Creator's image. As a part of creation, we are finite and temporal; but we are different than other parts of God's creation in that we bear His image, which in part enables us to know our imposed limitations.

Humanity was placed over creation. Humanity was the culminating act of creation and, hence, was given the unique purpose to "God blessed them, and God said to them, "Be fruitful, multiply, fill the earth, and subdue it. Rule the fish of the sea, the birds of the sky, and every creature that crawls on the earth. [A part of the human distinction is our place within the creation.] Rule over [it]" (Genesis 1:28). While God's creation was pronounced "good" on every day of creation (1:4, 10, 12, 18, 21, 25), after the creation of humanity—the man and the woman (1:26-30), He "saw all that he had made, and it was *very good*" (1:31a, emphasis added)—as echoed by the psalmist in Psalm 8. Humanity is the culmination of God's creative work.

All humanity, whether man or woman, is equally His image-bearer. Regardless of any perceived difference of familial or social roles of men and women, both the Old and New Testament affirm the image of God is equally present within men and women—without distinction. We all share in a common humanity—one that reflects God's image. Gender is not a part of the fall but a part of the created order—His intentional design within humanity. The *imago Dei* is not 50 percent male or 50 percent female but something the genders equally share 100 percent. It is not until after the fall that the differences between male and female are accentuated.[11]

The terms image and likeness are parallel, not totally synonymous; but both convey the notion that we are a representation of Him. Rather than trying to identify what particular element or dimension of human existence reflects the image of God in humanity, the language of both testaments (*tselem/demūth* and *eikōn/homoiōsin*) signifies a more holistic representation. The *imago Dei* is a holistic image—one which takes humanity in whole. We cannot separate our physical, material existence from our mental or spiritual life, nor can we regard one as being more "real" than the other.

In spite of sin and the fall, the image of God is still with humanity. Following the creation and fall narrative, the biblical authors continue to affirm humanity's worth and dignity as those who are bearers of God's image. Whatever was lost to sin in the fall of Adam and Eve, the *imago Dei* seems to have been left intact. Though humanity itself was broken and reflects that brokenness, God's image is still with us. Ronald Habermas identifies three "practical dimensions" of the *imago Dei*: (1) It facilitates a "transformed attitude" toward others; (2) it requires "transformed behaviors" as to how we treat others; and (3) it engenders a "greater appreciation for diversity" among all of humanity.[12]

The imago Dei is the basis for human dignity with accompanying ethical implications. Humans are to be afforded special consideration, ranging from proper affirmation in how we address one another, as noted in James, to capital punishment for the murder of another human being—one made in God's image, as first indicated in Genesis 9. Humans are not to be treated as animals—as if they were simply another part of God's creation. Humanity demands a baseline level of mutual respect and ethical treatment—regardless of social class, status, or stature—simply because we are God's image-bearers.

The imago Dei in the New Testament is not only anthropological but Christological and soteriological. The Scriptures affirm the core essence of humanity is the *imago Dei.* It is the centerpiece of a biblical anthropology. However, the imagery also is applied to the person of Christ Jesus and to those who follow Him as new creations, those who continue to pattern themselves after the image of their Creator—as depicted in Colossians.

From these biblical passages and themes, we now will turn to a more theological treatment of the subject. If the biblical passages provide the basic sketch of Christian anthropology, theology will provide us with a more complete portrait so as to gain a more thorough understanding of humanness from a Christian perspective.

Theological Portrait of Humanity as the Imago Dei

Scripture clearly affirms we are God's image-bearers, but what exactly is the *imago Dei?* Theologians have made an effort to identify the *imago Dei* in a variety of ways. Is it a part of what we are as humans, what we do, or something else?

Four general views have tried to capture the idea of the *imago Dei.* The most frequently articulated view is the *substantive.* It maintains that the *imago Dei* can be defined by one or more of its component parts such as the physical, psychological, ethical, or spiritual characteristics within humans. This is perhaps the most common means utilized for identifying the *imago Dei* within humanity. For example, the Hebrew term *tselem* ("image") in Genesis 1:26-27 generally denotes a physical representation—as would the phrase "the LORD God formed the man from the dust of the ground" in Genesis 2:7. Similarly, the rational or intellectual uniqueness of humanity is seen in Adam's ability to name the animals (Genesis 2:19-20) and the woman Eve (Genesis 2:22-24). Or the ethical-moral capacity of humanity—as demonstrated by the receiving of moral command (Genesis 2:7), expression of moral rectitude (Genesis 2:25), or demonstration of guilt after their transgression (Genesis 3:7). These characteristics do indeed make humanity distinct from the rest of

God's creation. However, of all these characteristics, perhaps the one most readily identifiable and distinguishable as being distinctively human would be our *spiritual capacity*. Our spirituality does indeed influence and interact with all of the other characteristics already identified. The substantive view seizes on one or all of these factors as defining the *imago Dei*. Humanity would be reflective of God's image in that we are a representation of Him in a temporal form—physical and otherwise.

Others have suggested a more *functional view*, identifying the *imago Dei* as the God-ordained purpose and work specified to humans, e.g., "They will rule . . . Be fruitful, multiply, fill the earth, and subdue it. Rule," (Genesis 1:26-28). This view emphasizes the idea of God installing an innate purposefulness to humanity. The God of the Bible is a working God. Though He completed His work of creation and rested, He is still working today in providence and governance (John 5:17; 9:3-4). The creativity, energy, and authority we exert in working reflect something of God's character in us."[13] The functional view sees our rule and oversight of God's creation as a reflection of the divine aspect of God as Ruler.

The *relational view* asserts that the *imago Dei* is seen in humanity's social or relational capacity. The *imago Dei* means the relational capacity between humans, e.g., male and female as a collective reflection of God's image. Adam and Eve were created together in His image (Genesis 1:26-28); they are conversant with one another (Genesis 2:18,23; 3:6-8; 4:1). Ultimately, it is expressed throughout the pages of Scripture in our relationship with God. In this view, we reflect His image by being in relationship with one another and Him.

Still others present a *teleological view* of the *imago Dei,* suggesting it is reflective of the ultimate objective of human existence. We are indeed God's image-bearers today, but this will not be fully realized until eternity. Hence, the *imago Dei* is both a current reality and an eschatological, future reality. This view may best be understood as a post-fall idea of the *imago Dei* since death, redemption, and eternity would pertain only to those who, in fact, were facing the deadly results of sin, need of redemption, and eternal destination—one who embraces the soteriological and Christological dimensions of the New Testament.

However, all of these separate approaches share a common fault—as assessed by Gregg R. Allison of Southern Baptist Theological Seminary:

> The problem is that all of these ideas tend to reduce the image of God to one particular part or aspect of our humanness; thus, they miss a key point: we human beings are not made in a piecemeal way and put together, like the many pieces of a jigsaw puzzle. Rather, in our humanness, we are constructed holistically with a wholeness and completeness that does not allow us to be divided into this part or that part. We are human beings in our entirety… are created in the image of God.[14]

Perhaps it is in this criticism that an answer is revealed. The *imago Dei* is not defined by its components, functionality, relational capabilities, *or* its teleological dimension. Perhaps all of these views are, in fact, pieces of the whole portrait of God's image in humanity with our spiritual capacity serving as the common denominator of them all. Could the *imago Dei*, in effect *all of the above*, reflect humanity's special inclusion into creation? We are God's image-bearer because, in our very essence, we were and are simply made distinctive from the rest of creation—what Stanley Grenz calls our "special standing" within creation.[15] It is an innate quality, which only human beings possess. God's image within humanity is what we *are* and, in turn, is reflected in the components of our existence, relational capacity with one another and God, in our function to fulfill God's expressed purpose for humanity, and even in the eschatological reality that awaits us (figure 1.1).

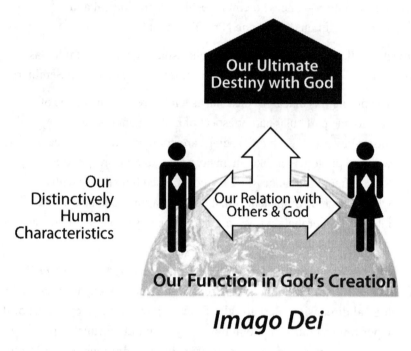

Figure 1.1: *Imago Dei* as Humanity's Special Standing

Because we possess a distinctive character, we are able to relate to one another and God—as well as fulfill the purpose for which God created us—and ultimately share an eternity with Him. If one element of human existence had to be identified as the *imago Dei*, perhaps the spiritual capacity of humanity, which directly influences all of the other dimensions of our existence, is indeed unique and innate to all people. Just as a mirror reflects our physical image, we serve as a mirror reflecting God's image— not merely in a physical sense but in our innate capabilities and capacities as humans, our sense of purposeful design, interrelatedness to one another, and the desire for ultimate spiritual wholeness. God's image in us is seen in who we are as humans, our connectedness to each other as humans, what we are designed to do, and what we are destined to ultimately become. We are *all* bearers of God's image—stamped by our Creator as made *imago Dei*.

Humanity as the *Imago Dei*: Created, Broken, and Redeemed

What happened? Watching cable news, listening to the radio, reading a newspaper, or even sharing over the fence with our neighbors is enough evidence to realize that humanity is *not* what it was created to be. The idyllic portrait of humanity as created in sinless perfection in God's image—where is it today? The biblical portrait of man is drawn, in fact, on three canvases (figure 1.2).

The first canvas is our *created* state. Adam and Eve were created in God's image; and in the absence of sin, their reflection of our Creator is unaffected—readily evident within humanity. They possess an intellect that is clear and unclouded. They are morally innocent, possessing an original righteousness (Genesis 1:31; Ecclesiastes 7:29), lacking even the knowledge of good or evil (Genesis 2:9,17; 3:5,22). Man and woman exist in harmony—different from one another—but equals before God as His image-bearers. They have a clear sense of God-given purpose and direction. In short, the *imago Dei* is fully reflecting God who created us.

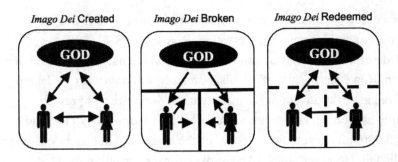

Figure 1.2

Sin is an unfortunate and inescapable reality. Genesis 3 describes the instance of sin's entry into creation, including humanity. After this point, humanity is not what God intended it to be. Several observations can be made about sin's impact on us from Genesis 3:

- *Sin was not God's invention or intention*—as evident in His conversation with Adam and Eve (3:9-13) and condemnation of Satan (3:14-15).

- *We knew better.* Eve knew what Satan was asking of her was wrong (3:2); and she, with Adam, hid from God after partaking of the fruit (3:8).

- Despite the deceptive enticement, *we are responsible for our sin*— as not only seen in the dialog with Adam and Eve (3:9-13) but the pronouncement to both Eve (3:16) and Adam (3:17-19).

- *Sin's effects were devastating.* We were physically (3:7,10-11,16); intellectually (3:6, 13); emotionally (3:10); and morally (3:7,12-13) compromised. Our relationship with one another (3:12, 16, 20) and God was broken. (3:8-9, 11,13) Humanity's God-given rule of the earth was made significantly difficult in the presence of sin (3:17-19), and we became moral—subject to death just as God had warned (3:22-24).

It seems every possible dimension or aspect of humanity was not spared the impact of sin's entrance into creation. Romans 1:18-23, 3:9-18, and 5:1-21 describe the effects of sin—not only upon the individual but all of creation. However, in spite of all this, humanity still possesses the *imago Dei*. Even after the advent of sin into creation, Scripture still presents humanity as God's image-bearers. Genesis 9:6, 1 Corinthians 11:7, and James 3:9-10 all attest to the presence of the *imago Dei* in humanity—even after the fall. However, much like a broken mirror can still reflect an image, humanity still possesses the *imago Dei* but as a poor reflection of the One whose image we bear. Whatever sin's effect on humanity, it did not discount our special standing or remove God's image from us. For example, Mark Mangano, Professor of Old Testament at Lincoln Christian University, maintains that because of the presence of the *imago Dei*, "Old Testament legislation" does indeed reflect a "high regard of personhood"—even in matters of male-female, slave-free, parent-child, and Israelite-Gentile relations.[16] The theological debate is not over the total loss of the *imago Dei* but the *degree to which* Adam and Eve's sin affects humanity and the individual even today.

Genesis 3 does not leave us without hope. Genesis 3:15 is regarded as a gospel prototype, giving the promise of a Redeemer and redemption from Satan's deceptions and sin's devastation: "And I [God] will put enmity between you [the serpent] and the woman, and between your offspring and hers; he [the woman's offspring] will crush your [serpent's] head, and you will strike his [offspring's] heel." Humanity is not destined to exist hopelessly in its fallen state. God has provided the opportunity for redemption through Jesus Christ who "is the image of the invisible God" (Colossians 1:15a). In this regard, Jesus represents the perfect prototype and the archetype of humanity. What was marred in the fall of humanity is now reclaimed by Christ who came as "the image of the invisible God" to restore us to our Creator in whose image we were created.

As previously noted, the New Testament adds new dimensions to the anthropological portrait of humanity made in the image of God. Christ in Colossians 1:15 is said to be "the image of the invisible God."[17] Perhaps this was the idea behind the author of Hebrews when he wrote, "The Son is the radiance of God's glory and the exact representation of his being, sustaining all things by his powerful word" (1:3). George Carey contends that Jesus is the "paradigm man ... the revelation of what man should be."[18] However, the *imago Dei* imagery also is employed to describe the process of salvation, particularly sanctification, in the life of the new believer. Whatever was lost in the fall of humanity—in whatever way the *imago Dei* was tarnished by sin, it is redeemable in Christ Jesus. Once again, returning to Colossians 3, following a list depicting the old life in sin, Paul writes to the Colossian Christians, "...you have taken off your old self with its practices and have put on the new self, which is being renewed in knowledge in the image of its Creator" (Colossians 3:9-10). The verbs "have taken off" (*apekdusamenoi*) and "have put on" (*endusamenoi*) are both aorist tense, signifying completed actions. Yet the verb "being renewed" (*anakainoumenon*) is, in fact, a perfect participle, connecting the two points of the past and present status of humanity.[19] We are continually being renewed because we already have removed the old and accepted the new.

This parallels other sentiments expressed by Paul such as "You were taught, with regard to your former way of life, to put off your old self, which is being corrupted by its deceitful desires; to be made new in the attitude of your minds; and to put on the new self, created to be like God in true righteousness and holiness" (Ephesians 4:22-24). Salvation is, in part, a process of restoring the *imago Dei* in its fullest expression of God's reflection. This process is expressed throughout the New Testament (cf. Ephesians 5:1-2, 1 Corinthians 11:1, Philippians 2:5-11). This restoration is *not* a return to the garden—a return to Adam, Eve, and Eden; rather, it is "a new creation" (2 Corinthians 5:17). Paul expresses this transformation toward redemption in Ephesians 2:1-10, paralleling our fallen state with our redeemed one (figure 1.3).

Ephesians 2:1-3	Ephesians 2:4-7
"you were dead" (2:1)	God "made us alive with the Messiah" (2:5)
"trespasses and sins" (2:1)	"by grace you are saved" (2:5)
"walked according to this worldly age" (2:2)	"raised us up with Him" (2:6)
"fleshly desires, carrying out the inclinations of our flesh and thoughts" (2:3)	"seated us with Him in the heavens" (2:6)
"by nature we were children under wrath" (2:3)	"display the immeasurable riches of His grace in [His] kindness to us in Christ Jesus" (2:7)

Figure 1.3: Humanity in Sin and in Christ

Because of this restoration, we are found "in Christ," which essentially changes our nature and spiritual status. Because we are now in Christ, believers view humanity beyond the dimensions that typically separate us, e.g., ethnicity, culture, social, or gender divisions (Colossians 3:11; Galatians 3:23). Ultimately, this new creation and new community will be realized only from an eschatological perspective.[20]

The Human Condition: Just How Broken Are We?

Adam sinned, Eve sinned, and we have all sinned—but how broken is humanity due to sin? The degree of sin's contamination is not just a theological matter but one that has enamored philosophers as well. English philosopher and scholar John Locke (1632-1704) spoke of humanity as a *tabula rasa*—a blank slate, innocent, morally neutral. Borrowing his metaphor of a slate board, the human condition has been conceived in three ways (figure 1.4):

Figure 1.4: The Human Conditions

Locke's *tabula rasa* is in the center—represented by a blank slate and by two other "slates" flanking it. On the left would be those who maintain that humanity is not only born innocent but actually born with a predisposition toward moral goodness such as described by the French philosopher Jean-Jacques Rousseau (1712-78) in *Emile*. To the right of Locke are those who believe sin's impact is inescapable, leaving an innate mark on all humanity, making us to some extent born depraved.

However, in light of this, just how broken are we? This is a matter for centuries-long theological debate. For Augustine vs. Pelagius (5th century

AD), Calvin vs. Arminius (16th century AD), and even today, the question remains of how much Adam's sin has impacted the human condition. Pelagius would maintain that Adam's sin had little direct affect upon humanity—that we are born innocent or unmarred by sin. In so doing, we denied such ideas as original sin and the necessity of grace and predestination; and we affirmed the totality of human freedom. Opposing this idea, Augustine, and later John Calvin, would advocate the opposite— that humanity is totally depraved, inescapably marred by Adam's sin, guilty from birth, partakers of a fallen humanity, and in absolute need of the unconditional election of God. James Arminius held a moderating view. Often called semi-Pelagianism, Arminius maintained that Adam's sin, in fact, did impact humanity and that, from birth, humans are partakers of a fallen humanity but not guilty of Adam's sin. The original sin of Adam does impact us, biasing us toward evil, but not in itself condemning us.

Appropriation of Original Sin?

How would Adam's sin still impact humanity today? How does his sin become imputed to us? And to what effect? Perhaps the main passage in this regard is Romans 5:12-21, but it is still open to the question of the actual mechanism by which Adam's sin is appropriated by the human race.

One response is to view Adam's sin as an *example* of our own sin, maintaining that Romans 5:12 refers to the sins committed by each individual, which are reflective of Adam's original sin. We *like him* have all sinned, and we *like him* are guilty.

A more commonly held view is that of *solidarity*. This view maintains that humanity is somehow connected to the sin of Adam—either through a biological or genetic connection between Adam and humanity (seminalism) or because Adam is regarded as the representative head of the human race (federalism).

In either of these two solidarity variants, humanity appropriates Adam's sin, and his sin becomes our sin. In any case, whether by example or solidarity, humanity cannot escape the effects of original sin. As humans, we are indeed unable to escape the ramifications of Adam's act of rebellion against his Creator.

Once again borrowing from Locke's tablet illustration, perhaps the depiction of the human condition could be made of a clean, but broken, tablet. Humanity, in one sense, is born in innocence; the slate is clean. Yet the slate itself is broken, having been tainted by original sin that permeates all of humanity. We are born broken but still blank. We bear the marks of humanity's brokenness and the consequences of Adam's sin. As humans, we are not directly guilty of the original sin, but we are indeed directly impacted by it. As individuals, we are a *tabula rasa*; but as humans, the slate itself is broken.

The Human Constitution

Of what are we composed? What constitutes a human being? This simple question evokes some theological debate within Christian circles and also distinguishes the Christian faith from other world religions and even Christian cults. For example, Christian theologians recognize we are more than physical, more than flesh; but what else is there to us? Dichotomists believe we are body and soul, meaning we are twofold beings, regarding the soul and spirit mentioned in Scripture to be merely synonymous terms—even used interchangeably. On the other hand, trichotomists affirm the threefold constitution of humans as body, soul, and spirit, regarding the soul and spirit to be distinguishable from one another. Additionally, while Christian theology affirms the physical, bodily reality of humanity—that flesh is a real, tangible part of our existence—this fact would be denied by many eastern religions, such as Hinduism, which denies the reality of physical existence, regarding it to be an illusion. Similarly, the Christian Science cult rejects the reality of bodily or physical existence, regarding the affirmation of it to be a sin. So of what are we made?

Both dichotomists and trichotomists affirm the reality of physical existence, i.e., humans have bodies. The debate is over the nature of humanity's *nonmaterial components*. This debate itself is, in part, a matter of scant passages, semantics, and very dependent on scriptural inference since we are asking a question that the Bible itself does not claim to be directly answering. Paul wrote, "May God himself, the God of peace, sanctify you through and through. May your whole *spirit* [*pneuma*], *soul* [*psychē*] and *body* [*sōma*] be kept blameless at the coming of our Lord Jesus Christ" (1 Thessalonians 5:23, emphasis added). In this passage, Paul would seem to affirm a threefold constitution—body, soul, spirit. Similarly, the author of Hebrews, who may well have been Paul, contended, "For the word of God is living and effective and sharper than any two-edged sword, penetrating as far as to divide soul *(psychē)*, spirit *(pneuma)*, joints, and marrow; it is a judge of the ideas and thoughts of the heart" (Hebrews 4:12, emphasis added). The distinction between the dichotomists and trichotomists is the distinction between the soul and spirit. Dichotomists believe there is no distinction—that, in effect, the terms are interchangeable; whereas trichotomists affirm the distinction of soul and spirit.

It is difficult to conceive of Paul simply being redundant in his use of terminology and the author of Hebrews simply speaking of dissecting something that does not require separation (if, in fact, the soul and spirit are synonymous). Perhaps it is in the notion of viewing humans as twofold vs. threefold in their existence. In some respects, we are a dichotomy—material and immaterial; but the question remains: Is the immaterial divided? Scripture would seem to indicate that our immaterial component is indeed divided into soul and spirit. The soul is the dominant element; and hence, in some respect, we are body and soul. As Jesus once said, "...rather, fear Him who is able to destroy both soul and body in hell" (Matthew 10:28). However, the spirit is not a wholly separate component but one within the soul, which would explain the seemingly interchangeable terminology in the Scriptures—as illustrated in figure 1.5.

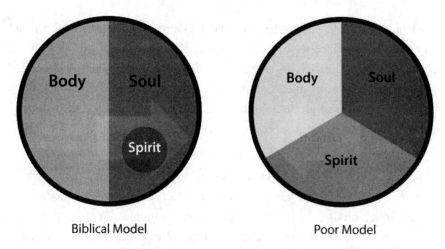

Figure 1.5: Trichotomy Models

Representing the human constitution as having three distinctive pieces—as shown on the right—is a Poor Model since we would be physical (body), nonphysical (soul), and ... what? The model on the left affirms we are physical and nonphysical but with the nonphysical partitioned into soul and spirit. This seems more consistent with the biblical witness. Robert L. Saucy notes the idea of soul is "broader than that of spirit" since its use typically refers to "the total person," explaining "the spirit is thus a metaphysical entity, namely, the principle of life which empowers, while the soul is the individual subject or bearer of that life."[21] Hence, the language and idea of the soul and spirit are compatible and complementary but not simply synonymous. The human constitution is one of body and soul-spirit.

The *Imago Dei*, Human Development, and Christian Formation

What makes us human? The biblical portrait of humanity—and especially the *imago Dei*—reminds us the root of our humanity is found in our Creator in whose image we were created. We are human because we are God's image-bearers. Christian anthropology provides a theological context in which the social sciences (especially those most relevant to

Christian educators such as learning theories and human development) can be effectively utilized in the service of ministry. In this section, we will itemize some of the insights provided by theology for the use of the social sciences by Christian educators so as to demonstrate that theology can provide the essential grounds for constructively using developmental and learning theories in Christian education.

First, we cannot substitute the *imago Dei* with any number of developmental theories. As humans, we develop throughout our lifespan and in various areas of measurable progress such as cognitive, social, moral, or personality—as reflected by numerous theories. Yet innate to our humanity is that we are God's image-bearers. We do not *develop* into the *imago Dei*; we *are* the *imago Dei*. However, developmental theories do provide a lens through which to see growth of many distinctly human dimensions within individuals—from infancy to elderly. For example, a better understanding of how humans develop cognitively would provide insight for a children's minister to express theological truths to young minds or help struggling adolescents find their identities in light of personality development theories while always affirming their innate value to God as His image-bearers.

Second, Christian anthropology affirms that humanity's constitution is both physical and nonphysical—not one or the other. Humans cannot be reduced to either physical *or* nonphysical; we are inseparably both. Though distinguishably different, we cannot be separated in our thinking.[22] Monism, affirming the existence of *either* the physical *or* the nonphysical, and dualism, arguing for the absolute independence of the physical *and* nonphysical, are simply insufficient. Hence, Christian theology views humanity holistically as material and immaterial, body and soul-spirit— not one or the other. Developmental theories, likewise, explain human development as a part of our physical makeup and yet moving beyond the physical. For example, Piaget advanced structuralism, wherein cognitive development was attributed to the actual development of the brain's net of neurons, but Vygotsky understood cognition or intellectual development to move beyond the mere physical "wiring" of the brain.

Third, males and females share in a common humanity, both having been made in God's image; yet they are distinctly different from one another. Developmental theories reflect this common-core humanity but affirm distinctive, yet parallel, developmental processes. For example, the development of moral reasoning has been studied by Lawrence Kohlberg in male subjects and in females by Carol Gilligan. While their results are similar—with males and females equally capable of all levels of moral reasoning, the developmental process itself is different, resulting in an ethic of justice in men and one of care in women. However, realizing the common element between justice and care, both place the needs of another individual first—before self-interest, showing a common moral center with two equally valid expressions.[23]

Fourth, Christian anthropology understands the limitations of developmental theories in regard to our Christian formation. While developmental theories can aid in understanding the human aspect of spiritual formation, they cannot address the Divine aspect of it. For example, developmental theories are very helpful when used to explain the difference between an individual's understanding of God at ages five, ten, and fifteen—in part due to differences in their achieved stages of cognitive development. However, developmental theories cannot explain the work of the Spirit in the life of a believer (e.g., Romans 8). The innate developmental processes within humanity cannot overcome sin's effect. Salvation is not a mere matter of cognition or moral reasoning since Adam's problem was not simply one of ignorance.[24] No Gnostic approach to Christian formation would be acceptable when compared to the biblical teaching on human nature.

Fifth, Christian anthropology understands the *imago Dei* to be innate to the individual. Hence, we do not develop into the image of God; we *are* the image of God. The developmental processes are innate to our humanity—a part of the Creator's design within the human genome. Therefore, it is no surprise to learn that many developmental theories parallel those dimensions of humanity that are associated with the *imago Dei* (figure 1.6).

Imago Dei as...	Scriptures	Developmental Theories
Physical	Luke 2:52; terms in Matthew and Luke's birth narrative of Jesus	Most commonly identified developmental feature of humanity
Intellectual	Genesis 1:26-28; Psalm 8:4-9	Cognitive Development, e.g., Piaget and Vygotsky
Moral	Genesis 1:31; 2:17,25; 3:7; Ecclesiastes 7:29	Moral Development, e.g., Piaget, Kohlberg, Gilligan
Social/Personality	Genesis 2:18,23; 3:8; 4:1	Psychological Development, e.g., Erikson, Marcia, and Kegan
Purposeful	Genesis 1:26,28	Psychological Development, e.g., Erikson, or Lifespan Development, e.g., Levinson
Spiritual	Genesis 3:8-10	Spiritual Formation or Faith Development, e.g., Fowler

Figure 1.6: The *Imago Dei* and Developmental Theories

The centerpiece of Christian anthropology is humanity as the *imago Dei*, God's image-bearers. Developmental theories recognize the uniqueness of humanity, which Christians attribute to being God's image-bearers. For the Christian educator, the better understanding of human development can provide keen insights into the process of Christian formation. When placed alongside the insights from theology, they provide a more accurate picture of humanity. We can say with the psalmist, "I will praise You because I have been remarkably and wonderfully made. Your works are wonderful, and I know this very well," (Psalm 139:14).

Reflection Questions

1. How would you define the *imago Dei* in your own words?

2. How did the chapter challenge your thinking about theology and education? More specifically, how does your belief in the *imago Dei* shape your approach to education?

3. While we have used the *imago Dei* in an educational context, what might its implications be for social ministry, outreach / evangelism, or missions work?

4. How might you communicate this biblical principle to those who teach in your congregation?

ENDNOTES

[1] "Ape to Man," History Channel documentary (Arts & Entertainment Television Network, 2005). www.historychannel.com

[2] Ibid.

[3] Cf. Francis Brown, S. K. Driver, and Charles Briggs, *Hebrew and English Lexicon*, 198, 854; *PC Study Bible V5 Beta* (2008) edition.

[4] Cf. Gordon J. Wendham, *Genesis 1-15, Word Biblical Commentary*, Volume 1 (Waco, Texas: Word Books), 29-33; Edward M. Curtis, "Image of God (OT)," *Anchor Bible Dictionary*, Volume 3, 389.

[5] Anthony A. Hoekema, *Created in God's Image* (Grand Rapids: Eerdmans Publishing Company, 1986), 13. See Gerhard Von Rad, *Genesis* (Philadelphia: Westminster Press, 1972), 58-9 for a discussion on the physicality of the image of God.

[6] Curtis, 390-1; Von Rad, 58.

[7] Wenham, 194.

[8] *IVP Bible Background OT,* Psalm 8:4-6 in *PC Study Bible V5 Beta* (2005).

[9] Some commentators regard this statement to be a reflection of the Corinthians' attitude or position, a Corinthian slogan, or a reflection of Jewish rabbinical tradition but not necessarily the opinion of the apostle Paul, especially in light of 11:11-15, which is described by Paul as being the more Christlike approach to gender relations in the church. See Gordon Fee, *The First Epistle to the Corinthians* (Grand Rapids: Eerdmans Publishing, 1987), 491-512 and David E. Garland, *1 Corinthians: Exegetical Commentary of the New Testament* (Grand Rapids: Baker Book House, 2003), 505-23 in regard to the exegetical difficulties of this passage.

[10] Cf. Markus Barth and Helmut Blanke, *Colossians: The Anchor Bible* (New York: Doubleday, 1994), 194-5; Curtis Vaughan, "Colossians *The Expositor's Bible Commentary: Ephesians-Philemon,*" *Volume 11* (Grand Rapids: Zondervan Publishing House, 1978), 181.

[11] Cf. Allan F. Johnson and Robert E. Webber, *What Christians Believe: A Biblical and Historical Summary* (Grand Rapids: Zondervan Publishing Company, 1989), 191-2.

[12] Ronald T. Habermas (1993), "Practical Dimensions of the *Imago Dei,*" *Christian Education Journal,* 13 (2): 90-1.

[13] John S. Hammett, "Human Nature," *A Theology for the Church,* Daniel L. Akin, ed. (Nashville: Broadman-Holman, 2007), 362.

[14] Gregg R. Allison, "Humanity, Sin, and Christian Education," *A Theology for Christian Education*, James Riley Estep, Jr., Michael J. Anthony, and Gregg R. Allison, eds. (Nashville: Broadman-Holman, 2008), 180.

[15] Stanley J. Grenz, *Theology for the Community of God* (Grand Rapids: Eerdmans Publishing Company, 1994), 171, 177-80.

[16] Mark J. Mangano, *The Image of God* (New York: University Press of America, 2008), 44-7.

[17] Cf. Kurt Anders Richardson, "*Imago Dei*: Anthropological and Christological Modes of Divine Self-Imaging," *The Journal of Scriptural Reasoning*, 4.2 (2004), 1-11; http://etext.lib.virginia.edu/journals

[18] George Carey, *I Believe in Man* (Grand Rapids: Eerdmans Publishing Company, 1977), 63, 67.

[19] Hoekema, 25.

[20] Ibid., 30; Grenz, 180.

[21] Robert L. Saucy, "Theology of Human Nature," *Christian Perspectives on Being Human,* J. P. Moreland and David M. Ciocchi, eds. (Grand Rapids: Baker Books, 1993), 33. Saucy, likewise, would affirm the idea of the soul is so all encompassing that it also may include the body, making soul the life which is comprised of body and spirit within the context of the soul. Hence, soul refers to the whole person, not simply a part.

[22] Cf. J. P. Moreland, "A Defense of a Substance Dualist View of the Soul," *Christian Perspectives on Being Human,* J. P. Moreland and David M. Ciocchi, eds. (Grand Rapids: Baker Books, 1993), 55-79.

[23] Cf. James Riley Estep, "Education and Moral Development," *Christian Ethics: The Issues of Life and Death*, Larry Choinard, David Fiensy, and George Pickens, eds. (Joplin, Missouri: Parma Press, 2004), 33-7; James Riley Estep and Alvin W. Kuest, "Moral Development," *Introducing Christian Education: Foundations for the 21st Century,* Michael Anthony, ed. (Grand Rapids: Baker Book House, 2001), 75-7.

[24] Cf. Calvin Linton, "Man's Difficulty—Ignorance or Evil?" in Millard J. Erickson, ed., Readings in Christian Theology, Volume 2: *Man's Need and God's Gift* (Grand Rapids: Baker Book House, 1976), 125-30.

CHAPTER 2

DEVELOPMENTAL THEORIES:

FOE, FRIEND, OR FOLLY?

The Role of Developmental Theories in Christian Formation[1]

By James R. Estep Jr.

What makes spiritual formation *Christian*? This question has been the focus of attention by the Christian education community throughout the 20th century and even today. However, the community has indeed responded with a resounding voice: Theology! Within the Christian education community, there would be little resistance, if any, to the notion that our theological convictions should influence our approach to education and spiritual formation. Hence, we have Catholic, Lutheran, Wesleyan, Reformed, and Baptist approaches to education and spirituality. Arguing for the inclusion of theology into this dialogue is much like preaching to the choir. What about flipping the question? What makes Christian education *education?* More specifically, do the theories of human development provide vital insights into the process of Christian formation? How eager is the Christian education community to embrace insights from the social sciences, i.e., theories of human development, learning, and lifespan? To echo the concern of Ted Ward, "Christian education is *neither*. In far too many cases, Christian education is neither thoroughly Christian nor soundly educational."[2] Could the same be said of our approach to Christian formation?

But what are developmental theories? Are they all alike—with the same assumptions, definitions, and outcomes? Timothy Jones of the Southern Baptist Theological Seminary (Louisville, KY) in figure 2.1 has captured the four basic approaches used by developmental theories: Hard, Soft, Functional, and Cultural-Age Models—with a basic description, definition of *stages*, the influence of culture, and examples for each model (most of which are discussed in the latter chapters of this book).

Developmental Theory	Soft Developmental Hard Theory	Functional Model of Development	Cultural-Age Model of Development
Each stage represents an integrated set of cognitive-neural operations that result in qualitatively different approaches to the same tasks.	Each stage represents an integrated set of cognitive-neural, social, affective, and self-reflective operations that result in qualitatively different perceptions of and responses to the same realities.	Each style or stage represents the individual's primary form of ego-functioning in response to culturally rooted tasks or crises that emerge within the individual's life story.	Each style or stage represents a shift in how the individual's socio-cultural ecosystem perceives and presents his or her role.
Stages are hierarchical and invariant. Each stage develops out of the previous stage; persons do not regress or skip stages.	Stages are sequential and invariant. Each stage develops out of the previous stage; persons do not regress or skip stages.	Stages or styles are psychosocial and phenomenological—rooted in the unfolding narrative of the individual's life and arising from interaction between biologically rooted growth and culturally rooted expectations.	Stages or styles are cultural—rooted in social expectations that are often marked by rites of passage.
Cultural ecologies influence development, but every person—regardless of cultural context—experiences the same stages.	Cultural ecologies influence development, but every person—regardless of cultural context—experiences the same stages.	The individual may not completely leave behind one stage or style when moving to another; some aspects of stages or styles may differ from one culture to another.	Stages or styles vary from one socio-cultural system to another.

Developmental Theory	Soft Developmental Hard Theory	Functional Model of Development	Cultural-Age Model of Development
Examples	Examples	Examples	Examples
Jean Piaget, cognitive development	James Fowler, faith development	Erik Erikson, psychosocial development	**In Roman Catholic tradition:** Infant baptism, first communion, confirmation, marriage, holy orders, anointing of the sick, or last rites
Lawrence Kohlberg, moral development	Jane Loevinger, personality development	V. Bailey Gillespie, faith situations	
		Heinz Streib, religious styles	
Fritz Oser and Paul Gmünder, stages of religious judgment[3] (considered by some to be a "soft developmental theory")	Robert Kegan, equilibrium stages		**In Jewish tradition:** Brit milah [circum-cision], bar mitzvah [becoming "son of commandments"], kiddush'in [betrothal], nissu'in [marriage vows]
			In U.S. American society: Going to kindergarten, eighth-grade graduation, earning of driver's license, graduation from high school, turning 21, graduation from college, marriage, retirement

Figure 2.1: Jones' Typology of Developmental Theories [4]

Hence, before one can accept or reject the insights of *developmental theories*, the particular type of theory must be taken into consideration. Developmental theories are not all created equal and are diverse not only in the subjects they address but the way in which they address them.

This chapter will address the question of the appropriateness of using the social sciences—in particular, theories of learning and human development—in addressing the notion of Christian formation. It will address this question in three sections. First, it will provide an overview of the present debate within the Christian education community. Second, it will discuss how social science theories have influenced our understanding of Christian formation, especially in childhood, and offer an assessment of the developmental paradigm(s). Finally, the implications of utilizing social science theories in understanding Christian formation will be identified for the Christian educator.

The Present Debate

As you read this chapter, you are actually entering into the current historical debate within the Christian education community. It is historic because it has always been present within the Christian community and because it is a debate that continues today within evangelical circles. Over the centuries, the debate has taken many forms, but they all relate to the basic question of the relationship of Christianity to its culture. Within the Christian education community, the debate is far less esoteric and more tangible. It has been with us as far back as the 3rd century AD. Tertullian questioned the value of Christians learning "secular" teachings and Christian children attending Roman schools, *ludi*.[5] Today, in the Christian education community, the debate is more focused. What is the proper place of developmental theories in Christian education? Are they a foe— innately anti-Christian? Are they folly, having legitimate insights for Christian educators? Or might the social sciences be friends—beneficial and affable toward our faith? Respondents to such questions fall into three general camps, providing five options in regard to the use of the social sciences (figure 2.2).

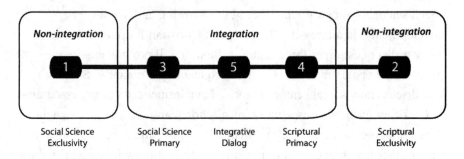

Figure 2.2: Spectrum of Integration

Option 1: Social Science Exclusivity?

On the far left of the figure is a position of non-integration, favoring the virtual exclusive use of the social sciences, i.e., social science exclusivity. In this view, Christian formation is understood from the perspective of the social sciences and theological insights are not necessary—in fact, they may even be considered a detriment. Non-Christian educators would comprise this camp, presenting a psychological or sociological model for spiritual formation that is indeed not distinctively Christian. For this reason, evangelical Christian educators would find it difficult to advocate such a position. As Romney Moseley observes, "It is not surprising, therefore, that Christian education would be criticized for confusing the goals of the Christian formation of persons with those psychological theories of human development."[6] Even when theology or Christian ideas are used within the framework of a social science-exclusivity framework, theology is warped into the shape of psychological or sociological conventions. For example, Susanne Johnson notes that such an approach would have erroneous results, such as equating Abraham Maslow's self-actualization with the final stage of human development. She continues with cautions against explaining the community of the Church and her practices, such as marriage or ritual, simply as the essential means of self-actualization—or even describes God in terms of psychological necessity, such as Karl Marx's opiate of the people.[7] Advocating the sufficiency of the social sciences to form a theory of education, there remains little need for the inclusion of *theological baggage*. Indeed, an educator in this camp would indeed not see the need or benefit of making use of theological insights on the matter of education or Christian formation.

What is the point? This approach to understanding Christian formation is inadequate for Christian educators. It would principally describe Christian formation, or more generically spiritual formation, as a wholly human phenomenon. Psychological and/or sociological phenomena comprise and define spirituality and its formation—with no significant place (if any at all) given for theological insights. As a science, it cannot rely on the supernatural or divine to provide insight into the subject of study.

Option 2: Scriptural Exclusivity?

On the opposite end of the spectrum is a mirror image of non-integration. The Scriptural exclusivity camp has no significant regard for the insights of the social sciences, favoring the sole voice of Scripture as the basis for formulating an approach to Christian formation. This view would be consistent with the perspectives of those extreme fundamentalists who see modern science as a foe or folly of Christianity. While this notion may sound preferable and is certainly enticing to the Christian mind and far simpler than an option requiring integration, it is no more viable than the social science-exclusivity position! It suffers from the mirror-imaged same faults as its antithesis; such a view typically has an insufficient view of Scripture and theology—let alone the social sciences.

The position is somewhat enticing and, in fact, simplistic or naïve. For example, the phrase "We accept scientific discoveries *in so far* as they agree with Scripture!" often brings praise from many evangelical Christians. While in presumption this is not incorrect, in practice it is simply impractical. The problem is the statement presupposes our *interpretation* of Scripture is, in fact, absolutely correct—without exception. To regard the Scriptures as inerrant does not mean that we regard our interpretations of Scripture as inerrant. Science often provides interpretive light on the biblical text. For example, when I read the phrase "the four corners of the earth" in Revelation 7:1 and 20:8—or similarly Isaiah 41:9, "I brought you from the ends of the earth and called you from its *farthest corners*," as a 21st century Christian, how do I interpret this imagery? I know it must be figurative or perhaps using the imagery of a map with four corners. Why? Because I know the world is spherical, resembling a three-dimensional ball (slightly compressed). My knowledge of the natural world, God's creation—as discovered by science's study of it—influences my interpretation of Scripture. If I were a Christian living in the 4th century AD, it is more likely I would have understood the passage literally since we live on a flat surface, a square. Similarly, when the phrase is read from Isaiah 40:22, "God is enthroned above the circle of the earth; . . ." some more modern interpreters see a reference to a spherical earth, which may indeed be the case; *but* no one accepted this interpretation—prior to science proving the world was indeed spherical.[8] Likewise, the church of the 16th century affirmed, as it had for centuries, that the earth was the center of the universe—consistent with the prevailing scientific view first advocated by Ptolemy in the 3rd century BC. However, when Galileo scientifically proved the geocentric universe was not possible and advanced the notion of a heliocentric model, the Church was resistant to give up its long-held interpretation of Scripture and the theological constructs dependent on this interpretation.[9]

What is the point? Scripture itself claims sufficiency (cf. 2 Peter 1:3; Mark 12:24; 1 Corinthians 2:13-16; Luke 11:28; 16:27-31; James 1:25; Hebrews 4:12; Psalm 119:1ff),[10] but it usually is accompanied by a qualifier or a specific situation or context in which it is sufficient. It does indeed; N*ot* claim exclusivity! In many regards, Scripture itself may be sufficient; but our interpretation of it may not be accurate! Scripture requires interpretation and *reinterpretation* in light of scientific discovery, including the social sciences. (Ironically, we do this all of the time with archaeological discoveries but rarely when a discovery is made from other scientific fields!) Additionally, Scripture is sufficient in all it addresses, but it quite simply does not address *every* question humanity has ever raised—perhaps just the most important ones. Scripture must always be a part of our thinking; theology must always provide a context for our discussions but not to the exclusion of other sources of truth.

In terms of Christian formation, it may well provide a strong voice as God's special revelation about Himself—humanity as the *imago Dei*, the innate need for salvation, and the general path of maturing in Christ. However, God's first revelation—His creation, which is the subject of the social sciences—must also be heard. Just as Christian formation is not wholly psychological or sociological; it is not wholly supernatural or divine. Perhaps the best illustration of this view is childhood spirituality— in which case one factor impacting their Christian formation is the fact they are children, not adults. For example, better understanding of the cognitive abilities of five-year-olds may be insightful as to how they conceive a concept of God, what teaching strategies are most useful, or what factors contribute most to their Christian formation.

Options 3-5: Integration!

If the first option is a no-book approach to Christian formation and education—devoid of biblical insight—and the second is a one-book approach—the Bible only—then these approaches are best described as two-book approaches to Christian formation and education.[11] Rather than choosing from either/or, this approach is both/and. It affirms the value of both the insights of Scripture as God's special revelation (2 Timothy 3:16, 2 Peter 1:20-21) *and* creation as God's general revelation (Job 38:1ff, Romans 1:18-22). Like David in Psalm 19, integrationists affirm, "The heavens declare the glory of God, and the sky proclaims the work of His hands. Day after day they pour out speech; night after night they communicate knowledge," (1-2) and likewise affirm, "The instruction of the LORD is perfect, reviving one's soul; the testimony of the LORD is trustworthy, making the inexperienced wise. The precepts of the LORD are right, making the heart glad; the command of the LORD is radiant, making the eyes light up" (7-8). Without belaboring the point, the integrationist position says the first two options discussed are, in fact, *insufficient* for a complete understanding of Christian formation. It affirms the centuries-old assertion: "All truth is God's truth"—regardless of whether its source is Scripture or creation. Insights from both theology and the social sciences are critical—each in their own way. Figure 2.3 illustrates this model of dual revelatory sources of truth.

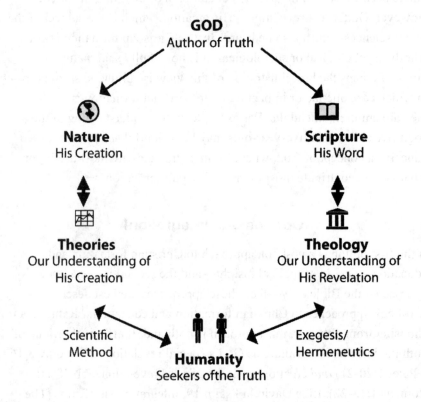

Figure 2.3: God's Two Revelations

In this model, God is the author of all truth. His truth is revealed through His creation, His nature, and His Word—Scripture. God's revelatory actions leave a deposit of information, a revelation—accessible to us in both sources of His revelation, nature, and Scripture. Humanity, seeking truth and understanding, studies God's revelations. The study of God's creation is called *science,* resulting in theories; whereas the study of His spoken revelation is called exegesis/hermeneutics, resulting in *theology*. Both science and theology are the results of human inquiry into God's revelations, human constructs of revealed truth. Since God is the ultimate source of truth, contradiction between creation and Scripture is inconceivable, but apparent contradictions can and do arise between theology and the sciences because of the fallible nature of human inquiry. Theology and science are *not* equivalent to God's revelations but represent the human appropriation and processing of God's revelations. To neglect science is to neglect what God has revealed to us through His creation, and to neglect theology is to neglect what God has revealed to us through His Word. Theology and science are in a continual interaction between their respective revelations, always endeavoring to better understand and glean new insight from what God has revealed to us through them. How does all of this relate to Christian formation? If we are to fully understand Christian formation—and, in particular, from a developmental perspective as it relates to lifespan, it will require the integration of both what God has revealed through His creation and His Word as well as our willingness and ability to engage both as we develop a complete portrait of formation in Christ.

As one looks at figure 2.2—unlike the previous options, integration is a spectrum of its own. On the left is social science primacy, indicating some integrationists, while utilizing both "books," which gives primary voice to the social sciences. On the right, Option 4 indicates primacy is given to Scripture—though not to the exclusion of social science insights. The fifth option is recognizably the most integrative, advocating a virtually equal balance between the two books.

Why three different integrationist approaches? Without sounding vague or intentionally simplistic, it depends on the question being posed. While endeavoring to use both books to inform our thinking, it is obvious that, on some occasions, one of the two books may have more relevant information. For example, if the question is asked, "How do the cognitive abilities of five-year-olds influence children's Christian formation?" or perhaps "How does the social development of fifteen-year-olds influence their Christian formation?," the *emphasis* of the question is on the individual's age being only five-or fifteen-years-old. Does Scripture or the social sciences more readily respond to these questions? You can scan through a concordance, but no specific references to five-or fifteen-year-olds are found—let alone a theory of cognitive development or social development. In this case, social science primacy may be the best position to use—perhaps gleaning insights from Jean Piaget's theory of cognitive development or William G. Perry's studies on adolescent development. However, if the question is: "What is the Holy Spirit's role in the Christian formation of a child?," Scripture (and theology) obviously speak more directly to this question—with only minimal insights (at best) from the social sciences. Thus, the Scriptural primacy option is best suited to answer the question. What if the question was a little more complex? What if the question is something that may draw almost equally from both Scripture and the social sciences? For example, perhaps one of the most common theological-developmental questions for the Christian educator involves the age of accountability, i.e., "At what age does a child become responsible for his/her actions in terms of legitimately recognizing the need to receive Christ?" Option 5, integrative dialog, would provide the most thorough response—one that examines Scripture to discern when God considers a child responsible (such as James 4:17; Isaiah 7:16; Numbers 14:29-31; Deuteronomy 1:39; Romans 14:12) *and* one that presents social science research regarding when a child becomes morally aware of wrongdoing and is capable of accepting personal responsibility.[12] In short, the integrationist's perspective simply does not close the door on either "book"—Scripture or the social sciences—but seeks to utilize both appropriately in response to what is being addressed about Christian formation.

An Illustration of Options 1-5: Paul and Piaget[13]

These five options are perhaps best illustrated by a student's term paper on a Christian educator's view of human development. If she has Paul's theology of humanity, as represented by any number of theological texts, and Jean Piaget's *The Psychology of the Child* (1966)[14], representing the social sciences, how does she integrate them? Picture this student at a desk armed with her copy of Piaget's work, representing the social sciences; a Bible commentary, representing theology; and her MacBook Pro on her lap. How does she proceed to address a human development question from a Christian perspective?

Option 1: The student uses Piaget—*unaware* of Paul's possible voice on the subject—or she regards him as irrelevant to the subject. Hence neglected, she removes Paul from the table, and she and Piaget interact. The paper is a summary and an application of Piaget due to her unawareness of Paul, i.e., Social Science Exclusivity.

Option 2: She uses Paul, but though aware of Piaget, she *rejects* Piaget as being incompatible with Scripture and subsequently removes him from the table. Then she and Paul interact. The paper is a summary and an application of Paul due to her rejection of Piaget, i.e., Scriptural Exclusivity.

Option 3: The student uses both Paul and Piaget somewhat *independently* but gives obvious primacy to the social sciences—with Scripture simply used in its support, i.e., Social Science Primacy. Hence, the paper reflects the social science sources, but this vignette from Scripture supports the social science portrait of human development.

Option 4: She uses both Paul and Piaget, but Paul is given priority, placing Paul's theology over Piaget's theory. Piaget is used sparingly and as theological form for the social science substance. Hence, she uses Paul for the primary substance—but Piaget later.

Option 5: The student uses both Paul and Piaget in the formation of a conceived conceptualization of human nature. At this option, both the form and substance of education are derived from theology and the social sciences. She endeavors to use Paul and Piaget simultaneously. All of the advantages of the previous options are present—without the limitations or inadequacies. Hence, the student's paper reflects Paul and Piaget together in terms of both analysis and application.

Figure 2.4 will further illustrate the progression of integrative levels described above.

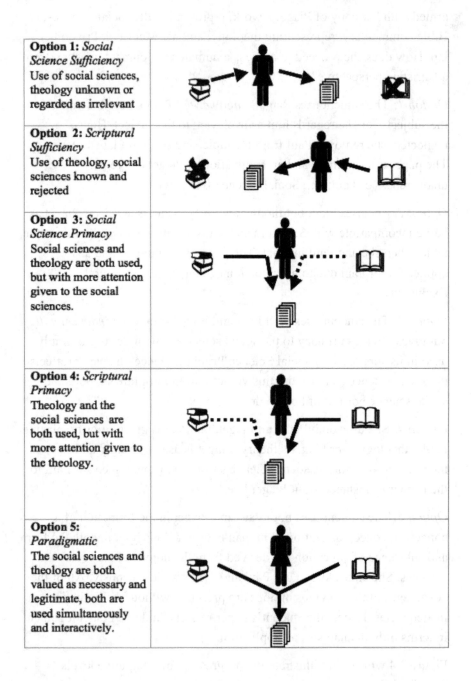

Option 1: *Social Science Sufficiency* Use of social sciences, theology unknown or regarded as irrelevant	
Option 2: *Scriptural Sufficiency* Use of theology, social sciences known and rejected	
Option 3: *Social Science Primacy* Social sciences and theology are both used, but with more attention given to the social sciences.	
Option 4: *Scriptural Primacy* Theology and the social sciences are both used, but with more attention given to the theology.	
Option 5: *Paradigmatic* The social sciences and theology are both valued as necessary and legitimate, both are used simultaneously and interactively.	

Figure 2.4: Student Integrative Endeavor

For a more complete portrait of Christian formation, we must not limit our search to the Scriptures alone but include God's creation as a source of revelation. We must integrate the truth of Scripture with that from within creation so as to provide an ample comprehension of Christian formation for the Christian educator.

Social Science Theories' Influence on Christian Formation

The Christian education community, particularly among evangelicals, frequently makes this affirmation: "Christian education is a theological discipline that draws upon the behavioral sciences."[15] Have social science theories made an impact on the Christian education community's understanding of Christian formation? Gabriel Moran commented, "The modern history of religious education can be read as a struggle around the idea of developmentalism," noting the early attempts at developmental approaches to Christian education by Bushnell and Coe.[16] Similarly, Richard Osmer comments that "the recent discussion of faith development has been sparked by advances in developmental psychology," citing the influence of "life cycle and the structural development" theories of Erikson and Piaget, respectively.[17] Susanne Johnson perhaps said it best when stating that the "foundational theory and practice in Christian education today are development theories rooted in psycho-dynamic thought (Freud, Jung, Erikson) and in structural-developmental theory (Piaget, Kohlberg, Fowler)."[18] Perhaps the most advanced example of the influence of social science theories on our understanding of Christian formation is that of James Fowler. In an essay for *Faith Development in Early Childhood*, Fowler provides an intriguing chart that presents his stages of childhood faith in relation to other developmental theories, e.g., Erickson, Piaget, Stern, and Rizzuto as a part of the "emergent self and the genesis of faith."[19] Indeed, social science insights have left their mark on the Christian education community's understanding of Christian formation.

It seems apparent the Christian education community maintains that social science theories provide a valuable lens through which to conceptualize an approach toward Christian formation. Ted Ward, professor emeritus at Michigan State University and Trinity International University, regards the various forms of human development (physical, intellectual, emotional, social, and moral) as a "spiritual ecology"—although he does not regard spirituality itself to be necessarily a developmental process. He comments that "a developmental perspective invites the educator to see each human life as a unique person emerging through common aspects that can be observed, measured, and evaluated, yet in essence a human soul, a soul with spiritual reality at core, alive through God's redemptive race or else spiritually dead in sin, unregenerated (Ephesians 2:1)."[20] Notice how his comments integrate both insights from the social sciences as well as theology; this is the integrative model.

Theology vs. Theory?

It is easy to perceive a vast gulf between theology and the social sciences—as if they originated in two different worlds. Alien from one another, what could they possibly have in common? However, nothing could be further from reality. Theology and the social sciences—and any science for that matter—have far more in common than their differences. In fact, they are indeed intellectual siblings—as figure 2.3 demonstrated. How close is their sibling relationship? Figure 2.5 provides a comparison of theology and the social sciences, demonstrating their distinctive commonalities.

	Theology	Theory
Revelation	Based on God's special revelation of Scripture	Based on God's general revelation of creation
Human Inquiry	The meaning of revelation discerned through human inquiry, i.e., logic, reason, critical thinking	The meaning of revelation discerned through human inquiry, i.e., logic, reason, critical thinking
Accepted Methods of Interpretation	Exegesis/Hermeneutics, e.g., literary or historical-grammatical approach to interpretation	Scientific method, e.g., qualitative and quantitative research
Responsible Community	The Church or specifically the academe, theologians	Scientific Community or specifically the educational community
Three-Tiered Development	Scripture Passages ⇩ Doctrines ⇩ Theology	Scientific Facts ⇩ Laws ⇩ Theory
Self-Correcting and Plural	Theologies; History of the church demonstrates the continual reform of theology in reaction to error in belief and practice with the development of different theological traditions, e.g., Wesleyan, Reformed, Baptist	Theories; History of the scientific community demonstrates the continual refinement of theory with the development of different theoretical camps, e.g., cognition, according to Piagetians, Vygotskyans, or Neo-Piagetians
Reason & Faith (epistemology)	Emphasis placed on faith and reason as means of knowing	Emphasis placed on reason and faith as means of knowing
Humanity	Recipient of Scripture, a subject of theology, i.e., Christian anthropology	Recipient (and part) of creation, a subject of science, i.e., human development

Figure 2.5: Theology and Theory

While they differ in specifics, they are indeed not alien from one another and, hence, should not be alienated from each other. That theology and social science theories share a common origin, i.e., human inquiry into God's revelation, provided adequate reason for the commonalities they share. Integration of these two is obviously plausible and possible.

Scripture and Human Development

Does the Bible reflect developmentalism? How is the scriptural portrait of life connected to the idea of lifespan development? John Dettoni and James Wilhoit have correctly identified four connections between developmentalism and Christianity, which contributes to the case in favor of integrating social science and Scriptural insights.[21] However, how does the Bible actually speak about human development? One could readily argue that Scripture has nothing to do with our understanding of human development since the Bible does not provide scientific insight nor use scientific language to articulate an approach to human development. However, this assumption and expectation are unreasonable. The Bible speaks volumes about human nature and the spiritual need of humanity, but how does it make mention of human development? The Bible is not a textbook on human development nor should it be made one. The language of Scripture in regard to human development can be summarized in four observations:[22]

1. Scripture does not use scientific language but popular language to describe human development. While Luke may be an exception, frequently using the medical terminology of his era,[23] most authors of Scripture use popular terms when describing humans.

2. Scripture also relies on phenomenological language, meaning it simply describes people as they appear on the surface—with no detailed explanations for why human development occurs.

3. Similar to the previous, Scripture does not postulate a theory of human development, meaning it does not always explain human phenomena.

4. Scripture is also culturally based—but not culturally bound—in its depiction of human development, meaning explanations for actions and activities are generally sociocultural rather than psychological or sociological.

While numerous passages could be used to illustrate these four observations, perhaps two will suffice in this instance. Luke 2:42-52 contains the only canonical narrative of Jesus' adolescence when He was 12 years of age in the Jerusalem temple. Luke, in part, records, "When he was twelve years old, they went up to the Feast, according to the custom. 'Why were you searching for me?' he asked. 'Didn't you know that I had to be in my Father's house?'... And Jesus grew in wisdom and stature, and in favor with God and men" (Luke 2:42,49,52). Notice that in verse 42, it was "according to the custom" that He was in the Temple. Also, in verse 49, Luke offers no explanation as to why Jesus *now* realizes—or at least articulates clearly for the first time—that He is God's Son. However, someone familiar with cognitive development may draw the connection to age 12 being the start of formal operations—the ability to comprehend abstract thoughts (such as the ability to begin capturing His identity as God's Son). Similarly, notice the final verse simply describes Jesus' growth from adolescence into young adulthood in generic, nonscientific terms—without postulating explanations of His development. In short, the four observations—made about how Scripture describes human development—are at least reflected in this short passage that most clearly addresses Jesus' growth.

Another passage that reflects this development is Paul's use of the image of a child, "When I was a child, I spoke like a child, I thought like a child, I reasoned like a child. When I became a man, I put aside childish things" (1 Corinthians 13:11). Paul makes the general observation that children think and talk differently than adults, which is essentially correct; but still the presentation is a popular, phenomenological, and nontheoretical portrait of childhood's transition into adulthood. He does not present a theory of cognitive development from childhood to adulthood, explaining the suppositions of structuralism (aka Piaget) and the necessity of sociocultural interaction (aka Vygotsky), nor does he engage in discussion akin to pedagogy vs. andragogy (learning in childhood vs. adulthood). Paul simply asserts this transition based on casual observation. In short, while mentioning human development, the Bible is indeed not a developmental textbook—nor should it be expected to be. Just because the Bible does not use the language of a 21st- century reader is no reason to think the Scriptures are mute on the subject or reject its insights.

Assessment of Integration

Are Christian educators in the practice of integrating human development theories into their discussions of Christian formation? Actually, the answer is almost self-evident. Gabriel Moran's *Religious Education Development* bases his approach to religious development primarily on theories of Erickson, Piaget, Kohlberg, and Fowler.[24] Similarly, Iris Cully approaches the subject of spiritual growth in children with a heavy dependence on Erickson and Piaget.[25] More recently, such works as Catherine Stonehouse's *Joining Children on the Spiritual Journey* (1998) likewise demonstrate reliance upon human development to help explain and define spiritual formation in children. Perhaps Westerhoff's four-stage theory is the least directly dependent on the influence of formal developmental theories—though he does relate the formation of faith in terms of four sequential, progressive stages of development.[26] One final example is Perry Downs' *Teaching for Spiritual Growth*. He devotes an entire chapter to the explanation of developmentalism and its role in the instructional process, outlining 10 assumptions upon which developmentalism is based and advocating its role in forming an approach to Christian education[27]— followed by chapters summarizing and critiquing several major developmentalists. It appears the approach to human development—e.g., that of Piaget, Vygotsky, Gilligan/Kohlberg, Fowler—has a dominant voice in the theorizing of an approach toward Christian formation. However, what are the pros and cons of such an approach? What are the benefits and cautions we must maintain when engaging in the integrative task?

John Yeatts regarded a developmental paradigm of Christian formation to be "helpful, but inadequate."[28] In a phrase, he has captured the full assessment of integrating human development theory into an approach to Christian formation. What is *helpful* about the inclusion of human development theories in our understanding of Christian formation? While an ever-increasing list of items could be provided, the four main positive contributions can be readily summarized. First, a developmental approach provides a new perspective on the question of faith, religious life, and how one grows in Christ—one that is more precise and technical. Second, it allows the Christian educator to better address Christian formation at various stages of life, e.g., formation in children is quite different than in senior citizens—in part because of the inherent developmental differences between a seven-year-old and a seventy-year-old. Third, it makes Christian formation, in part, a human process—something that can be nurtured, cultivated, and taught, meaning it highlights the human dimension of Christian formation. Finally, it does provide the Christian educator with a deeper appreciation for the necessity of sociocultural context as an environment for Christian formation since developmental theories are increasingly recognizing the influence of the individual-in-context as a factor in growth, i.e., the necessity of the church in relation to the individual Christian.

However, the other end of Yeatts' phrase also must be considered—"but inadequate." We cannot simply *equate* Christian formation with one of the prevailing theories of human development. If an approach toward Christian formation was purely a fabrication based on human development theories, it would simply be inadequate for the Christian education—and the Christian! This caution is raised, e.g., by Richard Osmer of Princeton University, questioning "whether a developmental pattern per se is adequate to describe the Christian life" and specifically regarding Fowler's theory "that his use of structuralism [i.e., stages of development based primarily on the development of the brain] to describe human faith distorts this phenomenon" of Christian faith.[29] This signals the cautionary note mentioned previously. Christian educators must not mistake the formation of a Christian as a mere developmental process or an aspect of humanity.

Hence, when Christian formation is defined as a development or by sequential progressive stages—especially when removed from the context of the Christian community, the Church, Christian educators must remember the witness of theology—social sciences' counter balance—to level out their approach to Christian formation. A solely developmental paradigm would not be beneficial—any more than a solely theological paradigm—for the Christian educator.

Implications for Christian Educators

An integrative approach—one that values both theological and theoretical insights into the process of Christian formation—carries implications for participants in the Christian education community. First, Christian educators must acknowledge, value, and utilize the revelation of creation—God's first revelation—the study of which results in the theories of human development that inform our conceptualization of Christian formation. We cannot be just students of theology; we also must be students of the social sciences. Second, this approach facilitates integrative thinking between the truth of Scripture and creation, calling Christian educators to affirm the assertion that all truth is God's truth. This view results in the Christian educator having a consistent worldview, addressing the truth of God revealed in Scripture and creation as *one*—not variant from each other. Third, the inclusion of human development in our approach to Christian formation fosters respect for people throughout their lifespan. For example, Christian educators are compelled to understand the developmental processes innate within humanity—especially in regard to the Church's ministry to children and adolescents who are the most developmentally distinct from adults. Fourth, Christian educators can express Christian formation as being both a very personal phenomenon *and* yet one that does, in part, progress in somewhat predictable patterns along developmental lines as our human development interacts with the work of God throughout our lives. Finally, acknowledging the interrelatedness of Christian formation and human development encourages the Christian educator to provide an age-appropriate ecology for Christian formation to occur rather than a generic pattern of adult education being inappropriately applied to believers of all ages.

Conclusion

Robert Frost's "Mending Wall" (1949) perhaps has a message for us. In this poem, he muses as to the reason we build fences, stone walls, making the observation:

Something there is that doesn't love a wall,... .

And on a day we [neighbors] meet to walk the line

And set the wall between us once again.

We keep the wall between us as we go.

Before I built a wall I'd ask to know

What I was walling in or walling out,

And to whom I was like to give offense.

Have we built an unnecessary wall between theologies of the Church and the social science theories? Have we regarded the theories of human development as foes or folly—irrelevant to our task as Christian educators? Even if a wall is needed, should it be built so high? Frost also says, "Good fences make good neighbors"—but only when necessary. Theology and theories can be neighbors and friends and perhaps do not need a fence to keep them so. While a fence may allow us to keep the distinctiveness of theology and theories, the fence need not separate us entirely. What we may be "walling in or walling out" may, in fact, be beneficial to our understanding of Christian formation.

ENDNOTES

[1] I have previously written on the necessity of integrating theoogy with education theory so as to provide an approach to education that is consistent with Christian belief and suitable for use in the church. Hence, some of my remarks in this chapter may bear similarity to those in previous materials published by Broadman & Holman, cf. James Riley Estep, "What Makes Education Christian?," A Theology for Christian Education, James Riley Estep, Gregg R. Allison, and Michael J. Anthony, eds. (Nashville: Broadman and Holman, 2008), 25-43.

[2] Ted Ward, "Facing Educational Issues (1977)," *Reader in Christian Education Foundations and Basic Perspectives*, Eugene Gibbs, ed. (Grand Rapids: Baker Book House, 1992), 333.

[3] Some consider this to be a soft developmental theory. For discussion of whether Fritz Oser and Paul Gmünder have developed a hard or soft developmental theory, see C. Power, "Hard versus Soft Stages of Faith and Religious Development," *Stages of Faith and Religious Development*, J. Fowler, K. Nipkow, F. Schweitzer, eds. (New York: Crossroad, 1991).

[4] Timothy Jones produced this chart – developed and adapted from several sources, including J. Snarey, L. Kohlberg, G. Noam, "Ego Development in Perspective: Structural Stage, Functional Phase, and Cultural Age-Period Models," *Developmental Review* 3 (1983): 303-38; J. Snarey and D. Bell, "Distinguishing Structural and Functional Models of Human Development," *Identity* 3 (2003): 221-30.

[5] Tertullian, *On Idolatry*, 10.

[6] Romney Mosley, "Education and Human Development in the Likeness of Christ," *Theological Approaches to Christian Education*, Jack L. Seymour and Donald E. Miller, eds. (Nashville: Abingdon Press, 1990), 147.

[7] Susanne Johnson, "Educating the *Imago Dei*," *Theological Approaches to Christian Education*, Jack L. Seymour and Donald E. Miller, eds. (Nashville: Abingdon Publishing, 1990), 127-8.

[8] Cf. Bernard Ramm, *The Christian View of Science and Scripture* (Grand Rapids: Eerdmans Publishing, 1955), 125-36; Harry Rimmer, *The Harmony of Science and Scripture* (Grand Rapids: Eerdmans Publishing, 1944), 119-57 for a full discussion on these and other instances of similar interpretations.

[9] Cf. "The Universe: Beyond the Big Bang," A&E/History Channel Documentary, 2007.

[10] These passages are regarded as supporting scriptural sufficiency as presented in John MacArthur, "Embracing the Authority and Sufficiency of Scripture," Think Biblically! Recovering a Christian Worldview, John MacArthur ed. (Wheaton, Illinois: Crossway Books, 2003), 21-35.

[11] Cf. Taylor B. Jones, "Why a Scriptural View of Science?" *Think Biblically! Recovering a Christian Worldview*, John MacArthur, ed. (Wheaton, Illinois: Crossway Books, 2003), 233-7 for the illustration of the no-one- and two-book approach. However, Jones advocates the one-book approach.

[12] Cf. James Riley Estep, Jr., "Childhood Transformation: Toward an Educational Theology of Childhood Conversion and Spiritual Formation," *Stone-Campbell Journal* (Fall 2002), 5 (2): 183-206.

[13] Adopted from James Riley Estep, Jr., "What Makes Education Christian?," *A Theology for Christian Education*, James Riley Estep, Michael J. Anthony, and Gregg R. Allison, eds. (Nashville: Broadman & Holman, 2008), 32-7.

[14] Jean Piaget and Bärbel Inhelder, *The Psychology of the Child* (New York: Basic Books, 1966).

[15] D. Campbell Wyckoff, "Theology and Education in the Twentieth Century," *Christian Education Journal* (15.3), 12.

[16] Gabriel Moran, Religious Education Development (Minneapolis: Winston Press, 1983), 21.

[17] Richard R. Osmer, "Faith Development," *Harper's Encyclopedia of Religious Education* (New York: Harper and Row, 1990), 249.

[18] Susanne Johnson, *Christian Spiritual Formation in the Church and Classroom* (Nashville: Abingdon Press, 1989), 106.

[19] James W. Fowler, "Strength for the Journey: Early Childhood Development in Selfhood and Faith," *Faith Development in Early Childhood*, Doris A. Blazer, ed. (Kansas City: Sheed and Ward, 1989), 8-9.

[20] Ted Ward, "Introduction," *Nurture That Is Christian*, James C. Wilhoit and John M. Dettoni, eds. (Wheaton, Illinois: Victor Books, 1995), 16.

[21] James Wilhoit and John Detonni, Nurture That Is Christian (Wheaton, Illinois: Victor Books, 1995), 27-30.

[22] This section gleans insights from Ramm, 66-76, regarding the language of the Bible and science.

[23] Cf. William Kirk Hobart, *The Medical Language of St. Luke* (Grand Rapids: Baker Book House, rpt. 1954). However, his findings have been challenged in more recent years as being overstated but not necessarily incorrect.

[24] Moran, 29-126.

[25] Iris V. Cully, *Education for Spiritual Growth* (New York: Harper and Row, 1984), 125-46.

[26] Gwen Kennedy Neville and John H. Westerhoff III, *Learning Through Liturgy* (New York: Seabury Press, 1978), 161.

[27] Perry Downs, *Teaching for Spiritual Growth* (Grand Rapids: Zondervan Publishing Company, 1994), 69-80.

[28] Cf. John R. Yeatts, "Helpful but Inadequate: A Critique of the Developmental Paradigm," *Christian Education Journal*, 13 (1): 49-60.

[29] Osmer, 252-3.

CHAPTER 3

INTELLECTUAL DEVELOPMENT AND CHRISTIAN FORMATION[1]

By Jonathan H. Kim

From the inception of the church to the present, Christians have incessantly engaged in a comprehensive study to provide an accurate exposition of the intellect as it relates to Christian formation. Undoubtedly, the discussion surrounding intellectual development and Christian formation has gained its momentum due to the church's recent surge of interest in Christian formation. The time has come, and the church needs to tend to the assumptions underlying contemporary views of the relationship and offer accurate insights to its members.

This chapter presents an overview of the relationship between intellectual development and Christian formation. The chapter focuses on the rational and relational (i.e., empirical) functions of the human intellect as they relate to the development of Christian faith. It suggests an integrative way of understanding Christian sanctification by situating human intellectual capacities in the context of faith formation. Since faith and the intellect are in a complementary relationship with one another, understanding their interrelatedness will provide a holistic picture of Christian spiritual growth. The chapter divides into four distinct yet interrelated sections. Subsequent to the introduction, the first chapter presents the theoretical overview of cognitive development theories—principally those of Jean Piaget and Lev Vygotsky. This is followed by a study of intellect and its development in the Scriptures. The third section presents a Christian perspective on intellectual development—with implications for our understanding of Christian formation and ministry.

Theories of Intellectual Development and Theorists

In general, the intellect divides into rational and relational dimensions— schema and thema, respectively. Schema refers to a rational structure of the mind; it represents the prototype of the mind that has a generative and normative power in the conception and validation of analytical knowledge. It indicates the rational embeddedness of the mind that serves as a basic starting point of and catalyst to knowing. In a general sense, schema denotes mental form, shape, or figure. However, in a specific sense, it refers to the character or characteristic property of a thing or mind (figure 3.1).[2]

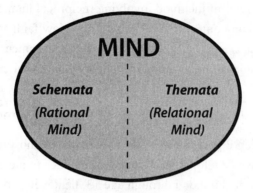

Figure 3.1: Dimensions of the Mind

Those who understand the critical function of *schema* (i.e., rational mind) contend that a logical formalization and employment of knowledge involve assimilation and accommodation —assimilation involving the theoretical inception of new information and accommodation involving the internalization process by which newly received information is dialectically synthesized to the preexisting *schema*. This formalization then results in a reconfiguration of *schema* where faith emerges. As will be demonstrated later in this chapter, this has implication for Christian formation and education.

The second dimension of the mind is called *thema*, which represents the relational epistemic function of the intellect. The term *thema* basically means to *that which is placed under or laid down*; technically speaking, *thema* denotes the *primary (nonderivative) element or property* of a mind.[3] Thema represents the empirical dimension of the mind that has a constructive and normative power in the apprehension and validation of empirical knowledge.[4] Thema is the archetype of the praxis-relational mind or a deep structure of empirical knowledge such as first principle, primary conception, or preconception as a belief, maxim, or deep ideological category of the mind.[5] Those who understand the critical function of thema (i.e., relational mind) relate Christian formation to the inter-mental activity of the mind involving reciprocal human-God, human-human, and human-context interactions.[6] They view faith as something people construct as an empirical experience, a development of ideas, and the comprehension of the meaning of their spiritual experiences.

Schematic Perspective: Piaget's Theory

Swiss genius Jean Piaget (1896-1980) is perhaps the most recognized name in cognitive development. Using mathematics to measure cognitive development from childhood through age 13, he developed a theory of intellectual development that has essentially been unchallenged. His theory is presented in these two principal works: *The Psychology of the Child* and *Genetic Epistemology*.[7] Without over simplifying, Piagetian theory can be characterized in three words: Organization, Adaptation, and Stages.

Piaget postulated that humans have an innate desire for *organization*, meaning we try to systematize our reasoning such as making categories, patterns, connections between ideas. This may be most evident in the observation of a two-year-old continually asking, "Why?," trying desperately to understand their surroundings. This is assumed by Piaget's theory because it is rooted in the Kantian synthesis of rationalist and empiricist ideas. The focus of Piaget's theory was on the quality output of the mind utilizing various forms of knowledge such as percepts, symbols, concepts, and hypotheses/theories.

How is this achieved? Through the process of *adaptation*. This process is comprised of three interrelated components: (1) assimilation, (2) accommodation, and (3) equilibration (and disequilibration). Figure 3.2 will illustrate and explain the process of adaptation.

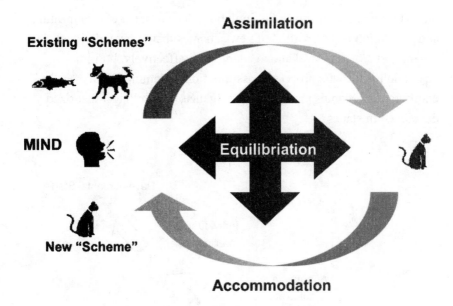

Figure 3.2: Piagetian Thinking[8]

This child can recognize two animals—fish and dog—because in his mind, two "schemes," or brief descriptions that allow an individual to categorize reality, already exist. Fish have scales, swim in the water, and have gills; whereas dogs have four legs, fur, and walk. As long as these are all the animals he sees, equilibration is achieved; i.e., everything is in balance. But what if he sees a cat for the first time? It is definitely not a fish; but it has four legs, fur, and walks. He exclaims to his parents, "Doggy!" The parents explain, "This isn't a doggy. It's a cat. Cats go meow. Dogs go bark." Now the child's definition of dog has expanded; but more importantly, a new scheme—that of cat—has been added to his mind. Now balance is restored, equilibration has replaced disequilibration, and the child grows intellectually.

Snowman and Beihler summarize, "In their drive to be organized, individuals try to have a place for everything (accommodation) so they can put everything into its place (assimilation). The product of organization and adaptation is the creation of new schemes that allow individuals to organize at a higher level and to adapt more effectively."[9] From adaptation—with the process of assimilation-accommodation-equilibration—comes increasing intelligence, which Piaget theorized developed in stages (figure 3.3).

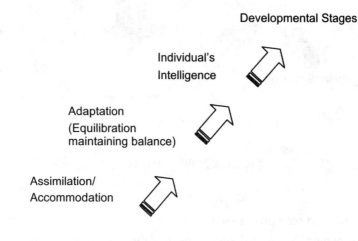

Figure 3.3: Piagetian Intelligence[10]

Ultimately, Piaget's theory of intellectual development is expressed in a series of developmental stages. The Piagetian theory explains the function and development of the human intellect at four stages or levels of thought (figure 3.4):

1. Reflexive Thinking (Sensorimotor Stage)

2. Intuitive Thinking (Preoperational Stage)

3. Concrete Thinking (Concrete Operational Stage)

4. Abstract Thinking (Formal Operational Stage)

Although Piaget divided these cognitive abilities according to four chronological stages, these types of thinking also can be understood as people's innate intellectual ability—regardless of where they are chronologically.

Cognitive Ability	Form of Knowledge Best Utilized	Description
Reflexive Thinking Sensorimotor Stage Ages 0 - 2	Percepts (Sense Impressions)	•Able to develop understanding primarily through visual, auditory, and tactile experiences •Sensorimotor problem solver •Early likes and dislikes appear •Affect invested in the self, ego-centric
Intuitive Thinking Pre-operational Stage Ages 2 - 7	Symbols (Psychological and Emotional Impressions)	•Able to think symbolically, according to psychological categories •True social behavior begins •Intentionality absent in moral reasoning
Concrete Thinking Concrete Operational Stage Ages 7 - 11	Concepts	•Able to formulate concepts and basic categories •Able to understand logical relationships among concepts but only by generalizing from concrete experiences •Logic applied to problems •Autonomous will appears •Intentionality is constructed
Abstract Thinking Formal Operational Stage Ages 11 - 15	Hypotheses and Theories (Logical assumptions or speculations)	•Think critically •Solve problems systematically •Able to deal with abstractions to form propositions •Emergence of personality formation •Adaptation toward adulthood

Figure 3.4: Piaget's Theory of Intellectual Development

Reflexive Thinking. The first level of intellectual function describes how the mind coordinates sensory experience to apprehend knowledge and organized them according to a set of ideological system. Usually, reflexive thoughts are generated based on the sensory intake of information, involving visual, auditory, and tactile experiences. The primary form of knowledge utilized in reflexive thinking is impression (e.g., sensory data of experience). Impressions, functioning as mnemonic means of sensory experience, aid the person and elicit ideas. While the reflexive form of knowing mainly involves actual seeing, hearing, and feeling, when the person is able to make sense of their sensory experiences, ideas emerge as knowledge. At the reflexive stage, knowledge is derived from percepts, and percepts are obtained through sensory experiences.

Intuitive Thinking. The second level of intellectual function describes how the mind perceives knowledge intuitively and organizes it according to the system of symbols. That is, the person learns to detach their ideas from the physical world and then organizes them to a set of psychological systems. Here observations and emotional impressions are converted into a set of mental symbols and then into a set of ideas. Thinking at this stage is highly egocentric and perception bound and lacks inferential support.

Note there are two different types of intuition: sensible and intellective. Most people understand intuition as direct knowledge of an object gained with noninferential knowledge, which we call sensible intuition. However, there is another type of intuition that has a conceptual foundation; it is called intellectual intuition. While sensible intuition is generated by the outer (i.e., physical) senses, intellective intuition is engendered by the inner (i.e., nonphysical such as psychological and emotive experiences) senses owned by the soul.

Concrete Thinking. The third level of intellectual function describes people's ability to reason and conceptualize. This stage marks the beginning of logical thinking in that people become relatively free from the perceptual dominance and are able to form ideas inductively—a major turning point in human intellectual development. Although people at this stage have a limited abstract thinking ability to process multiple ideas, they are still capable of recognizing their logical relationship to one another (i.e., transitivity), sorting them out (i.e., seriation), and classifying them (i.e., categorization). With the ability to understand the logical dimensions of the physical and perceptual experiences, people at the concrete operational stage expand their mental capacity to a conceptual horizon.

Abstract Thinking. The fourth and final level of intellectual function describes people's ability to deal with abstract ideas, think critically, systematically solve problems, and form hypotheses and/or theories. Abstract thinking includes: (1) abstract reasoning—the ability to fully process theoretical concepts; (2) inductive reasoning—the ability to observe/evaluate ideas and generate hypotheses; and (3) deductive reasoning—the ability to consider various propositions and formulate a solution, e.g., theory. The main characteristic of thinking at this stage is that thoughts are exclusive of physical/perceptual constraints and employ full use of abstract reasoning. When faced with a problem, people often formulate a hypothesis or theory to resolve the issue. One thing to note here, however, is that because people are at this stage does not mean their minds are only confined to abstract thinking. Although abstract thinking can dominate their thoughts, people still make use of the three former thinking abilities in construct knowledge (see figure 3.4). For this reason, thinking becomes much more holistic in that people learn to fuse percepts, symbols, concepts, and hypothesis in learning; the four functions of the mind work complementarily with one another. Endowed with the aptitude and potentiality to expand their epistemic horizon, people at the abstract thought stage learn to fully utilize logic for default reasoning.

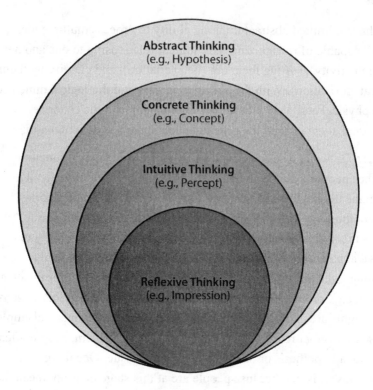

Figure 3.5: Intellectual Development Overview

Thematic Perspective: Vygotsky's Theory

The perspective of Russian theorist Lev Vygotsky (1896 - 1934) on intellectual development was different from that articulated by Jean Piaget. Vygotsky's idea of intellectual development is grounded in the assumption that intellectual development is dependent on the social-historical of the individual. This is, in part, due to the fact that Vygotsky used language acquisition as the means of assessing intellectual development, i.e., from where does someone learn language? (See figure 3.5.)

Pre-exists the Individual	Individual grows up within the culture	Emergence of Individual Mental Process within

Figure 3.6: SocioCultural Development[11]

The Society or Culture in which They Live. Such an approach is often labeled as "sociohistorical," "sociocultural," or a part of "social reconstruction-ism."[12] In essence, Vygotsky argued, "Society precedes the individual and provides the conditions that allow individual thinking to emerge."[13] Thus, "development, far from being teleological or unidirectional, must be viewed as context-dependent."[14] Unlike the stage theory presented by Piaget, Vygotsky perceived development as uneven and contingent on the environment.[15] How does culture get into the mind of the individual? It is through what Vygotsky called mental tools. Tools are mediators between the individual and "external activity" which develops higher cognitive functions.[16] Mental tools are such items as language, symbols, writing, concepts, or art since each of these conveys ideas from the culture to the individual. Just as physical tools expand the physical abilities of humanity, so the mental tools expand the mental abilities and capabilities.[17]

Vygotsky maintained that development occurs in a variety of "zones." The term *zone* intentionally implies a nonlinear area of development, and *proximal* is limited by behaviors that are developed or that will develop soon. He identified three zones of development:

Zone of Actual Development: The student's actual developmental level. How capable of independent action is he/she?

Zone of Potential Development: The students' achievable potential. What should the individual be able to do independently but cannot presently?

Zone of Proximal Development: The amount of assistance required for a student to move from the Zone of Actual Development and the Zone of Potential Development. How much assistance does the student need to move from what they can presently do to what they should be able to do?

This final zone, the Zone of Proximal Development (ZPD), best captures and represents Vygotsky's contribution to developmental theory. He described the ZPD as a "new approach" since it explains the interrelatedness of learning, teaching, and development.[18] He defined the ZPD as "the distance between the [child's] actual developmental level as determined by independent problem solving and the level of potential development as determined through problem solving under adult guidance or in collaboration with more capable peers."[19] Hence, the limits of the ZPD are based on the individual's (1) ability to perform independently and (2) performance requiring assistance.[20] As stated previously, Vygotsky was convinced that development was dependent on learning/instruction. Vygotsky stated:

> From this point of view, learning is not development; however, properly organized learning results in mental development and sets in motion a variety of developmental processes that would be impossible apart from learning. Thus, learning is a necessary and universal aspect of the process of developing culturally organized, specifically human, psychological functions. To summarize, the most essential feature of our hypothesis is the notion that developmental processes do not coincide with learning processes. Rather, the developmental process lags behind the learning process; this sequence then results in zones of proximal development. Our hypothesis establishes the unity but not the identity of learning processes and internal developmental processes. A second essential feature of our hypothesis is the notion that, though learning is directly related to the course of child development, the two are

never accomplished in equal measure or in parallel since development is dependent on learning.[21]

But what is developmental about Vygotsky's theory? No stages, levels, or progression? In order to understand the developmental dimension of the ZPD, two basic functions of the mind need to be understood: Lower/Spontaneous Thought and Higher/Scientific Thought (figure 3.7).

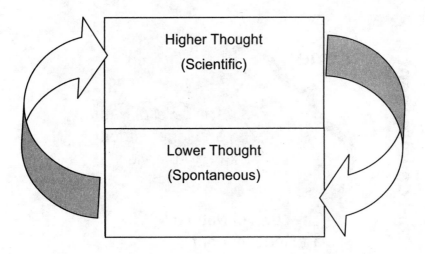

Figure 3.7: Higher and Lower Thoughts[22]

The lower function refers to the individual's analytical cognitive ability related to the function of *schema*, while the higher mental function refers to a reflective-active cognitive process involving *thema*. In other words, the lower mental function produces a theoretical knowledge, which is static and contemplative; while the higher mental function produces a so-called praxis knowledge, which is dynamic and transformative. The lower mental function is usually subject to one's convergent thoughts, whereas the higher mental function is subject to both divergent thoughts and contextual influences. When the idea of lower/higher thought is combined with the Zone of Proximal Development, this concept describes the additional level of development/learning achieved under adult guidance or in collaboration with more capable others[23] (see figure 3.8). Taken in a theoretical sense, the ZPD indicates the amount of influence that significant others can have on intellectual development.

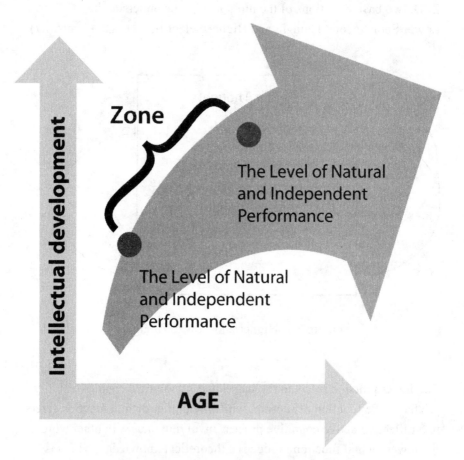

Figure 3.8: Zone of Proximal Development (ZPD)

In summary, Vygotsky's relational epistemic (or *thematic*) view of intellectual development highlights the process of dialogic induction, promoting thinking and growth. It explains how—through the dialogic experience of generating higher thinking skills (i.e., cognitive scaffolding)—a person can develop intellectually.

Biblical/Theological Insights on Intellectual Development

As indicated in chapter 1, our capacity for rational thought can be directly attributed to the *imago Dei*, the human distinction within God's creation. According to biblical anthropology, the intellect is viewed as a rational property or a thinking agent of the soul. It comes from a Hebrew word *lebh* (Proverbs 4:23) and two Greek words *nous* (1 Corinthians 2:16) and *dianoia* (Matthew 22:37; Mark 12:30; Luke 10:27). Though a wide range of expressions and connotations are associated with these words, they are generally translated as the intellect or mind in the Bible, signifying the ratiocinative activity of the heart. It refers to the activity of conceiving and perceiving ideas based on the use of reflection, reasoning, and judgment. As understood in Christian theological literature, faith is closely related to the output of the intellect, legitimating the truth of Scripture.

Scripture does witness to the intellectual development of individuals. For example, this truth is observed by Paul when he wrote, "When I was a child, I spoke like a child, I thought like a child, I reasoned like a child. When I became a man, I put aside childish things" (1 Corinthians 13:11, as well as Luke's summative observation of Jesus' youth, "And *Jesus increased in wisdom* and stature, and in favor with God and with people" (Luke 2:52, emphasis added). However, these are simply passing observations regarding the growth of individuals from childhood toward adulthood. To really get a biblical portrait of how individuals grow in the intellectual capacity requires a far more in-depth study.

While Scripture does not provide a theory of intellectual development, it does indirectly bear witness to it.[24] When Scripture presents a model of instruction or series of instructions to teachers, these instructions are based on perceived progression of the students' mind, i.e., their intellect. Much attention has been given to the educational theory contained in the wisdom literature of the Old Testament. For example, Daniel Estes,[25] James

Crenshaw,[26] Charles Melchert,[27] and Donn Morgan[28] have identified the broad spectrum of learning methods specified in the wisdom literature in ancient Israel, reflecting a spectrum of understanding of the student's intellectual capacity. Teaching methods range from teacher-centered indoctrination of students to teachers as facilitators, e.g., Ecclesiastes, Proverbs, and Job encourage students to wrestle individually with the text. This would certainly reflect a teacher's appreciation that younger or less advanced students were capable of mere rote memorization while acknowledging that students grow intellectually and become capable of independent thought.

Proverbs and Ecclesiastes use very descriptive terminology—"verbs, phrases, and idioms relating to learning," which seem to provide insight into "stages in the learning process" as understood by the Israelites.[29] Nili Shupak of the University of Haifa (Israel) "tries to reconstruct the progressive stages of learning from the first, passive step to the last, more active and creative step"—based on the usage of such vocabulary in Hebrew wisdom literature, which is illustrated in figure 3.9 as follows:[30]

Passive Learning		
Listening, Obedience	Šm⁽, šyt, lēb, and synonyms (first meaning)
Observance	šmr, ns.r, s.pn + objects relating to h.okmâ
Assimilation	qnh + objects relating to h.okmâ, bqš + objects, relating to h.okmâ (first meaning)
Understanding	Šyt lēb and synonyms (second meaning), lqh. mûsār, lmd
Mastery	byn, śkl (hiph⁽il)
Searching, Pondering	Leqah. (noun), h.qr (verb, noun), bqš (second meaning), ntn ʾel lēb, ntn ʾet lēb lᵉ
Active Learning		

Figure 3.9: Learning in Old Testament Wisdom Literature

The wisdom literature of ancient Israel, produced mostly during the monarchical period, observes that learners move from content mastery toward higher levels of learning and living.

While the New Testament does not have a corpus parallel to the Old Testament's wisdom literature, it similarly utilizes various terms to describe the learning process, all reflecting a different level of intellectual development.[31] For example, note the following list of terms used in the New Testament that describe intellectual ascent:

Be prepared to learn, pay attention (Gk. *prosechō,* e.g., Acts 8:6,;16:14; 1 Timothy 4:1; Hebrews 2:1; and Gk. *epechō,* e.g., 1 Timothy 4:16);

Know (Gk. *ginōskō,* e.g., Acts 8:30-31,17:20; 1 Corinthians 2:12) or Known (Gk. *gnōstos*);

Memory (Gk. *mnāmoneuō*, e.g., 2 Timothy 2:8);

To think, comprehend, or understand (Gk. *noeō*, e.g., 2 Timothy 2:7 and Gk. *logidzomai*, e.g., 2 Corinthians10:11);

To decide or conclude (Gk. *krinō*, e.g., Romans 14:5); and

To evaluate and judge (Gk. *krisis*, e.g., John 7:24, Gk. *krima*, e.g., Hebrews 6:2).

While the Scriptures do not provide a comprehensive theory of intellectual development, the language used within educational contexts in both the Old and New Testaments reflects a progression of intellectual thought.

Intellect and Faith

Without faith, it is impossible to please God (Hebrews 11:6). But what is faith? Is it the same as belief or trust, or is it more than that? There seems to be a great deal of confusion among Christians regarding the definition of faith, so understanding the proper meaning of faith is essential before we explore its relation to the intellect. Faith consists of two parts: belief and trust.

Belief, as a mental act of faith, is an intellectual recognition and acceptance of the truth, which we affirm and accept. Belief can be childlike, but it also can be adult like; the difference is a matter of complexity in logic. Although we could trust in spite of the evidence, we cannot believe unless the mind comprehends and/or apprehends that which is true.

Trust, as a volitional act of faith, is the confident expectation about something or someone. It is a generalized expectancy that we can rely on the word or the character of another person. Trusting requires the choice and the willingness to give one's self to the possibility that what we know is indeed true. It generates confidence in or reliance on something or someone that we believe to be true or trustworthy.

This is the point: Faith involves both trust and belief but not to the exclusion of intellect. Jesus said, "And to love Him with all your heart, with all your understanding, and with all your strength" (Mark 12:33, emphasis added; cf. Matthew 22:37). Faith is the sum total of *belief* in the facts and truth of Scripture that produces the complete *trust* in the person and work of Jesus Christ. This faith requires "a firm and certain knowledge of God's grace toward us, found upon the truth of the freely given promise in Christ."[32] Biblically speaking, the formation of faith is anchored to the complex interworking of the Holy Spirit and the human intellect. The dialectic fusion between spiritual (i.e., supernatural) and intellectual (i.e., natural) forces generates a meta cognitive knowledge (Latin, *notia* [knowledge]), trust (Latin, *fiducia* [trust]), and deep-seated assurance/conviction (Latin, *assensus* [assent]) called faith when the human mind recognizes and responds to the effectual call of God grounded in His truth and grace.[33] On the one hand, faith is bestowed upon believers by a loving work of the Holy Spirit (John 6:44; Hebrews 11:1; Romans 1:8; 8:14; Jude 3; Ephesians 2:8-10; 1 John 2:14; Philippians 3:10-11; James 2:26; Hebrews 12:2). On the other hand, however, faith is rationally and/or experientially induced by the mind as it responds to the truth of Scripture (John 8:32; 14:16-17; 16:13). Faith then, as Calvin propelled us to believe, produces in the mind a sense of the Divine (i.e., *sensus divinitatis*) that engenders a desire to love, worship, obey, and serve God.

Intellectual Development and Christian Formation

How can Piaget and Vygotsky aid us in understanding Christian formation? Like the roof of a Gothic cathedral, it is upheld by flying buttresses coming from both sides of the building but meeting in the middle. In this instance, Piaget comes from the *schema* side and Vygotsky from the *thema* side, but their apparent opposition to one another is what actually provides support for the roof. With our study of both perspectives, we must understand that neither Piaget's nor Vygotsky's contention, by itself, provides an adequate explanation of the relationship between intellect development and Christian formation. Christian educators need the development insights from both the *schemata* and *themata* perspectives to more fully comprehend Christian formation (figure 3.10).

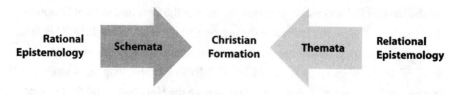

Figure 3.10: Schematic and Thematic Perspectives of Christian Formation

A Christian Approach to Schema and Christian Formation

On the whole, the Piagetian theory introduced a highly analytical and reductionistic paradigm of Christian formation to the church. The proponents of this view argued that the construction of knowledge takes place primarily in one's mental sphere as the individual assesses basic ideas (i.e., concepts) according to the pre-established criteria called *schema* (or *schemata* [plural]). By relying on the analytic functions of the intellect, those within the schematic tradition explained faith as an intellectual trust of God that rests exclusively upon a conception of analytical knowledge with the use of logic. Their analysis presupposes faith as employing an intra-process of the mind, viewing logical intelligence as a primary tool for conceiving, evaluating, and validating life in the Spirit. Their basic argument is viewing the successful obtainment of intellective knowledge as a necessary condition for the Christian formation process.

Although the schematic perspective, according to Piaget, was widely accepted and grew into a major paradigm in Christian education, we must understand that such a theoretical claim offers a limited description of the relationship between the intellect and faith. According to the Piagetian view, analytical logic is considered the primary component of faith and spiritual experience as secondary. This perspective not only confines faith to an analytic sphere but also limits the life in the Spirit to an intracognitive domain of the mind and produces a highly static view of spirituality. The subsequent result is equating faith to conceptual learning, depicting faith as nothing more than a set of rational determinants shaping spiritual life. Under the Piagetian perspective, faith becomes a mechanistic output of one's *schema*; and so called, the individual's analytic competency turns into an autonomous force that informs, shapes, and controls faith unidirectionally (i.e., unidirectional determinism).

Unidirectional determinism views faith as the work of a rigid, mechanistic mind in the sense of applying a fundamental lawfulness or order to faith. Thus, faith is understood in direct relation to or as a by-product of the rational mind. This is where the structure of faith is determined by the conception of analytical knowledge. So as the person receives information and acts upon it to make it known to himself/herself, the comprehension of that very information triggers some form of knowledge, which in return generates faith—like the concept of dialectics, the way that a learner reaches out and grasps knowledge through a critical process of analysis, evaluation, and synthesis. Under this view, analytical knowledge becomes a dependent cause of faith, and the human capacity for conscious and logical judgment enthrones as a singular determinant of faith formation.

To a large degree, the unidirectional view of Piaget advocates a one-sided perspective of faith development. For instance, faith is viewed as a feeble recipient of cognitive influence, and spiritual life becomes, to a large degree, mere intellectual experience as if Christianity was a theory to be studied. Many who are swayed by this perspective contend that mature faith would only exist if a person has a capacity for analytical induction. Does this mean that young infants and mentally challenged individuals cannot have faith? In the end, the discussions surrounding the schematic view will be reduced to an argument that says people who are incapable of processing abstract concepts cannot be saved. The schematic view of intellectual development explains just one aspect of the complexity and variability of the relationship regarding intellectual development and Christian formation.

Having discussed the schematic perspective of intellectual development and its relation to Christian formation, we now turn to the thematic perspective developed by the Vygotskian scholars. Christian formation, under this perspective, became the perceptual encounters of God and His truths that produce sensible and intellective knowledge engendering faith. Epistemologically, the thematic perspective is rooted in empiricism.

A Christian Approach to Thema and Christian Formation

As the intellectual trend emanating from Piaget's rationalist epistemology was dissipating in the field of Christian education, there emerged theoretical articulations of Vygotsky's relational epistemology.[34] Contrary to Piaget's schematic view, those within the Vygotskian tradition saw Christian formation being closely linked to the inter-mental activity of *thema* involving spiritual experiences.

By employing the concept of *thema* in the analysis of Christian formation, Vygotskian scholars argued that a person's relational situation is inseparable from the manner in which one thinks and interprets faith; thus, they asserted perceptual experience involving critical thinking as the source of spiritual knowledge and faith. This is where experience as a spiritually significant activity becomes a semiotic medium for spiritual knowledge when the related point of concerns obtained in critical reflection leads the learner to conceive faith. For example, as the learner proceeds through spiritual life, significant others—by providing a foundational consistency between theology (e.g., theology of prayer) and practice (e.g., daily prayer life)—help the learner grow considerably beyond the level naturally expected of him/her. This is where the relationship, whether spiritually overt or covert, becomes a dependent cause of faith formation –especially when the learner is able to generate sensible and intellective knowledge. According to this contention, what bridges knowledge and faith is the influence that significant others have on the learner through *koinonic* (from koinonia) encounters. Vygotskian scholars would describe this influence as semiotic mediation—like intentional mentorship whereby the spiritual reality of mature individuals (e.g., mentor, teacher, parent, etc.) is overtly passed on to the learner. In such a context, significant others, through their notable life in God, become the semiotic mediums, encouraging the learner to deepen the meaning of the spiritual truth/reality observed.

Reciprocal determinism, in essence, suggests that faith results from the interaction of content, reflection, and experience/action rather than from any one of these factors alone. The principle thrust of reciprocal determinism is the Socratic method of dialogue or also known as Socratic induction, which highlights relationally induced knowledge. This classical method of knowledge typically involves three stages: (a) Reflective Observation; e.g., perplexity and wonder, (b) Critical Analysis; e.g., question and doubt, and (c) Synthesis/Action; e.g., integrated knowledge. In the first stage, faith is conceived through observation—this is where the learner first seeks to understand both internal and external structures of the percepts (or perceptual lessons) being learned reflectively. In building the semiotic structure of percepts, the person first observes the orientation, value, and significance of a given environment and evaluates the prominence or estimable value of what is being offered by significant others. Then decisions are made about which aspect of the percepts should be adopted into his/her faith. Then a praxis action is carried out whereby the individual translates the percepts into an internal conviction that can guide faith through its formational process. During this stage, significant experiences are translated as sensible knowledge, which is later actualized as intellective knowledge in active experimentation, i.e., Synthesis/Action stage.

Having internalized perceptual experiences through reflective observation, the learner moves to the second stage of Christian formation, Critical Analysis. During this stage, previously conceived convictions are questioned, doubted, and criticized. The degree to which evaluation is made depends on the three following factors: (a) the relevance and credibility of the lessons being observed, (b) the prestige of the person who is teaching or embodying the concepts being taught, and (c) the satisfaction already present in the learner's situation where the lessons are being applied.

The third and final stage of Christian formation, according to the theory of reciprocal determinism, is Synthesis/Action. During this stage, a favorable experience becomes more tangible through application. Continuous interactions between the learner and situational experiences take place dialectically. This is where the learner develops praxis knowledge, which later serves as a cognitive framework to either validate or reject the sensible knowledge received earlier. If the knowledge is validated, it becomes intellective knowledge; if it is rejected, it then becomes insignificant information (e.g., semiotic data) in the learner's mind. However, one must note that the Vygotskian concept of reciprocity is grounded in cognitive control over its environment, not vice versa. Faith is induced as the learner selectively chooses and reflectively interacts with his/her spiritual environment.

On the one hand, Vygotskian scholars shied away from the *schematic* view of the mind, largely ignoring the cognitive individual-centered accounts of learning and faith formation. On the other hand, their theoretical position made an undeniable contribution to the faith development theory by introducing the structural relation between *thema* and faith. Their theory elucidated the intercognitive process of the higher mental function involving praxis knowledge and faith. Extrapolating from Vygotsky's framework, we could correlate Christian formation to the person's dialectic ability to (a) identify a significant experience on which to reflect, (b) examine underlying values associated with that understanding, (c) engage the specific process of critical reflection, and (d) arrive at a decision for a new meta-epistemic belief called faith.

Implications for Christian Formation

To seek an accurate understanding of the relationship between intellectual development and Christian formation, schematic (i.e., rational) and thematic (i.e., relational) contentions were examined in this chapter. As is evident in our analysis, an antithetical tension exists between the two. The *schematic* perspective confines faith to the pole of autonomy/analytic-rationality; while the *thematic* perspective, to the pole of interdependence/praxis-relationality. Being swayed by these two perspectives, Christian educators proposed two opposing views of Christian formation: one group asserting the human as the object of thinking who is capable of formulating faith analytically, while the other asserting the human as the subject of thinking who is under the influence of praxis-consciousness.[35] Although both contentions seem to offer clear systematic bases of the interface between the intellect and faith, neither perspective offers a complete picture of Christian formation.

Contrary to what Piagetian and Vygotskian scholars are contending, the antithetical tension indicates the dialectic of complementariness rather than of difference. In my opinion, the antithetical tension indicates larger cognitive functions associated with the mind. Between the poles, more than a simple division or conflict, there operates the dialectic of reciprocity between *schema* and *thema*.[36] So rather than trying to limit Christian formation to either pole, we need to understand their dialectic harmony and set forth a holistic framework of Christian formation —which, in my opinion, is possible under the conceptual framework of the dual knowledge theory.[37]

We need to understand that the dual knowledge theory will be an important interpreter of the relationship in that it provides detailed explanations of the relationship between analytic-rational and praxis-relational perspectives of Christian formation (see figure 3.11). Clearly, this idea here is still provisional and arguable. However, we could consider the insights gained from the dual knowledge theory to stabilize, if not deepen, our understanding of Christian formation. So to propose a broader framework to reconceptualize Christian formation, let's understand the dual knowledge theory[38] and discuss its implication to Christian ministry.

In essence, the theoretical underpinning of dual knowledge theory explains the genesis and function of spiritual thoughts; it elucidates how both rational (i.e., schematic) and relational (i.e., thematic) thoughts function in the Christian formation process. What this signifies is that faith, being anchored to the complex inter-working of *schema* and *thema,* is linked to both conceptual and perceptual ways of knowing. Here we need to presuppose two different spheres of reasoning taking place in the mind— the conceptual reasoning in the schematic sphere and the perceptual in the thematic sphere. Although there is a clear difference between the two spheres, we must recognize how they are dialectically related and complement one another in knowing. Philosophically speaking, it is true that both perspectives are antithetical; conceptually speaking, however, they elucidate how Christian formation is grounded in the configural dynamics of the deployment of both analytical and empirical knowledge.

For instance, when a person is growing in faith, two distinct yet harmonizing modes of reasoning work together—comprehension involving *schematic* knowledge where the interiority of truth is conceived based on mediating concepts and apprehension involving *thematic* knowledge where the exteriority of truth is perceived based on spiritual experiences. This is where the person consciously augments knowledge intake by the confluence of divergent intellectual functions: the rationalization process of recognizing the concepts presented before him/her and the empiricalization process of actualizing sensible knowledge obtained in spiritually significant experiences. Upon impression, the mind reacts—that is, intellectually objectifying knowledge of a particular concept or percept whose forms had been conceived or perceived prior; and the whole knowledge that has been internalized will produce meta-epistemic belief, which evokes faith to begin its formation process.

Corporate worship is a good example for us to consider. Besides the spiritual experience of honoring and glorifying God, worship, as a spiritually significant activity, provides in our consciousness a variety of conceptual (such as truth, value, idea, narratives, attitudes, music, etc.) and perceptual (such as motion, touch, interaction, people, objects, etc.) experiences, which come to us in a form of reality that can be conceived and perceived with our mind. As we experience the given spiritual reality, our mind naturally reflects, analyzes, and objectifies the worship experience as first sensible, then as intellective knowledge, which afterwards becomes a *source (or foundational) idea* for spiritual thoughts. After numerous verifications, spiritual thoughts are then converted to axiomatics, attributing to the genesis of faith.

To all intents and purposes, the dual knowledge theory clarifies some under-explored issues surrounding Christian formation; it explains the triadic relationship of *schema*, *thema*, and faith. The argument here implicitly suggests that spiritual life is not a mere intellectual or perceptual experience but both. It involves a holistic engagement of the mind and heart that allows us to anchor theoretical and praxis knowledge to our faith—theoretical knowledge generating the concept-driven faith and praxis knowledge, the experience-driven faith. It is through this process of anchoring holistic knowledge to faith that people experience spiritual growth. However, many Christian educators are still divided between rational and empirical persuasions, seeking to figure out what epistemic mode of thinking might best work for them. Many are wandering between reductionist and constructivist models of nurture—the former calls for a didactic, content-driven, teacher-centered, and highly rationalistic method of nurture; and the latter calls for a dialogic, context-driven, student-centered, and highly relational model of nurture, respectively (see figure 3.11). We must understand that neither position offers a complete picture of the relationship between the intellect and faith.

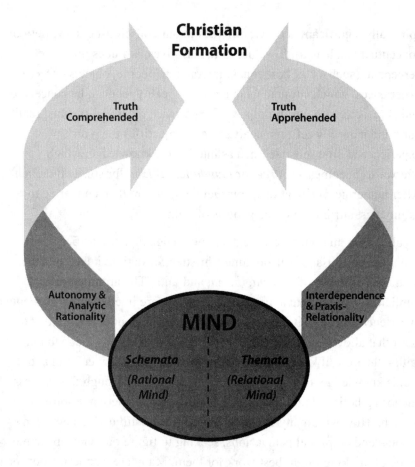

Figure 3.11: Model of Christian Formation

Pastoral and Educational Implications

Given the integrated approach to Christian formation discussed previously in this chapter, several implications for the education ministry of the church can be derived. The most obvious implication is a cautionary note. As tempting as it may be, we cannot equate intellectual development with Christian formation since this chapter has made it obvious that faith is more than intellect. Perhaps the most general is that teaching must be intellectually challenging. More specifically, teaching should aim at challenging the equilibration or balance in the mind of the student. This is a matter of engaging the existing schemes but also introducing new ones into the mind of the student. Likewise, teaching and learning are communal activities, requiring community interaction and participation to fully promote the formation of Christlikeness.

For Children:

Abstractions for a child under 12 must always be tied to a concrete point since cognitive stages control what the child can learn. Until children reach the final stage of logical thinking (i.e., around 12), the inception, retention, or even rejection of knowledge is limited by their cognitive capabilities. For this reason, the teaching materials and learning activities used in class should entail the appropriate level of cognitive and motor skills of which children are capable. Expecting children to learn what is beyond their existing cognitive abilities should definitely be avoided such as teaching the origin and nature of evil, the debate concerning the New Millennium (e.g., Postmil vs. Amil) or dichotomism vs. trichotomism.

Focus on one central lesson for children under seven, and avoid multi-symbolic abstractions. Young children's learning is limited by one-dimensional abstraction (e.g., God is my Father). The theological concepts that are highly abstract and symbolic, which often demand multi-dimensional abstractions, will be hence difficult for young children to comprehend (e.g., fire representing God's presence (Exodus 3:2; Hebrews 12:29); Christ as God's glory (Ezekiel 1:28; 2 Corinthians 4:6); water representing the Spirit (John 4:13-14, 7:37-39); the Four Horsemen (Revelation 19); the 144,000 (Revelation 7). Teachers should keep in mind children's inability to conserve highly abstract concepts.

Meaningful learning is necessary for later abstract thinking. Can you teach children deep theological concepts? Most likely NO; but you can teach meaningful Bible lessons, which enable them to develop theological constructs later in life. Unlike adults who categorize concepts around abstract principles (e.g., presupposition, thesis, belief, etc.), children organize concepts around a set of meaningful ideas, which functions as a frame of reference for classifying (e.g., good friends who play with me vs. bad friends who do not play with me). More so than in adults, meaning-laden lessons will increase children's Bible knowledge and engender the ideological basis of faith.

Use storytelling as a teaching tool. Storytelling is perhaps the oldest form of teaching technique. While there are many creative techniques available for teachers, the use of storytelling elicits a conscious understanding of the lessons being taught. Every culture, including that of the Ancient Hebrews, used storytelling as a main vehicle to transmit the tales of their history, traditions, and beliefs to succeeding generations (Deuteronomy 6:4-9). We ought to use this ageless tool when communicating truth to children. Storytelling is a power pedagogical tool that engages children's minds and enables them to make sense of seemingly arduous facts and principles.

For Adolescents and Adults:

Adult education concerns participants, not pails! Adults tend to prefer active participatory learning, which helps them move beyond a simple reception of ideas toward a new discovery. This idea is based on the adult learning theory, which assumes that adults are self-directed and tend to be less content-driven than children.[39] Although didactic teaching still has a role to play in adult ministry today, pastors/teachers should incorporate the curricula that integrates problem-solving lessons and interactions. A mere transmission of content will not help adults know and experience the truth of God.

Allow for questions and dialogue to correct misconceptions and to gain correct conceptions. Dialogue is a process of discovery and transformation. It entails an uninhibited flow of shared meanings and consequently enhances learning. Since dialogic learning challenges adults' assumptions, encourages critical thinking, and generates heartfelt knowledge, adult teachers should definitely utilize this informal method of teaching. After all, the pattern of Christ's discipleship ministry was highly dialogical.

Ask thought-provoking questions and encourage self-reflection. Self-reflection is the crux of adult learning. Self-reflection helps learners break away from a teacher-dependent mode to a dynamic, continuous mode of learning. Since Jesus, in His earthly ministry, asked countless questions and challenged people to reflect on the principles He taught (John 3:1-21; 4:4-42; Matthew 6:25-28,30; 16:13-15; Luke 2:41-52, 7:41-42; Mark 7:1-23),[40] we ought to do the same. Incorporate questions that prompt critical reflection, soul-searching, commitment, and application.

Lastly, focus on transformation, not just transmission. As Kingdom workers, the primary concern of our teaching ought to be on the transformation of lives, not just on the transmission of scriptural content. The goal of adult education is to cause a pervasive shift of perspectives and understanding, making a vital impact in people's lives.

Conclusion

In order to promote holistic Christian formation, nurture, denoting holistic pedagogy, has to become a central methodology in the church and school. One important feature of this pedagogy is on the dialogic impartation of the whole knowledge-involving theory (i.e., theoria), practice (i.e., poiesis), and critical-reflection (i.e., praxis). Teaching under this perspective focuses on dialogic learning where the synthesis of both conceptual and perceptual knowledge leads to transformation and growth.

Moreover, because the pedagogy of nurture is relationally driven, it demands, most of all, that teaching be done in a koinonic context, relationally—just as Christ, the master teacher, taught His disciples. In order to teach relationally, however, the institutional context of which students are a part needs to become a koinonic community where teachers function as mentors and role models rather than mere instructors. Such teaching then promotes interaction and cooperation between students and teachers, creating an unbreakable bond in Jesus Christ.

What people need is holistic nurture from which the complete knowledge of faith is conceived and perceived. Only then will our people understand the true picture of faith and be able to grow into the image and likeness of Jesus Christ who is the Source and Perfecter of our faith (Hebrews 12:2).

Reflection Questions

1. Explain the relationship between the essential and experiential domains of faith.

2. What is intellect and how does it grow? Explain based on Piaget's theory of cognitive development.

3. How does the Bible describe the human intellect? The Christian tradition typically contends that the human intellect has been hopelessly distorted by the fall, and we do not have the full capacity of the human intellect. Agree or disagree? Explain.

4. How do you think the human intellect functions in relation to the ministry of the Holy Spirit?

5. What is your view of the relation between intellectual development and Christian spiritual formation?

ENDNOTES

[1] The author originally published some portions of this chapter as "Cognition and Faith Formation," *Christian Education Journal*, 5 (2): 1-23. Copyright 2007, used here with permission of the publisher.

[2] Henry George Liddell and Robert Scott, *A Greek-English Lexicon* (Oxford, UK: The Clarendon Press, 1968), 789.

[3] Ibid.

[4] Gerard Holton, *Thematic Components: Thematic Origins of Scientific Thoughts* (Cambridge, Massachusetts: Harvard University Press, 1973, retrieved October 27, 2005, from http://www.autodidactproject.org/other/themata1.html.); Sergi Moscovici and Georges Vignaux, "The Concept of *Themata*" in K. Duveen, ed., *Social Representations: Explorations in Social Psychology* (Cambridge, UK: Polity Press, 2000), 156-83; Heinz Streib, "Faith Development Theory Revisited: The Religious Styles Perspective," *The International Journal for the Psychology and Religion*, 11 (3): 143-58.

[5] Moscovici and Vignaux, "The Concept of Themata," 177.

[6] James Balswick, Pamela King, and Kevin Reimer, T*he Reciprocating Self: Human Development in Theological Perspective* (Downers Grove, Illinois: IVP, 2005); James R. Estep, Jr., "Spiritual Formation as Social: Toward Vygotskian Developmental Perspective," *Religious Education*, 97 (2002): 141-64; Cynthia J. Neal, "The Power of Vygotsky," *Nurture That Is Christian*, James Wilhoit and John Dettoni, eds. (Grand Rapids: Baker, 1995), 123-37; Streib, "Faith Development Theory Revisited"; Heinz Streib, "Faith Development Research Revisited: Accounting for Diversity in Structure, Content, and Narrativity of Faith" *The International Journal for the Psychology of Religion*, 15 (2): 99-121.

[7] Jean Piaget, *The Psychology of the Child* (New York: Basic Books, 1969); Jean Piaget, *Genetic Epistemology* (New York: Columbia University Press, 1970); Jean Piaget, *The Child and Reality: Problem of Genetic Psychology* (New York: Grossman, 1972).

[8] James Riley Estep, Illustration from CE605: Human Development and Ministry (2009), Lincoln Christian University (Lincoln, Illinois).

[9] Jack Snowman and Robert F. Beihler, *Psychology Applied to Teaching* (New York: Houghton Mifflin Company, 1994), 39.

[10] James Riley Estep, Illustration from CE605: Human Development and Ministry (2009), Lincoln Christian University (Lincoln, Illinois).

[11] Ibid.

[12] Cf. Serge Moscovici, "The History and Actuality of Social Representations," *The Psychology of the Social* (Cambridge: Cambridge University Press, 1998), 209-47.

[13] William Frawley, *Vygotsky and Cognitive Science: Language and the Unification of the Social and Computational Mind* (Cambridge, Massachusetts: Harvard University Press, 1997), 89.

[14] Jonathan Tudge, "Vygotsky, the Zone of Proximal Development, and Peer Collaboration: Implications for Classroom Practice" *Vygotsky and Education: Instructional Implications and Applications of Sociohistorical Psychology,* Luis C. Moll, ed., (Cambridge, New York: Cambridge University Press, 1990), 158.

[15] Frawley, *Vygotsky and Cognitive Science*, 90-1.

[16] Uwe Flick, *The Psychology of the Social* (Cambridge: Cambridge University Press, 1998), 98-9.

[17] Alex Kozulin, *Vygotsky's Psychology: A Biography of Ideas* (New York: Harvester Wheatsheaf, 1990), 110-50.

[18] Lev S. Vygotsky, *Mind in Society: The Development of Higher Psychological Process*, M. Cole, V. John-Steiner, S. Scribner, and E. Souberman, eds. (Cambridge, Massachusetts: Harvard University Press, 1978), 84.

[19] Vygotsky, *Mind in Society*, 87.

[20] Elena L Grigorenko, "Mastering Tools of the Mind in School (Trying Out Vygotsky's Ideas in Classrooms)" in *Intelligence, Instruction, and Assessment: Theory into Practice*, Robert J. Sternberg, ed. (New Haven, Connecticut: Yale University, 1998), 211.

[21] Vygotsky, *Mind in Society*, 90-1.

[22] James Riley Estep, Illustration from CE605: *Human Development and Ministry* (2009), Lincoln Christian University (Lincoln, Illinois).

[23] Vygotsky, *Mind in Society*.

[24] The following few pages are an adaptation of a portion from James Riley Estep, Jr., "Biblical Principles of Christian Education," *A Theology for Christian Education*, James Riley Estep, Jr., Michael J. Anthony, and Gregg R. Allison, eds. (Nashville: Broadman & Holman, 2008), 55-62.

[25] Daniel, J. Estes, *Hear My Son: Teaching and Learning in Proverbs* (Downer's Grove, Illinois: InterVarsity Press, 1997), particularly 101-24.

[26] James A. Crenshaw, *Education in Ancient Israel* (New York: Doubleday, 1998), 115-38.

[27] Charles Melchert, *Wise Teaching: Biblical Wisdom and Educational Ministry* (Harrisburg, Pennsylvania: Trinity Press International, 1998), particularly 47-58, 91-101, and 134-38.

[28] Donn Morgan, *The Making of the Sage: Biblical Wisdom and Contemporary Culture* (Harrisburg, Pennsylvania: Trinity Press International, 2002).

[29] Nili Shupak, "Learning Methods in Ancient Israel," *Vetus Testamentum*, 53 (3): 416-26.

[30] Ibid., 424; cf. Roy B. Zuck, "Hebrew Words for 'Teach'," *Bibliotheca Sacra*, 121 (483): 228-35.

[31] Cf. Mark Wilson with Jason Oden, *Mastering New Testament Greek Vocabulary through Semantic Domains* (Grand Rapids: Baker Book House, 2003) for a complete listing of terms related to human psychological faculties, including those related to learning.

[32] John Calvin, "The Way We Receive the Grace of Christ" in *Calvin: Institutes of Christian Religion*, J. T. McNeill, ed. (Philadelphia: The Westminster Press, 1960), 551.

[33] J. P. Moreland and Klaus Issler, *Releasing Faith: Transforming Belief into Confident Expectation* (Downers Grove, Illinois: InterVarsity, 2008); Wolfgang Pannenberg, *Systematic Theology*, G. Bromiley, trans. (Grand Rapids: Eerdmans, 1991).

[34] Estep, 2002; Neal, 1995, 2003; Streib, 2001, 2005.

[35] David Elkind,, *The Child and Society: Essays in Applied Child Development* (New York: Oxford University Press, 1979); Estep, "Spiritual Formation as Social"; James W. Fowler, *Stages of Faith* (San Francisco: Harper and Row, 1981); Neal, "The Power of Vygotsky"; Cynthia J. Neal, "A Parenting Style for Nurturing Christian Wisdom" in *Limning the Psyche: Explorations in Christian Psychology*, R. Roberts and M. Talbot, eds. (Eugene, Oregon: Wipf and Stock, 2003), 165-85; Streib, "Faith Development Theory Revisited"; Streib, "Faith Development Research Revisited"; M. M. Wilcox, *Developmental Journey* (Nashville: Abingdon, 1979).

[36] Elkind, *The Child and Society*; Estep, "Spiritual Formation as Social"; Fowler, *Stages of Faith*; Neal, "The Power of Vygotsky"; Neal, "A Parenting Style for Nurturing Christian Wisdom"; Piaget, *The Mind of the Child*; Piaget, "Genetic Epistemology"; Streib, "Faith Development Theory Revisited"; Streib, "Faith Development Research Revisited"; Vygotsky, *Mind in Society*; Wilcox, *Developmental Journey*.

[37] Ann C. Baker, Pamela Jensen, and David Kolb, *Conversational Learning: An Experiential Approach to Knowledge Creation* (Westport, Connecticut: Quorum Books, 2002); William James, *Essays in Radical Empiricism* (New York: Longmans, Green and Co., 1947).

[38] Baker, Jensen, and Kolb, *Conversational Learning; James, Essays in Radical Empiricism*.

[39] Malcolm M. Knowles, *Andragogy in Action* (Houston, Texas: Gulf Publishing, 1984).

[40] Roy B. Zuck, *Teaching as Jesus Taught* (Grand Rapids, Michigan: Baker Books, 1995).

CHAPTER 4

PERSONALITY DEVELOPMENT AND CHRISTIAN FORMATION

By Jonathan H. Kim

In a conversation some years ago, I recall a church member expressing disdain for people's overuse of the word *personality*. We hear this buzz word often. He asked, "What is personality? What does it really mean?" And he also added, "The word is used a lot both inside and outside the church, but I really do not know what it truly means." Due to people's overuse and, in many cases, blatant misuse, the concept of *personality* has become elusive and meaningless.

Most people, including Christians, do not realize the significance of the term—especially in relation to human nature. Misguided by secular psychology, people view personality as temperament or character traits, which is partially correct but not sufficiently so. To our amazement, the same confusion exists—even among Christian teachers and pastors. Variations exist along denomination lines and across ministry lines. Rarely do people apply an accurate definition to explain the concept. While a growing number of Christians are engaged in the study of personality as a broad psychological category, there is an urgent need to understand this concept in relation to the theology of anthropology.

Personality—as will be explained later—denotes the characteristic attribute of the human soul in its natural state, representing the enduring personhood that typifies a person from another. We will study this concept in relation to spirituality, which is the characteristic attribute of the regenerated soul. For the sake of clarity, we will refer to personality as the innate attribute and spirituality as the imputed attribute of the soul. Additionally, the term *attribute*—as used in this chapter—will mean an "essential characteristic" of a being that is either inherent or ascribed by God.

This chapter, which is conceptual in its nature, seeks to bring into focus an idea of personality as the substantial domain of the soul. The structure of knowledge considered in this paper is built on the Christian doctrine of humanity and sanctification. The purpose is to understand the quintessential meanings of personality and spirituality as they relate to

Christian formation. Although the chapter discussion might sound premature and overly broad in scope, it is, however, a starting point to guide our study of personality—especially its relation to spirituality.

The chapter divides into six related sections. Following the introduction, the first section presents a theoretical overview of Erikson's and Marcia's theories of personality development. The second section offers biblical and theological insights on personality and spirituality. The third section elaborates on the interrelationship of personality and spirituality in Christian formation. The fourth and fifth sections provide ministry implications. Then the final section concludes the chapter discussion.

Theory of Personality Development

Erik Erikson's psychosocial development theory offers an important overview of personality development. In his book *Child and Society*,[1] Erikson provides helpful insight into how a person develops an understanding of self as a unique individual—i.e., sense of self—and finds identity as he learns to manage various challenges that life brings. To a large extent, this theory is about the ontological quest of self in search of its personhood.

Although various concepts are associated with Erikson's theory, the term *psychosocial* is mainly used to describe his theory—*psyche* referring to the rational dimension of a person [Gk. *psyche* means "soul"] and *social* referring to the relational dimension of a person. The theory is not about mere description of personality growth; it asserts the development of a person is correlated to the interaction between one's mind and experiences. This premise offers an ontological perspective regarding the nature of a person as a self-conscious being who is capable of thinking, feeling, and willing—just like the biblical notion of the human soul.

While the age division for each stage may vary considerably from person to person, the general tendencies and characteristics of personality development seem appropriate for the majority of people. According to

Erikson, a successful growth of person involves eight developmental outcomes (i.e., categories): (1) self-awareness, (2) self-autonomy, (3) self-worth, (4) self-confidence, (5) self-definition, (6) self-competence and intimacy, (7) self-fulfillment, and (8) self-integration (see figure 4.4a). Each outcome corresponds to the eight life stages noted in figure 4.1 It is critical to note, at this point, that the definition of stages in Erikson is different than those in Piaget (chapter 3). While both men used the term *stages*, Erikson's stages were not as uniform as Piaget's. In Erikson's stages, one can emerge in ascendency to one of two general poles. For example, in stage 1, a child emerges either leaning psychologically toward trust or leaning toward mistrust; whereas in Piaget, a child's cognitive ability is static and uniform and each individual progresses through the same stages, emerging with the same level of cognitive ability. Hence, Erikson's theory claims an individual has to successfully complete each life stage to progress toward the next one; otherwise, the unsolved issues from the previous stage will reappear as problems in life. The following section summarizes the main features of Erikson's theory. To aid a succinct understanding of the theory, each developmental stage will be interpreted.

Self-awareness Stage (Infancy). Developing a sense of self (i.e., self-awareness) and trust is the first formational outcome of personality development (see figure 4.1). As explained by Erikson, infants during the first 18 months of life learn to understand their selfhood and its relatedness to others. During this stage, infants' understanding of selfhood is directly related to the quality of the relationship they have with parents. Consistent, reliable, and responsive parental love will allow infants to develop a deep-seated sense of self and trust. According to Erikson, if infants do not have affirming relationships with parents, there will be a false sense of self, which leads to self-doubt, frustration, and mistrust. A healthy outcome is forming a trusting relationship with parents. Developing a positive sense of self during infancy sets the stage for a life-long trusting relationship.

Life Stage	Basic Conflict	Outcome	Description
Infancy	Trust vs. Mistrust	Self-awareness	Develop a sense of self and trust
Toddler	Autonomy vs. Shame/Doubt	Self-autonomy	Develop a sense of independence
Early Childhood	Initiative vs. Guilt	Self-worth	Develop a sense of significance
Childhood	Industry vs. Inferiority	Self-confidence	Develop a sense of social competency
Adolescence	Identity vs. Role Confusion	Self-definition	Develop a sense of identity
Young Adulthood	Intimacy vs. Isolation	Self-competence & Intimacy	Develop a sense of intimacy
Middle Adulthood	Generativity vs. Stagnation	Self-fulfillment	Develop a sense of altruism
Late Adulthood	Integrity vs. Despair	Self-integration	Develop a sense of coherent and integrated self

Figure 4.1: Erikson's Psychosocial Development

Self-autonomy Stage (Toddlerhood). Developing a sense of autonomy is the second formational outcome of personality development (see Figure 4.1). Autonomy means responsibility, and responsibility means self-reliance and independence. During this stage, toddlers learn to think, will, and act based on self-directed ideas and opinions. As they progress through this life stage, the positive sense of self (i.e., self-esteem) will generate self-confidence and serve as an impetus toward self-autonomy. If toddlers are denied their autonomy, shame and doubt will emerge in life with a sense of inadequacy.

Self-worth Stage (Early Childhood). Developing a sense of worth is the third formational outcome of personality development (see figure 4.1). Younger children, during this stage, embark on a series of initiatives to master the world. They learn the basic principles and skills necessary to understand the relationship between intent and initiatives and between purpose and action. Based on social relationships, children will soon realize this world has the capacity to grant a sense of purpose and significance or to thrust them into a state of confusion and inferiority. As the world unfolds before their eyes, children learn to actualize all of their potential and exercise their will to develop a sense of worth.

As suggested by Erikson, the articulated knowledge of self and measures of self-worth exist alongside the attainment of purposeful goals, so children need to be nurtured with affirmation and the meaningful goals that can be attained.

Self-confidence Stage (Childhood). Developing self-confidence is the fourth formational outcome of personality development (see figure 4.1). Children, during this stage, become more aware of their individuality and seek to deepen their personhood by undertaking and accomplishing various challenges that come their way. Given that confidence is dependent upon the level of competency generated by and situated in positive peer group relationships, friendships become all the more important. As the social world of children expands, parents—although still important—no longer play a major part in children's personality development.

Self-definition Stage (Adolescence). Developing self-identity is the fifth formational outcome of personality development (see figure 4.1). A primary task during this stage is to establish self-definition and form a philosophy of life. Adolescents learn to establish a coherent sense of self as they seek to define who they are and will be in relation to their desired ideological, moral, and sociocultural identities. This includes examining the self-concept infused by parents from the earlier stages of life and examining and experimenting with different self-concepts as they explore to add a proper definition to their existence.

Up to this stage, personality development was relatively passive; they were mostly passive recipients of the outside influence. However, from here onward, adolescents move toward a self-initiated process of managing and defining life. Life definitely becomes more complex and challenging as teens try to grapple with their existential, social, moral, and spiritual questions.

Though adolescents' life patterns are generally idealistic—somewhat removed from reality, they gradually learn to translate ideals into workable actions and experiences. According to Erikson, if self-identity is not successfully established, the identity diffusion will occur. Teen's identity diffusion is characterized by the high degree of confusion over one's identity, of one's beliefs, and of what larger social group one is/will be a part.

Self-intimacy Stage (Early Adulthood). Developing intimacy is the sixth formational outcome of personality development (see figure 4.1). During this stage, young adults' major concern is on establishing independent lives and finding healthy and mutually satisfying relationships. Unlike previous stages, young adults seek to find selfhood in a process of building committed relationships with significant others such as marital partners and close friends. According to Erikson, it is important for young adults to develop deep relational intimacy; otherwise, emotional and relational isolation will occur.

Self-fulfillment and Generativity Stage (Middle Adulthood). Developing self-fulfillment is the seventh formational outcome of personality development (see figure 4.1). Out of concern for others and the world, adults seek to attain an appropriate sense of self. Occupying and focusing on productive work and having meaningful family relationships are the major concerns of mid-lifers. Focuses of midlife are on establishing themselves in society, finding purposefulness and fulfillment, nurturing and contributing to the next generation, and having an ability and a commitment to care for others.

To a large degree, middle adults' life satisfaction and fulfillment depend on the influence they have on family, society, and culture. During these adult years, the inner quest of self-discovery and the outer quest of fulfillment allow adults to find the ontological significance and wholeness in life. If adults face inactivity and purposelessness in life, self-absorption and stagnation will lead to midlife crisis.

Self-integration Stage (Late Adulthood). Developing and experiencing the integration of self are the final formational outcomes of personality development (see figure 4.1). Wisdom marks a new and an important way of thinking about this stage of personhood. Erikson believed that late adulthood is a culmination of personal and social experiences, which result in increased wisdom and self-integrity. Accepting responsibility and facing the consequences for their life decisions and actions are done with life-induced humility.

Significant events, during this stage, are being able to retrospect and find the meaning of life. While accepting the inevitability of death, older adults seek to find a deep sense of contentment with all that is offered by life. A major transition takes place as they introspect, in a positive manner, their life goals and accomplishments. Adults will eventually realize the ultimate meaning of life lies not in external matters but in internal contentment. If older adults feel they have made a significant contribution in life, a sense of integrity will emerge. If, however, they sense their life is marked by purposelessness and incompleteness, existential despair will overcome them. Parenthetically speaking, elderly people who are unable to obtain a sense of meaning will not be able to embrace death with courage and dignity.

James Marcia's Identity Statuses

More current than the work of Erikson is that of James E. Marcia. He represents the next generation of theorists in the Eriksonian camp.[2] While not as elaborate or exhaustive as Erikson's theory, Marcia poses a four-stage progression through which individuals may (or may not) achieve a strong sense of identity.[3] Unlike Erikson, Marcia's theory is not cradle-to-grave but rather deals with the emergence of identity in adolescence through adulthood. Similar to Erikson, Marcia's four stages are driven by psychological crisis and combined with pendulum swings of weak-to-strong commitments of ideas—with the pendulum swing providing the opportunity to advance the identity achievement of the individual—as reflected in figure 4.2.

Identity Status	Description	Identity Crisis Level	Commitment to Ideals
Diffusion	Avoidance of responsibility; impulsive; Low self-esteem; avoids commitments to parents, school, and work	Low due to avoidance of responsibility	Weak; subject to impulse, current situation, and positive/negative feedback
Foreclosure	Adopts the values and goals of others such as parents or significant other; very assured due to affiliation with others; authoritarian and sense of superiority over others	Low due to attaching identity to that of others, especially parents or guardians	Strong; having adopted and affirmed the commitments already made by their parents

Identity Status	Description	Identity Crisis Level	Commitment to Ideals
Moratorium	Begins to have thoughts of uncertainty; rejection or weakening of parental commitments; begins to exhibit short-term commitments to relationships, school, tasks	Moderate; begins to ask identity-related questions to self	Weak; the previous answers from parents no longer provide a response to all of their life questions
Achievement	Makes their commitments on their terms; determines their values, establishes commitments and relationships, and assumes responsibility for decision making	High due to complete engagement with identity crisis; has resolved it by assuming responsibility for making choices—given multiple alternatives	Strong; has made commitments by individual choice

Figure 4.2: Marcia's Identity Statuses[4]

Marcia's work has proven helpful for those who serve in high school and higher education since much of what he describes is encountered during the advising process with students, e.g., choosing or changing an academic major or describing an indecisive career path—as opposed to those who have wrestled and chosen a direction in life. His theory reminds us we are not just academic advisors but advising adolescents and young adults about their personality development, the shape of their personal identity.

Biblical and Theological Insights on the Human Person

The Bible teaches us the human person—made up of body and soul—is an embodiment of distinct attributes and capacities that reflects the image of

God (Lat., *imago Dei*, Genesis 1:26-27). The centrality of this doctrine serves as the key indicator of human personhood in that it explains rational, personal, moral, and spiritual characteristics within the human soul.[5] Similar to the notion of communicable attributes of God, the four attributes, which are unified by the higher order of internal relations, characterize and constitute human personhood. In the remainder of this chapter, we will discuss two of the four attributes (i.e., personality and spirituality). The issues of intellect and morality are discussed separately in chapters 3 and 5.

Human Soul

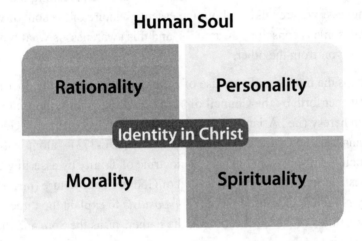

Figure 4.3: Characteristic Attributes of the Human Soul

Personality as the Innate Attribute of the Soul

Biblically speaking, the word *personality* comes from two Greek words, *prosopon* (2 Corinthians 1:11; 10:7) and *hypostasis* (Hebrews 1:3). *Prosopon*, which means persona, face, or person in Greek, refers to the extrinsic nature of a person—i.e., the *manifested image* or *countenance* of a person. In general, *prosopon* suggests the outer appearance or form in which one's nature is manifested[6]; it implies a more outward appearance or external conception of one's individuality, namely personality.

Hypostasis is another concept that explains the notion of personality. *Hypostasis*—from which we get the English words *substance* and *subsistence*—is a compound word in Greek: *hypo* means "under" and *stasis* means "standing." The word literally means "that which lies under" or "something that supports from below." *Hypostasis* signifies the *characteristic attribute of a person* that underlies all of his ontological manifestations. Theologically speaking, personality indicates a constitutive element that lies under and defines what we are like, meaning our beingness. We are talking about the essential nature of the soul of which the person has conscious awareness, and this awareness is what typifies one person from the other.

Perhaps the most significant use of *hypostasis* is found in the doctrine of Trinity set forth by the Council of Nicaea (AD 325). In response to the Arian heresy (i.e., Arianism), which denied the triune nature of God, Athanasius, the Greek Bishop of Alexandria (296-373)—along with the council members—established the doctrine of Trinity by asserting three subsistent personalities (*hypostases*) of God with one nature (*ousia*). The early church leaders used the word *hypostasis* to explain the three distinct personalities of the Godhead: God the Father, Jesus the Son, and the Holy Spirit.

Concisely summing, personality represents the characteristic attribute with which all humans are born. It is a distinct individuality that constitutes and typifies one person from another.[7] This distinctiveness persists over time and space—even into our eternality.

Now that we understand the meaning of personality, we will shift our focus to the concept of spirituality, the *pneuma* domain of the soul that is engendered when a person repents and invites Jesus Christ to be his Lord and Savior. Unlike personality, spirituality is not innate to humans; it represents the imputed attribute of the regenerated soul following justification (see figure 4.4b).

Spirituality as the Imputed Attribute of the Soul

Before we move further with the chapter discussion, we must remember the scope and extent of the term *spirituality* is so vast and varied that it is difficult to define it in a few words. It is amazing how frequently the term is used (or overused) and could mean so many different things. While a full examination of the term would be a great benefit, due to the limited focus of the chapter, our discussion will be confined to the attribute aspect of spirituality.

One of the important truths about the human soul is that it is not only personal but also (can be) spiritual. Sometimes spirituality is described as a separate nature within a person, while others consider it as one of the characteristic attributes within a regenerated soul. For your information, the perspective of spirituality being asserted in this section is based on the dichotomous view of human nature. Dichotomism explains spirituality as not a separate part of the person but as a characteristic attribute ascribed to a soul by the Holy Spirit at conversion.

Although we do not want to sound too presumptuous, suffice it to say that spirituality is the characteristic attribute of the soul that is imputed to those who are born of the Spirit through the atoning work of Jesus Christ and who are grounded in God's grace (John 6:44; Hebrews 11:1; 12:2; Romans 1:8; 8:14; Jude 3; Ephesians 2:8-10; 1 John 2:14; Philippians 3:10-11; James 2:26). As a person invites Christ to be his Lord and Savior, the soul, which was dead in sin, is revived and begins to experience the transforming work of the Holy Spirit who comes to indwell within a person. For the sake of clarity, let's use two "C" words, *condition* and *connection*, to understand the nature and relational components of spirituality.

Concerning the human spiritual *condition*, while the term *spirituality* means "wind" (Genesis 8:1), "breath" (Genesis 2:7; 6:17; Isaiah 40:7), "divine power" (Judges 3:10), or "spirit" (Genesis 1:2; Matthew 12:18; Romans 8:9; Ezekiel 37:5-6), the term generally signifies the imputed property of the soul (*psuche*) (1 Thessalonians 5:23; Luke 8:55) in its *pneuma* state.8 The term spirit—in many incidents in the Bible—signifies the substance nature or the spiritual condition of the regenerated soul[9] (Genesis 35:18; Psalm 31:5; Luke 23:46; John 12:27; 13:21; Acts 15:26).

Concerning the spiritual *connection*, the term *spirituality* refers to the spiritual relationship between God and human beings. It indicates, as defined by Robert Saucy, "an intimate, personal, and experiential relationship with God that is attained through an individualistic contemplative development of the interior life that makes significant use of various ascetical disciplines."[10] Basically, spirituality here refers to the quality of the *pneuma* relationship that allows people to experience their ontological wholeness through God.

The above views of spirituality are consistent with what evangelicals have been asserting for centuries, noting immaterial and relational dimensions of the soul. Assumed in the definition is the biblical stance on conversion (i.e., justification) through which spirituality is gained. In what follows, we will explore Christian formation by examining the growth that the Holy Spirit facilitates in personal and spiritual dimensions of the soul.

A Christian Approach to Personal and Spiritual Development: Christian Formation

Grounded in the image of God, the human soul has the nature that reflects the essential characteristics of the tri-personal God. Applied uniquely to the constitution of the human being, the soul represents the essential "*whoness*" of the person, while personality and spirituality represent the characteristic "*whatness*" of the soul. For example, how we perceive others is largely due to the individual soul projecting its statehood through the identifiable qualities such as personality and spirituality. Without personality, an individual would be a being without the particular quality that makes him a person; and without spirituality, an individual would be an unregenerated soul—lost and destitute, being apart from God.

Relating our discussion to the Christian sanctification process, the union leading the increasing synthesis between personality and spirituality is what we mean by Christian formation. As an unregenerated soul seeks to find its essential statehood through Jesus Christ and repents, God redeems the person and attributes a new property (i.e., spirituality) to a person and sends His Spirit to come and indwell in the depth of the human soul (Ezekiel 36:26). At the root of this ontological mystery lies the unitive condition to which personality and spirituality proceed; they begin a mutually supporting relationship with one another, thus giving a new consciousness (i.e., new heart) and statehood (i.e., new spirit) (Ezekiel 36:26; John 3:3; 2 Corinthians 5:17) to the person. This gaining of new consciousness and statehood, where the old self becomes the new self, is what we mean by conversion (Galatians 4:6; Romans 5:5; 8:14-17; Colossians 3:9-10; Ephesians 4:20) (see figure 4.4b).

At conversion, a person, who was in a stage of spiritual deadness (i.e., natural [*psuchikos*] person, 1 Corinthians 2:14), becomes alive; regains his spiritual consciousness (i.e., spiritual [*pneumatikos*] person, 1 Corinthians 2:15); and begins to commune with God (Romans 5:12,14-21) (see figure 4.3c). As the person seeks to walk with God, the Holy Spirit—with the goal of fully restoring the cohesive selfhood—works directly within the person's heart (Romans 8:16,9:1). The Holy Spirit constantly communicates God's intent and purpose and draws the person close to God (John 12:32; 14:16; 16:13; Romans 8:14-17,26-28; Ephesians 3:16).

The end result of the lifelong process of formation is the full fusion of personality and spirituality (see figure 4.4d) where the totality of personhood is finally achieved and realized. The regaining of this totality implies that the soul's attributes and capacities are now fully restored. This momentous moment is where the soul, which was fragmented under the original sin and existed in a natural state, becomes the completely renewed self who reflects the personhood of Christ (Hebrews 5:14; 1 John 3:2) (see figure 4.4c). Being in such a statehood, the person now realizes his whole self—a complete-I (i.e., new self) who resembles Jesus Christ in every aspect of humanity (likeness, Gk. *homoios*, of Christ, 1 John 3:2) (see figure 4.4c).

Now free from the bondage of sin, he enjoys the fullness of Jesus Christ (Colossians 2:9; Ephesians 3:18-21; Romans 8:17; John 1:16). We are talking about the end result of Christian formation called glorification where sanctification finds its ultimate fulfillment.

Until we reach the heavenly realm, Christian formation will continue. As long as we are living here on Earth, there will be a continuous responsibility to get involved in the process of renewal and formation. With God-induced humility, we need to daily move forward until our personhood is fully restored. Listen to Paul's message to Philippians in Philippians 3:12-14. How we desperately need the perspective that he had toward Christ-centered spiritual formation.

"Not that I have already reached [the goal] or am already fully mature, but I make every effort to take hold of it because I also have been taken hold of by Christ Jesus. Brothers, I do not consider myself to have taken hold of it. But one thing I do: Forgetting what is behind and reaching forward to what is ahead, I pursue as my goal the prize promised by God's heavenly call in Christ Jesus."

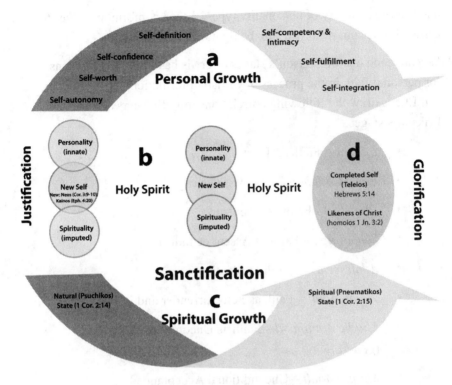

Figure 4.4 Christian Sanctification

Having established the biblical knowledge of personality and spirituality, we now turn to ministry implications and elaborate on implications for Christian formation and ministry.

Implications for Christian Formation

The implications of personality development theory and Christian formation can be centered on four intersects. *First*, Christian formation does not mean the omission of one's personality. Far too often individuals are convinced that, to become a Christian, means one gives up their individuality, their personality. This is simply untrue. We see many different personality types in the Scriptures. Even among Jesus' disciples, one can see a variety of personality types. As we conform ourselves to Christ, it does not mean we stop being ourselves.

Second, each one of Erikson's stages of crisis has direct implications for personal faith in the process of Christian formation. Aden, Benner, and Ellens draw the following correlations to faith from each of Erikson's stages.[11]

- *Infancy*—Faith as Trust

- *Early Childhood*—Faith as Courage

- *Play Age*—Faith as Obedience

- *School Age*—Faith as Assent or Industry

- *Adolescence*—Faith as Identity

- *Young Adult*—Faith as Self-Surrender and Intimacy with God

- *Middle Adulthood*—Faith as Unconditional Caring (*generativity*)

- *Mature Adult*—Unconditional Acceptance

Such an understanding of faith is dynamic in its development—with a distinctive form of faith emerging from each of the stages of personality development throughout the lifespan of the individual.

Third, James Marcia's identity statuses have some bearing on one's commitment to Christ. While not intending to address Christian commitment specifically, as one reviews the four identity statuses outlined by James Marcia, one can see how, as one develops a genuine relationship with Jesus Christ, that his commitment and identity achievement likewise increase. Similar to faith development, identity is first seen in relation to parents and significant others in one's life but later must be adopted by the individual for himself or herself. In this matter, Marcia's approach to achievement of identity status somewhat correlates to the four stages of faith development proposed by Neville and Westerhoff.[12] Ultimately, the individual who reaches identity achievements makes his own commitment, having his own relationship with Jesus Christ.

Fourth, Christian formation may, in part, arise from crisis. The Scriptures don't actually refer to psychological crises—as in the sense Erikson or Marcia described, but frequently it speaks of the growth potential of overcoming temptation (1 Corinthians 10:13) and trials (James 1:12; 2 Corinthians 8:2). While doubt is never spoken of in a positive light, it is always acknowledged as a reality we all face but must overcome to move on to higher levels of faith (Matthew 21:21; Mark 11:23; James 1:6; Jude 22). When individuals are asked to relay their personal testimonies, how many times do some of the most compelling testimonies come from those who have seemed to overcome obstacles in their lives, both external and internal, and presented a distinctive Christian witness? While crisis is not the only means of facilitating Christian formation, it is indeed at least one contributing factor of not only our identity achievement but also of our faith formation as Christians.

Implications for Christian Education and Ministry

Perhaps the most immediate implication in reference to this dimension of development is that the church must provide guidance for individuals. Individual need mentors, examples, and corrective discipline to navigate through the stages of identity achievement. The church stands in a unique position to provide such counsel—whether it be provided directly or indirectly through other caregivers. These mentors should understand the frustration innate to each level and be able to give wise counsel to individuals as they traverse through each stage of life.

A second implication is that we are all engaged in navigating these stages of crisis. No one is exempt from them. As such, as Christian educators, we should demonstrate respect for the person and his present level of psychological crisis. We can do this by providing guidance through questions and issues of life, working with his experience, *not* negating it. For example, if children are adopted into a family out of the foster care system, they come into the family not as infants but as youths with memories, traumas, moral dilemmas, etc. A parent cannot simply dismiss these earlier experiences but must help his child address them in a positive light and learn from his past as a means of providing strength for his future.

Third, permit success! The classic Chucky Cheese commercial "Where a kid can be a kid!" speaks it all. Children need to experience positive achievement and feedback to feel "good" about one's self. This does not mean we do not discipline or criticize; but it must be constructive discipline and criticism, not physically abusive or badgering of a child, which only degrades one's personal development.

Fourth, each stage provides the Christian educator with an opportunity to point him toward God. With each stage of psychological crisis, we can remind the individual that: "For no matter how many promises God has made, they are 'Yes' in Christ. And so through him the 'Amen' is spoken by us to the glory of God" (2 Corinthians 1:20). As such, Christ becomes our constant counselor and guide through the various stages of identity achievement. Christian educators must point people toward Christ as a consistent focus of their life and identity as individuals.

Next, recognize that behaviors, both good and bad, often reflect an identity issue. It is too cliché to say, "It's just a phase"; but in some cases, that is it. Regardless, even if it is just a developmental phase of identity achievement, individuals need to recognize the basis of their actions and have corrective counsel or affirmation provided by a more mature other. An adolescent, who is encountering an extreme measure of identity crisis, is likely to exhibit some antisocial behavior, rebellion against parents, etc. This does not make such occurrences acceptable, but Erikson and Marcia would agree that the individual should be informed of why he has such a disposition and aid him in resolving the root cause of his actions.

Finally, parental training is essential. A church once sponsored a support group for parents. It was called "P-nuts, Parents going Nuts"! Most parents of children or adolescents have not studied the stages of psychological development or have done so but forgotten them by the time they were parenting. The church could provide developmentally sound advice to parents regarding how to relate, direct, correct, and even instruct their children in such a manner as to promote healthy personality development.

Conclusion

In light of biblical anthropology, we studied two characteristic attributes of the soul—personality and spirituality. Given the complexity and grand scope of these concepts, it was difficult to pin down their accurate meaning. Personality and spirituality are definitely far too complex to explore adequately in the limited space allotted in the chapter.

Also, beyond the scope of the chapter discussion is the debate surrounding the effect of the fall upon the essential nature of the human person. Since the totality of a person was affected by the fall, it raises fundamental questions about the degree of limitation that sin places on the attributes and capacities of the human soul. More precisely, how much did the fall affect the personal and spiritual dimension of the soul? This question, which is beyond the scope of this chapter, remains to be answered.

Reflection Questions

1. How does the Bible describe a person? Explain the general makeup of a person.

2. What exactly are the capacities of personhood that constitute the image of God (i.e., *imago Dei*) in us?

3. What do the words "image" and "likeness" mean in Genesis 1:26? Can we identify the element or elements of personhood that constitute the image of God? What is the essence of the image? Which attribute of God does the image reflect?

4. What is personality, and how does it develop?

5. Review and criticize Erikson's and Marcia's theories of personality development.

6. What is spirituality, and how is it formed and developed?

7. What is the relation between personal development and Christian formation?

ENDNOTES

[1] Erik Erikson, *Child and Society* (New York: W. W. Norton & Co., 1950, 1963, 1985, 1993).

[2] Cf. James E. Marcia, "Why Erikson?," *The Future of Identity: Centennial Reflections on the Legacy of Erik Erikson,* Kenneth Hoover, ed. (Oxford: Lexington Books, 2004), 44-53.

[3] Dan Bilsker and James E. Marcia, "Adaptive Regression and Ego Identity," *Journal of Adolescence,* 14 (1): 75-84; Kenneth Hoover, James E. Marcia, Kristen Parris, and James Marcia, *The Power of Identity: Politics in a New Key* (Chatham, New Jersey: Chatham House Publishers, 1997).

[4] Based on Dan Bilsker and James E. Marcia, "Adaptive Regression and Ego Identity," *Journal of Adolescence,* 14 (1): 75-84; Jack Snow and Robert Biehler, *Psychology Applied to Teaching* (New York: Houghton Mifflin, 2000), 32.

[5] Based on the substantive view of *imago Dei* noted in Millard J. Erikson, *Christian Theology* (Grand Rapids: Baker Books, 1985), 498-502.

[6] Paul Carus, *Personality* (Chicago: The Open Court Publishing Co., 1911), 14, 18.

[7] Ibid., 15.

[8] G. Kittel, G. Friedrich, and G. W. Bromiley, *Theological Dictionary of the New Testament.* Translation of *Theologisches Worterbuch zum Neuen Testament* (Grand Rapids: W. B. Eerdmans, c1985, 1995), 876.

[9] Ibid.

[10] Bob Saucy, *Spiritual Formation in Theological Controversy* [paper presented at meeting of the Evangelical Theological Society (ETS), Toronto, Canada, 2002], 2.

[11] Leroy Aden, David Benner, and J. Harold Ellens, *Christian Perspectives on Human Development* (Grand Rapids: Baker Book House, 1992), 10.

[12] Gwen Kennedy Neville and John H. Westerhoff, III, *Learning Through Liturgy* (New York: Seabury Press, 1978), 163.

CHAPTER 5

MORAL DEVELOPMENT AND CHRISTIAN FORMATION[1]

By James R. Estep Jr.

It is impossible for Christians to avoid or dismiss themselves from the moral discourse in our world. African genocide, international conflicts, domestic political issues, medical decisions, ratings on movies and television, even the books selected for a school's literature course all raise the level of moral debate. A Christian's involvement in moral discourse—both within the church and in the community—is essential. But what are morals? How are they formed? What can the church do to promote moral formation? The responses to these questions often separate educators but nonetheless must be answered.

This chapter will review the contemporary theories of moral development, focusing on those that are most relevant to Christian educators. It will then offer a critique of these theories—as well as Christian alternatives and adaptations of those based solely on the social sciences. Finally, the chapter will present an agenda for the ministry of the congregation to promote the formation of moral believers as a part of our Christian life.

Theories and Theorists of Moral Development

Contemporary moral development theories can be divided into four major approaches, representing a different definition of morality and descriptions of its development: Psychoanalytical, Conditioning, Moral Potential, and Cognitive/Moral Reasoning.[2] The first approach, *psychoanalytical*, was first articulated by Sigmund Freud and perpetuated by his successors. In it, morality develops through psychological conflict among the ego, superego, and the id—elements of the conscious and subconscious mind. Hence, moral development is a psychological process of creating mental balance, harmony. The *behaviorist* approach—advocated by B. F. Skinner and subsequent behaviorist theorists—maintains that moral development occurs through external stimuli. Hence, morality is understood as a behavioral reaction produced through external stimuli in any given situation. Rather than a principally internal process, it is morality as a conditioned response to external stimuli. Morals are developed as a result of positive rewards and negative punishments consistently applied to given behaviors. Humanist theorists, such as Carl Rogers and Abraham Maslow, regard the basis for morality as the *human moral potential*. Morals are regarded as innate to human beings, developing as one's fundamental and advanced needs are fulfilled, and results in one advancing toward self-actualization. As advanced beings, we are capable of making moral determinations and decisions so as to become whole people, self-fulfilled.

However, educators, Christian and otherwise, tend to lean more heavily on those theories that are allied more closely with theories of cognitive development—*cognitive-moral reasoning*. This approach unites cognitive development theory—particularly that of Jean Piaget (chapter 3)—with the advancement of moral decision-making. In so doing, educators are provided with familiar territory—theories of human development—as a means of describing moral formation. Three main theorists represent the cognitive-moral reasoning approach to moral development: Jean Piaget, Lawrence Kohlberg, and Carol Gilligan (figure 5.1).[3]

Age	Piaget's Modes	Kohlberg's Levels	Gilligan's Levels
13+	Moral Autonomy	Level 3: Postconventional Stage 5: Social Contract Orientation Stage 6: Universal Moral Principles	Level 3: Postconventional Morality (interdependent concern for self and others)
13		Level 2: Conventional Stage 3: Good-boy/girl Orientation Stage 4: Authority Orientation	Level 2: Conventional Morality (concern for others)
12			
11			
10		Level 1: Preconventional Stage 1: Punishment Orientation Stage 2: Naïve Reward Orientation	Level 1: Preconventional Morality (concern for self)
9	Transitional Phase, both modes present		
8			

7	Hetronomy (Moral Realism)		
6			
5			
4			
3	"Pre" or "Proto" moral development; foundations for development being established		

Figure 5.1: Moral Development Theories

This section will briefly summarize each of their theories and then provide a general critique of the cognitive-moral reasoning approach to moral development.

Jean Piaget (1896-1980) postulated that "all morality consists in a system of rules, and the essence of all morality is to be sought for in the respect which individuals acquire for those rules."[4] For Piaget, two general modes or stages of moral cognition were present in children between the ages of six and twelve: heteronomy, or moral realism, and moral autonomy. In the first stage, rules are immutable and external—established by an outside authority figure—such as parents, teachers, civic authorities, or religious authorities. However, the second stage of moral development signals the internalization of these rules. The rules are adopted and accepted as one's internal morality; and rather than being obeyed simply as the orders of a superior, they are accepted as a necessity for maintaining relationships and community life.[5]

Lawrence Kohlberg (1927-87) based his moral development theory, not on the acquisition of rules, but on the moral reason behind human behavior. He did not ask, "Is an action moral or immoral?" or "Is a motive moral?" or even "*Why* is something moral or immoral?" Rather, he asked, "At what level of reasoning does one justify or explain one's moral decisions?" Traditional categories, such as right/wrong or moral/immoral, simply do not apply to Kohlberg. Rather, it is simply a matter of level of moral reasoning. To ascertain this, Kohlberg used moral dilemmas to facilitate moral reasoning in a given moral predicament. It was not the answer provided by the subjects that made it right or wrong but why they believed it to be right or wrong. For example, "Is it right or wrong to steal?" Kohlberg offers no answer. However, he would argue the reason to steal or not to steal would reflect a different level of moral reasoning; but the act, motive, or reason would not be regarded as moral or immoral—regardless of the response. Hence, no judgment was made on the decision or the outcome but simply on the presumed level of moral reasoning.

Kohlberg proposed three basic levels of moral reasoning—with each level composed of two stages. Level 1: moral reasoning, preconventional morality, bases moral decision on a personal criteria. It is divided into two stages: Punishment Orientation and Naïve Reward Orientation. On this level, right or wrong is determined by the personal implications of the decision. For example "Should I cheat on the ethics exam?" Once again, for Kohlberg, this is not a yes-or-no subject. Rather, it is the reason provided for the decision. "Yes because I need to pass the exam!" or "No because I'd get caught and be in trouble!" Notice the active word in both is "I." Right and wrong is determined by the individual on the basis of the positive or negative effect on the individual.[6]

The second level, conventional morality, contains the elements associated with level 1, but another line of thought is added. Level 2 maintains that moral decisions are dictated by an outside authority, i.e., laws, rules, guidelines. Adherence to these dictates will gain favor from another. It, too, is divided into two stages: Good-boy/Good-girl Orientation and Authority Orientation. The individual focus in level 1 is replaced by a concern for being regarded as "good" or "bad" by an authority figure—such as parents, teachers, or pastors—seeking the affirmation of a respected individual. For example, "Should I cheat on the ethics exam?" Such a dilemma might be answered in the affirmative, "Yes, think of what my frat buddies would think of me!" or in the negative, "No, think of what

Professor Tanner would think of me." In short, the keys to right and wrong are the opinion of a respected other and the desire to gain approval from them.[7]

Kohlberg's level 3, postconventional morality, is one of individual moral autonomy. Unlike the previous two levels, which were always dependent upon the response or affirmation of another individual, moral decisions at level 3 are based on individually applied principles. It is divided into two stages: Social Contract Orientation and Universal Moral Principles. These principles are beyond personal self-interest (level 1) or laws (level 2), calling for selflessness and reasoning beyond the limitations of the law. For Kohlberg, the ultimate moral principle was *justice*, a personal commitment to fairness to all—regardless of personal loss/gain or legalities. "Should I cheat on the ethics exam?" "No because, regardless of the impact on my grade or what Dr. Tanner thinks of me, it is simply wrong. It is a matter of personal honor and trust between the professor and students, and the integrity of the institution is more important than my grade." Or, an admittedly more difficult answer to conceive: "Yes because, regardless of the possibility of getting caught or what Dr. Tanner thinks of me, if I don't, I'll let down the whole class and reflect poorly on Dr. Tanner's abilities as an instructor." Level 3 almost always carries with it a sense of inner conflict between the universal principles and the lower levels of moral reasoning (i.e., self-interest and permissible requirements). It represents a laying aside of the thoughts of personal gain or acceptance to follow a higher ethical principle.

Is there a seventh stage to morality? Kohlberg himself, after publishing his theory but prior to his death, raised the possibility of a seventh stage of morality.[8] In part, he hypothesized a seventh stage—based on the faith development theory of James Fowler (chapter 6) and on the philosophical theology of Pierre Teilhard de Chardin (1881-1955).

Carol Gilligan (1936-), Kohlberg's assistant, applied his research methodology to the study of women's moral development, which Kohlberg had inadvertently omitted from his studies. Her critique of

Kohlberg was not only gender-based but stemmed from advances in Kohlberg's own test instruments that later challenged his original findings and conclusions.[9] Unlike Kohlberg, with his principle-centered moral reasoning, Gilligan favored one that was more affective—a moral reasoning of the heart. "Men feel secure alone at the top of the hierarchy, securely separate from the challenge of others. Women feel secure in the middle of a web of relationships; to be at the top of a hierarchy is seen as disconnected."[10] Without dismissing Gilligan too rapidly, her proposed levels of moral reasoning in women parallel the same levels for Kohlberg's moral development in men. Perhaps the one significant distinction is that the ultimate moral principle for women was not justice, as with men; rather, it was caring. However, justice and caring have one common thread that does signal a moral tone. The ultimate moral principle is to regard others before oneself—whether that is expressed in terms of justice or caring. As Feldmeier surmises, "For males, it is legitimate to fracture relationships if this means embracing a greater principle of justice. For females, such a fracture represents a failure, not an increase in sophistication."[11]

Biblical and Theological Insights into Moral Development

For the Christian educator, Scripture and theology have supplied the foundation for espousing an approach toward moral development. Dirks notes, while Scripture does not present a theory of moral development, it does provide a developmental *framework* in the metaphor of moral growth articulated throughout the New Testament (1 Corinthians 2:1ff; 13:11; Hebrews 5:12-14; Philippians 2:14; Ephesians 4:15)—as well as the concepts of internalization of values (Ephesians 6:6; Matthew 5:1ff) and that of moral transformation (Romans 12:1-2).[12]

The Scriptures do speak of morals as multidimensional. Scripture connects morality and moral formation to cognition, affect, and action—as seen in the stated connection between morality and knowledge or cognition in Scripture (Psalm 119:34; John 13:7, Ephesians 2:12; Philippians 4:9;

James 3:17). However, morals are more than decision making, more than cognition. Morals also are connected to affect, i.e., disposition or emotions (Galatians 5:22; 1 John 4:7-8) and to expected or approved behaviors—as indicated by standards of conduct (Psalm 15:1-4; Amos 5:11-12,21-22; James 1-2; Matthew 25:31-40).

Additionally, several central theological tenets have been advanced as sustainable bases for moral development within the Christian community. For example, Bonnidell Clouse has suggested the *imago Dei* provides a theological foundation for moral development theory, maintaining that his level 3/stage 6 can be tied to an unrestricted respect for humanity due to the *imago Dei*.[13] Similarly, Joel Brondos maintains the doctrine of sanctification is a suitable theological premise upon which to draw the portrait of moral growth in the New Testament. However, he cautions not to equate sanctification with moral development since morality is driven by the individual and society; whereas sanctification requires the direct involvement of God.[14] He regards moral development theory as beneficial, "but every precaution must be taken that such usage [of Kohlberg's theory] does not assume to impinge or improve upon the sanctifying work of the Holy Spirit through the Word."[15] Similarly, Samuel Rowen identifies the process of conversion and creation as a means of integrating Christian faith and moral development theories into a motivation to facilitate the moral developmental process.[16]

An underlying principle of Christian moral formation is our acknowledged dependence on the influence of the Holy Spirit in the life of the individual to aid in the process of moral formation. He is influential within the individual prior to conversion (John 16:8); in conversion (Acts 2:38; 1 Corinthians 2:10-16, Romans 8:1ff); and after conversion (1 Corinthians 12:1ff, 2 Corinthians 13:14, Galatians 5:2; Ephesians 4:3; Philippians 2:1). As Ferré describes Him, the Holy Spirit challenges the spiritual *status quo*, "Behind all pedagogy is the prompting of the Spirit."[17] While spirituality and morality are indeed two different concerns, they are not independent from one another.

Kohlberg and Scripture?

Is this approach to moral development alien to the Christian community?
While this section will endeavor to provide a general critique of the
cognitive-moral reasoning approach to moral development, it will tend to
focus on Kohlberg's theory since his is considered the most advanced and
the most widely recognized. This approach to moral formation does find
some warrant in Scripture since the Bible recognizes the connection
between knowledge and moral behavior is evident in the Scriptures (Psalm
119:34; John 13:7, Ephesians 2:12; Philippians 4:9; James 3:17—not to
mention the Old Testament's Wisdom Literature).

Some Christians see parallels between Scripture's depiction of human
morality and the moral stages suggested by Kohlberg. These parallels are
then used as a means of critically appropriating Kohlberg's moral
development theory. For example, Dirks finds general compatibility
between Kohlberg and Scripture, stating:

> Kohlberg's concept of autonomous moral judgment supports the
> biblical concept that the mature believer should not require moral
> decision to be propped up by external authority figures. . . . A
> biblical understanding of morality would suggest that self-chosen
> commitment to the values revealed in the image and character
> of God defines the essence of what is moral, e.g., Romans 8:29,
> 2 Corinthians 3:18, Ephesians 4:24, Colossians 3:10, and
> Philippians 3:21.[18]

Perry Downs regards Kohlberg as having "compatibility with Scripture,"
noting that "clearly Scripture makes appeals on all three levels of moral
development," i.e., conditional promises, appeals to authority, or universal
principles (Hosea 6:6; Matthew 9:13; Micah 6:8; Romans 7:6;
2 Corinthians 3:3).[19] Figure 5.2 contains a catalog of Scriptures that
generally reflect the moral development theory presented by Kohlberg
and Gilligan.

Kohlberg / Gilligan's	Kohlberg's Stages	Scripture References
Level 1	Stage 1: Punishment Orientation	"I will bless those . . . I will curse those . . ." (Genesis 12:3,6:11, 9:11; Deuteronomy 28:1-3,8,11, 15-16,20; 2 Chronicles 7:14; Job 4:7-9; Matthew 6:14-15).
Preconventional	Stage 2: Naïve Reward Orientation	
Ages 4-10		
Level 2	Stage 3: Good-boy/Good-girl Orientation	"Thus saith the LORD . . ." "It is written . . ." (Exodus 20:12; Psalm 19:7-8; Matthew 16:24; 1 Corinthians 10:32-11:1, Ephesians 6:1-3; Colossians 3:20; 1 Thessalonians 5:22).
Conventional	Stage 4: Authority Orientation	
Ages 10-13		
Level 3	Stage 5: Social Contract Orientation	"For I desire loyalty and not sacrifice, the knowledge of God rather than burnt offerings" (Hosea 6:6; cf. Matthew 9:13; 12:17; Isaiah 11:9; Micah 6:8; Matthew 22:36-40; Mark 2:27; Luke 4:18,10:25-27; John 14:15; Romans 7:6,13:8; 1 Corinthians 13:13; Galatians 5:14; Colossians 1:15-20).
Postconventional	Stage 6: Universal Moral Principles	
Ages 13+		

Figure 5.2: Kohlberg/Gilligan and Scripture

Additionally, Duska and Whelen comment, "If the highest level of moral reasoning is on a principled level, and if the highest principles are justice and love, one is hard pressed to find a more consistent statement of such principles than in the New Testament."[20] Hence, such theories as presented by Piaget, Kohlberg, and Gilligan may be *critically applied* to Christian education without a loss of theological integrity.

Some Christian authorities have affirmed Kohlberg even further, using it as a means of interpreting Scripture and even history. For example, Dan Motet comments, "Kohlberg's approach is analogous to what we find in

Scripture, where we can follow God's work to raise human moral judgment through the six stages [of Kohlberg]," using a survey of Moses and the Israelites during the Exodus, the life of King David, and finally the teaching of Jesus to demonstrate Kohlberg's compatibility with it.[21]

More recently, R. G. Shepherd's "Integrative Model" reflects Kohlberg and Gillian's levels in an almost dispensational fashion, noting that eras from biblical times to the present era follow the line of moral development theory.[22] Most recently, Timothy Gibson modified Kohlberg and Gilligan's theories for Christian use, rewording or illustrating the levels with more familiar Christian terminology and adding a fourth level, Kingdom-Centered, which is almost reminiscent of Kohlberg's suggested seventh stage.[23]

The teachings of Jesus are likewise subject to review with a moral development lens. Clouse identifies parallels between the teachings of Jesus and Kohlberg's six stages of moral development, particularly in regard to Jesus' "Law of Love" (Matthew 22:36-40) and Kohlberg's third level of development. Clouse asserts that "Jesus' Law of Love is representative of Kohlberg's highest level, namely that of principled or postconventional moral thought."[24] She cites three reasons for this conclusion:

1. Jesus understood the importance of law and submitted Himself to its jurisdiction.

2. Jesus showed there is a better way than the rigid observance [of the Law].

3. Jesus gave dignity and respect to every person.[25]

Similarly, Stonehouse suggests the Christian idea of "*agape* [Gk. *love*] does not compete with justice principles; rather, it inspires one to go beyond the demands of justice. Acts of *agape* are acts of grace to the recipient."[26] Dirks presses this even further, seeing a trajectory of moral formation in Scripture and Kohlberg. For example, Jesus' statement—"If anyone wants to come with Me, he must deny himself, take up his cross, and follow Me" (Matthew 16:24)—could be regarded as a Kohlberg level 3 thought, wherein the egocentric or judicious basis of morality is trumped by principles.[27] Provided such a spectrum of moral development, it could be argued that Jesus met with individuals on their level of moral development and made moral appeals to them, according to their ability to morally comprehend it.

Christian Critique of Moral Development Theory

However, many evangelicals are cautious about the wholehearted, uncritical acceptance of the cognitive-moral reasoning approach to moral development. While numerous authorities have critiqued Kohlberg's approach to moral development, three general criticisms seem to be frequently raised. *First*, Kohlberg's severe limitation imposed on his definition of moral development is a concern. While morality must include motive or decision-making, as this approach suggests, morality cannot be limited exclusively to moral reasoning. As will be demonstrated later in this chapter, morality is multidimensional, including more than just the cognitive reasoning process of moral decision-making. Moral *reasoning* is not comprehensive to address moral formation—more to morality than just reason. This critique has not only been voiced by Christian educators but also by others, e.g., Mary Francis Callahan of University of California at Santa Barbara, assessing that Kohlberg's theory and that of Gilligan are "limited—limited in the sense that it focuses on reasoning to the exclusion of feelings and behaviors."[28] While all morality may reflect a moral decision, there is more to morality than cognition. If Kohlberg's definition is limited or even incomplete, then his entire approach is similarly limited in its ability to address the subject of moral development comprehensively. This critique arises not only from theological concerns but by similarly voiced concerns provided from the social sciences. Hence, moral formation cannot be conceived as consisting of just a process of cognitive-mental reasoning but must include the dimensions of moral affect and behavior.

The *second* general criticism does arise from philosophical concerns. Kohlberg's moral development theory is not simply the product of empirical evidence but ideological assumptions.[29] For example, James Michael Lee notes that Kohlberg's rejection of religion as a positive influence on moral development was not done on the basis of empirical evidence or social science precedent but philosophical bias against it.[30] One factor, which is emphasized by Christian educators but minimized by non-Christians, is the role of religious belief in the formation of morals. Also, Iris Cully notes, "The Christian could not affirm, with level [stage] five thinking, that the social contract is an ultimate form of morality" since Christian convictions are often countercultural and reflect a higher allegiance.[31] Additionally, due to the affirmation of human brokenness, or sin, Christian educators tend to present moral development more as a formative process than one of a sequential, automatic developmental process innate to human beings, such as physical development or structuralism in cognitive development. In short, Kohlberg's basis for moral decisions is incomplete for the Christian educator. This does not mean his theory is categorically wrong, but rather it applies to only one aspect of moral formation and cannot explain all of it.

Third, and perhaps most enlightening, is Kohlberg's own admission that his theory was impractical, proving not to be viable in actual community situations. In 1978, he wrote for *The Humanist* magazine:

> Some years of active involvement with the practice of moral education at Cluster School have led me to realize that my notion that moral stages were *the* basis for moral education, rather than a partial guide to the moral educator, was mistaken. . . . It is not a sufficient guide to the moral educator who deals with the moral concrete in a school world in which value content as well as structure, behavior as well as reasoning, must be dealt with. In this context, the educator must be a socializer, teaching value content

and behavior, and not only a Socratic or Rogerian process-facilitator of development. In becoming a socializer and an advocate, the teacher moves into "indoctrination," a step I originally believed to be philosophically invalid. . . . I believe that the concepts guiding moral education must be partly "indoctrinative."[32]

In this admission, Kohlberg acknowledges the limitations of his theory. It simply cannot produce the moral objectives that it purports to deliver. It is, indeed, in need of additional measures—for example, indoctrination—to ensure the formation of morals.

Christian Perspectives on Moral Development

Morality is not a monodimensional concept but rather is multidimensional. Based on insights from theology and the social sciences, Christian educators have presented morality as having three interrelated dimensions: cognitive, affective, and behavioral (figure 5.3).[33] As one may see of the biblical references used to illustrate each of these dimensions, the Holy Spirit is indeed involved in bringing about the conviction for change, affirmation of life values, as well as guidance and direction for the journey.

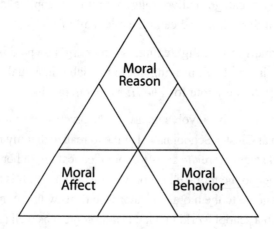

Figure 5.3: Three-Dimension Morality

The *moral reasoning* elements of morality have been described as moral judgments, choices, decisions—all of which reflect the mental or thinking aspect of morality.[34] Developmental theorists, such as Jean Piaget and Lawrence Kohlberg, would represent models of moral development exclusively focused on this dimension.

Second, *moral affect* refers to the sense of valuing and character formation, addressing the affective domain. This is perhaps the most neglected aspect of moral formation. As Robert Cooper observes, "[Moral] formation is not only a matter of forming thought but is also *a matter of forming affect*, of forming feeling among a community of persons, of forming ourselves in accordance with a vision of the God, who, in Jesus, has made us friends, who has given us to each other as gifts."[35] While not addressing the subject of moral development, educational theorist David Krathwohl's learning taxonomy describes the third level of affect as "Valuing," which is "sufficiently consistent and stable to have taken on the characteristics of a belief or an attitude. . . . At this level, we are not concerned with the relationships among values but rather with the internalization of a set of specified, ideal values."[36] Scripture does indeed reflect such a moral affect (Galatians 5:22; 1 John 4:7-8). Theorists such as Carol Gilligan, Anna Freud, Erick Erikson, and Robert Coles would represent those advocating this dimension of moral development.

Finally, *moral behavior* refers to moral actions—the behaviors of an ethical person.[37] This is perhaps the most commonly held concept of morality, particularly in regard to children. Being "good" is a matter of having the proper and expected behaviors. For example, an individual's strong character "gives the power to do what one believes is right."[38] Hence, behavior is the exhibitor of both moral reasoning and moral affect. Understanding morality as a three-dimensional paradigm provides a comprehensive concept of morality as being a matter of ethical cognition, affect, and behavior that is sound scripturally and consistent with the social sciences.

Christian Theories of Moral Development

A distinctively Christian approach to moral formation requires more than just foundational premises. It requires the articulation of a comprehensive approach to facilitate the process of moral formation as indicated in Scripture and observed through the social sciences. The following section provides summations of the most significant contributors to the formulation of a Christian theory of moral development in the Christian education community. The summations are, by no means, comprehensive but provide a representation of the contributors and the perspectives they bring. For example, Joy provides a stage theory of moral formation in a Christian context, whereas Moran and Dykstra give a more theological driven. Clouse endeavors to provide a broad portrait of moral formation, adapting the four major theoretical approaches to moral development into a single approach that is Christian. Similarly, Ward develops the metaphor of a bridge that affirms the tripartite nature of moral formation, explaining the relationship of the cognitive, affective, and behavioral.

Donald M. Joy affirms the value of Kohlberg's insights on moral development and his levels of moral reasoning (but not necessarily the stages). However, he regards the social sciences as "myopic, if not blind" to what "ought to be," being only phenomenological and, hence, requiring theological insights to establish morality.[39] Therefore, moral development must have the insights from theology, not just the social sciences, to provide a comprehensive view of the process. Theologically, Joy maintains the incarnation was "an adventure of reverse transformation," wherein Jesus breached the developmental process of humanity. "Hence, an entry station is opened at every stage and level by which any person might encounter and engage the redeeming Prince."[40]

For Joy, moral development must be understood through the metaphor of a pilgrimage, which "consistently is dynamic, relational, aspirational, epochal, and cumulative."[41] He comments that "ethical development on the pilgrimage tends to be characterized by two features: (1) an eagerness to move ahead to better perspectives and solutions . . . and (2) a magnetic attraction for advanced ways of interpreting reality . . . in which the 'vision' is embraced well before matching 'performance' is attained."[42]

Joy's model of Christian moral formation (figure 5.4) illustrates this moral pilgrimage as one moves from such moral "controls" as taboos, terror, and fear through an approach to morality typified by law (e.g., the Decalogue); then principles (e.g., the Greatest Commandment); and ultimately values (e.g., faithfulness, steadfastness, love, righteousness) that reverence (rather than terror) and respect (rather than fear) God.[43]

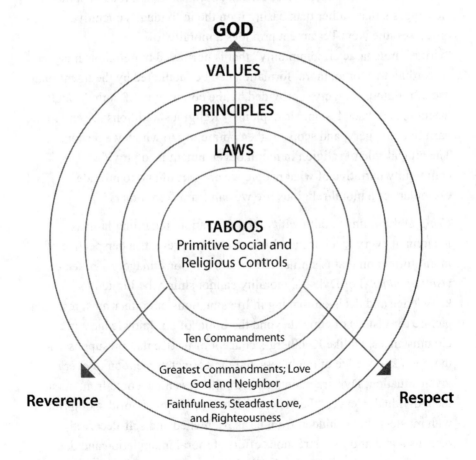

Figure 5.4: Donald Joy's Paradigm of Moral Development[44]

What he depicts as concentric spheres of moral levels, readily paralleling Kohlberg's levels, we progress through these stages: [45]

- Egocentrism − centering morality on self-interest, e.g., taboos.
- Heterocentrism − centering morality on external authorities, e.g., laws.
- Logocentrism − centering morality on the principles/values of the Logos (Christ).

Gabriel Moran advocates a less formal approach to moral development. He suggests that, rather than basing it on the individual's cognitive processes, the New Testament provides a morality of "virtue/care/character/community" that is portrayed by religious imagery.[46] According to Moran, moral formation can be facilitated by the intentional use of religious imagery − provided by the community of faith through teaching and discipleship. He explains, "Religious traditions . . . enrich the narrative, imagery, and scope of the community to which we respond. . . . The crucial role of religion in moral development is to provide a community narrative of what people we are part of and to provide exemplars of a moral/religious life we can learn from others."[47]

Craig Dykstra unites faith with moral formation, regarding faith as inherent at every level of moral formation. He presents a perspective of moral formation that is similar to Moral's religious imagery—based on *visional ethics.* For Dykstra, morality cannot simply be limited to knowledge and decision-making in life situations but rather must rest on a picture (or vision) of ethics beyond the limits of our knowledge and circumstances. Unlike Kohlberg's concept of justice that presupposes a thorough knowledge of oughtness and the correct perception of every given situation, Dykstra maintains the oughtness must come from outside the individual. Hence, "the visional picture is one of a world shot through with mystery that is hidden from us as frightened and self-deceived persons and that only a strenuous effort of moral imagination and deep discernment can begin to plumb."[48]

If vision is the foundation of moral development, the dynamics are *imagination* and *revelation*. Dykstra explains as follows:

> The function of revelation is to provide us with images by which to see truthfully and realistically. Revelation is not impersonal, however. Nothing is revealed when the images remain objects, part of an external cultural heritage. Revelation is the conversion of the imagination and takes place only when the revelatory images become ingrained in the psyche and provide the framework for all our seeing and living.[49]

What facilitates all of this? The individual and communal practices of the spiritual *disciplines* of repentance, prayer, and service are the instruments of moral formation. These disciplines are not just individually practiced; rather, they are likewise embodied by the community of faith as models of the disciplines.

Bonnidell Clouse, in her book *Teaching for Moral Growth*, presents a paradigm of moral formation that is intentional (i.e., psychoanalytic, conditioning, moral reasoning, and moral potential). According to Clouse, the biblical approach to moral formation is more inclusive and, hence, more comprehensive; whereas the four previous approaches are fragments of the whole (see figure 5.5). "Each of the major psychologies . . . emphasizes one of the four expressions of morality: conflict, action, knowledge, and potential. By contrast, the Bible stresses all of them, *thus presenting a more complete picture of what it means to be a moral person.*"[50]

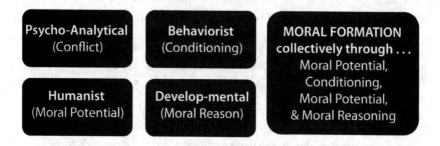

Figure 5.5: Clouse's Inclusive Moral Formation

Clouse, likewise, presents biblical passages in support of each of the four approaches to moral development—as provided below:

1. Conflict, which can be approach-approach (Joshua 24:14-18) or approach-avoidance (Romans 5:17; 7:21-24).

2. Action, which is an integration of personal and social morality (Psalm 15:1-4; Amos 5:11-12,21-22; Matthew 25:31-40; James 1-2).

3. Knowledge, which is linked to conduct (Psalm 119:34; John 13:7; Philippians 4:9; James 2:17; Ephesians 2:12).

4. Potential because of the *imago Dei* (Colossians 1:17; Philippians 2:7) and redemption (Psalm 138:8; Romans 8:17; 2 Corinthians 3:18; 1 Peter 2:2; 2 Peter 1:1, 3:8).

Hence, moral development is the combined result of psychological conflict, action, knowledge, and our potential as human beings—as theorized by the social sciences and demonstrated in Scripture.

Ted Ward (1930-) affirms the value of Kohlberg's findings—particularly the three levels of moral development—but regards his theory to be only one piece of the morality and moral formation puzzle. For example, according to Ward, one's view of authority is indicative of moral developmental level, i.e., obedience to law is a factor that allows and marks one's passage from level 1 to level 2; while trust does the same for level 2 to level 3.[51] Hence, he makes use of the three levels devised by Kohlberg but without limiting moral development to just a cognitive process.

Ward provides a metaphor of a "bridge" leading from "moral truth to moral action" as a more comprehensive concept of moral development.[52] The bridge itself has three parts: (1) Moral Reasoning or Cognition (ala Kohlberg), which leads to (2) Moral Will or Volition and leads to (3) Moral Strength to act upon the truth, which Ward calls "character."[53] According to Ward, the motivation to cross the bridge, moving from moral truth to moral action, are four life factors: (1) experience of justice, (2) experience of social interaction, (3) open discussions of moral concerns, and (4) opportunities for role play.[54] Hence, Ward provides a model of moral development that can make use of developmental insights but is not restricted to just their insights.

Toward a Christian Perspective of Moral Formation

Ethics are more than the mental process of our decisions; their scope includes affect and behavior. Ethics and morality imply the presence of norms. The prevalent questions become: *Who establishes the norms? From where do they come? How can we facilitate the process of moral formation?* For Christian educators, ethics and morality are not simply a human or societal product; rather, they are *dependent* on God. Figure 5.6 endeavors to illustrate the nature of Christian ethics and morality.[55]

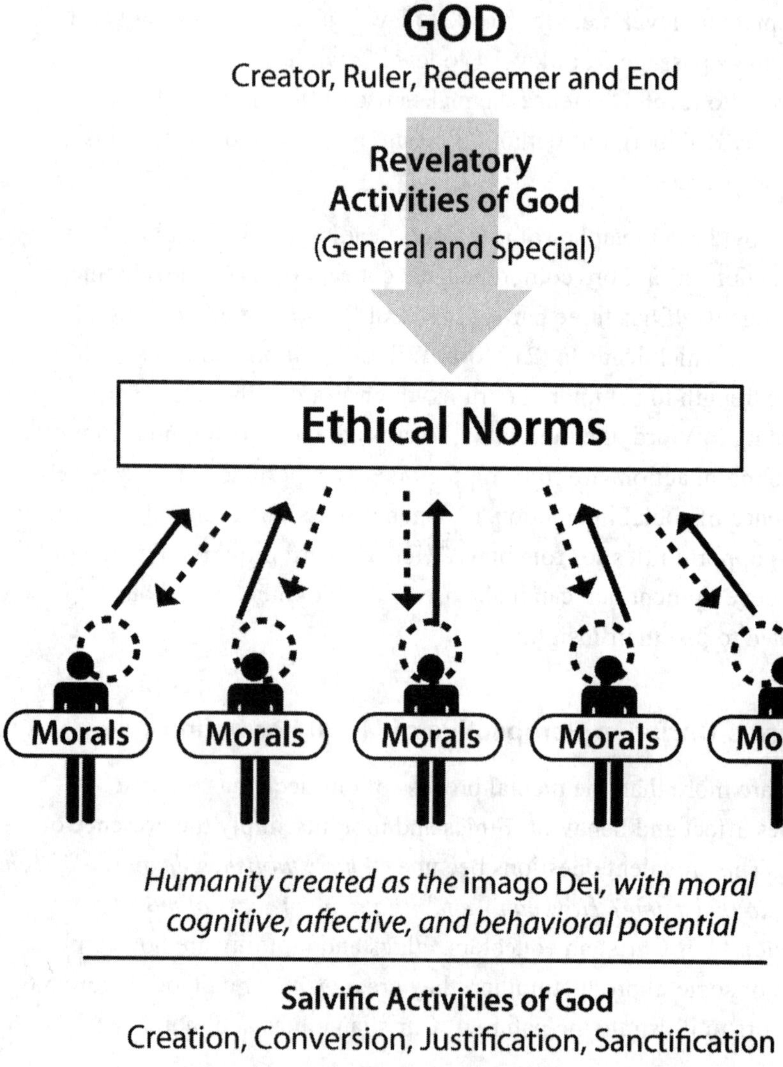

GOD

Creator, Ruler, Redeemer and End

**Revelatory
Activities of God**
(General and Special)

Ethical Norms

Morals   **Morals**   **Morals**   **Morals**   **Morals**

Humanity created as the imago Dei, *with moral
cognitive, affective, and behavioral potential*

Salvific Activities of God
Creation, Conversion, Justification, Sanctification

Figure 5.6: A Christian Approach to Ethics and Morals

Ultimately, ethical standards are attributed to God—revealed to humanity through creation and Scripture; but we, too, must be capable of discerning these ethical standards from His revelations. Morality is a process of internalizing these ethical principles. (See Ephesians 6:6, "doing the will of God from the heart;" Matthew 5:1ff.) Several theologically informed frameworks for ethics and morality have been presented by the community of faith—based on a variety of central Christian tenets, such as creation and conversion,[56] sanctification,[57] and as previously mentioned, the *imago Dei* and Revelation. Hence, the general concept of Christian morality is the integration of God-given principles into one's life and ultimately society and culture. This integration, likewise, implies a part of the concern for the process of moral formation.

The Process of Moral Formation: Scripture does present a metaphor of *growth* to denote moral formation and, hence, seems to favor the idea of formation rather than an innate process of development within the individual (1 Corinthians 2:1ff; 13:11; Hebrews 5:12-14; Philippians 2:14; Ephesians 4:15). Similarly, several passages denote the marks of an ethical person as one who is fruitful or demonstrates wisdom (Galatians 5:22-23; Colossians 3:12-13; James 3:17). Hence, the notion of a purely *developmental* approach to morality would be insufficient to the broader growth or formation approach presented in Scripture. The New Testament calls us to a *transformational morality*, such as Romans 12:2: "Do not be conformed to this age, but be transformed by the renewing of your mind, so that you may discern what is the good, pleasing, and perfect will of God." While this transformation is similar to what has been advocated by Piaget, Kohlberg, or Gilligan, it differs in that moral formation is not formless, having a pattern of individual or societal design. Rather, it is the integration of a transcendently prescribed pattern. Individuals must progress beyond their own ego (self) toward a societal or relational concern (often expressed in laws) and on toward the transcendent ethical principles universally applicable to everyone—the God-given ethical frameworks—as expressed in Joy's theory. Hence, it is a matter of using moral reasoning, affect, and behavior to integrate theologically derived ethical principles into one's life.

Moral Development, Christian Formation, and Educational Implications

The development of morals and faith are intertwined in the Christian approaches to development. Without over simplifying, you can be moral without being Christian, but it is inconceivable to be a Christian without being moral. As Perry Downs comments, "The church has always been concerned with morality because it is an important corollary to faith."[58] Such a relationship is exemplified by the obvious relationship between Kohlberg (and Gilligan) with Fowler's faith development theory—as is explained in the next chapter.

Moral formation—in almost every theory presented—has a common theme: It is a shift from egocentrism to other-centrism to principle-centered and ultimately toward a God-centered view of life. Christian formation is the broader context in which moral formation occurs. As with Christian formation, moral formation is not *naturally occurring*. It requires intentional engagement within the faith community, the Church. The Church, the ministry of Christian education, and the Christian educator are tasked with engaging in more than doctrinal indoctrination but moral discourse, deliberation, discernment, memory—remembering teaching.[59]

The implications of moral development (or formation) theory are numerous. However, they can be clustered into three general categories of implication: (1) general approach to the ministry of the church, (2) impact on the teaching ministry, particularly for the teacher and the task of teaching, and (3) how it relates to the communal aspect of the church.

Moral Formation and Ministry

Generally speaking, moral formation can be facilitated by three approaches—all of which are adaptable to a church setting. In fact, where many instances of moral formation attempts fail, it is because they do not use all three but limit the range of their endeavor. Peter Scharf identifies these three approaches to facilitating moral formation as indoctrination, values clarification, and developmental moral education (aka Kohlberg), favoring the last approach over the others.[60]

Indoctrination calls for the instruction of individuals to the ethical norms that already have been determined by the society or culture or, in our case, the church. These are best learned through repetition, association, modeling, reward, and example. As one may recall, the need for this approach was a later acknowledgment of Kohlberg.[61] It asks us where in our congregation do we actually share the ethical teaching of Jesus. Wherein do we provide direct instruction on moral expectations and standards? When done correctly, individuals acknowledge Scripture has a moral dimension that can form the basis for Christian ethics.[62] However, we must recognize that knowing the content of Scripture does not equal moral formation. Knowing what is right and actually living accordingly are indeed two different matters.

Values Clarification follows a period of indoctrination. While indoctrination can establish the "points," it cannot connect all the dots for us. Values clarification encourages the individual to make certain moral determinations. As Nels Ferré once critiqued, "The direct learning of social, moral, and spiritual wisdom is seldom applied by the learner because it has not been personally appropriated. Education suffers from a chronic indigestion of unassimilated propositional truths."[63] The same could be said of the church's endeavor to engage moral formation through indoctrination alone. Values clarification in the church is accomplished through reflection on alternative value premises—through self-analysis and awareness of implications of value choices *within the bounds of faith*. The use of values clarification also could be used as a means of assessing the current level of moral formation in individuals so as to better understand them and move forward. One could incorporate Scripture or theological insights into the moral determination. Hence, the individuals are reasoning through moral issues from a Christian perspective, not simply their own.

Moral Education is the capstone approach to facilitating moral development. Following indoctrination and values clarification, moral education is determined by philosophic rightness. Ethics principles should be universally valid, i.e., affirmed by the whole church. Generally, such principles are derived through periods of divergence of opinion, dialog within the community, role-taking, and moral interchange. This approach actually calls individuals into the process of determining the norms and connecting the dots and then moving beyond them to a statement of principles.

The combination of these three approaches within a Christian context is perhaps the most comprehensive and promising means of facilitating moral formation within the church. Figure 5.7 is an adaptation of a chart presented by Scharf in his *Readings in Moral Education,* demonstrating this combined approach for moral formation in the church—as one approach leads toward the validity of the next. Without using all of these approaches, each approach alone is insufficient to facilitate Christian moral formation.

	Indoctrination →	Values → Clarification	Development Moral Education
What is morally right?	Norms determined by congregational or denominational authorities upon biblical-theological basis	Norms determined by the individual Christian through critical examination of alternative biblical-theological perspectives	Norms determined by theological and philosophical oughtness. As such, ethical principles are universally and eternally valid within the kingdom of God.
How do children learn/change their moral ideas?	Conform to norms through repetition, association, reward and punishment, moral example, and modeling	Choice of norms through critical analysis, theological reflection, and awareness of moral implications	Established through debate, dialogue, role-taking/perspective changing opportunities, and moral transaction within the context of faith

	Indoctrination →	Values → Clarification	Development Moral Education
Stability of Church	Under pressure from congregational or denominational leadership; capable of returning or maintaining espoused norms	State of indecision or even confusion; morality in flux lowers ethical stability; affirmation of a minimal moral core but many moral options	While affirming eternal moral principles, their application and moral articulation vary between congregations and denominational traditions.
Biblical Example	"Train a child in the way he should go, and when he is old he will not turn from it" (Proverbs 22:6). "Then they can train the younger women to love their husbands and children" (Titus 2:4).	"Now fear the LORD and serve him with all faithfulness. Throw away the gods your forefathers worshiped beyond the River and in Egypt, and serve the LORD. But if serving the LORD seems undesirable to you, then choose for yourselves this day whom you will serve, whether the gods your forefathers served beyond the River, or the gods of the Amorites, in whose land you are living. But as for me and my household, we will serve the LORD" (Joshua 24:14-15).	"So whatever you believe about these things keep between yourself and God. Blessed is the man who does not condemn himself by what he approves. But the man who has doubts is condemned if he eats, because his eating is not from faith; and everything that does not come from faith is sin" (Romans 14:22-23).

Figure 5.7: Indoctrination, Values Clarification, and Moral Education in the Church[64]

Moral Formation and Teaching

Most moral development theories rely, in part, on the notion of cognitive dissonance. For example, as described in chapter 3, Piaget maintained that cognition seeks balance and order. When this cognition is absent, the mind enters into a state of disequilibration and, in turn, endeavors to reestablish the balance. Cognitive dissonance is basically the same process, wherein moral inconsistency cannot be tolerated. Hence, moral reflection, reasoning, and change are the results. figure 5.8 demonstrates how teaching can raise dissonance and, in turn, aid the individual in seeking a Christian resolution to the moral issue.

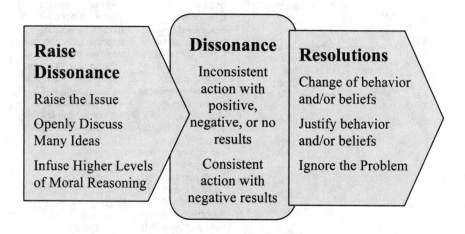

Figure 5.8: Creating Cognitive Dissonance[65]

Notice in the figure above that a teacher can raise dissonance by raising a pertinent issue, openly discussing it within the classroom, and aiding the students toward a higher level of moral reasoning—most certainly through the application of Scripture or theological insights, introducing God's perspective into the life situation. This causes the dissonance to become intolerable, and the individual is compelled to seek resolution—as depicted on the right side of the figure. But how can one teach so as to engage this process? Figure 5.9 may provide some insights on this matter.

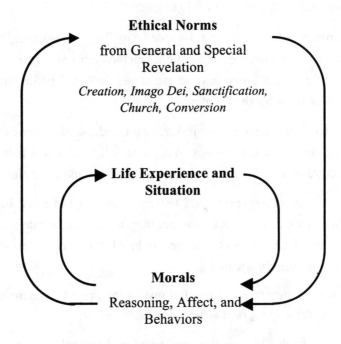

Ethical Norms

from General and Special
Revelation

*Creation, Imago Dei, Sanctification,
Church, Conversion*

**Life Experience and
Situation**

Morals

Reasoning, Affect, and
Behaviors

Figure 5.9: Teaching for Moral Formation

Teaching for moral formation involves an instructor who engages students in their real-life situations and experiences—not just in artificial discussions on political hot topics or sociocultural issues. They create a sense of dissonance by raising the inconsistencies between their lives and the espoused morals. Once the dissonance is inescapable, the instructor can guide the student to God's Truth as a means of assessing their morals and life situation, endeavoring to restore the harmony and balance. Hence, teaching for moral formation is a cycle of interaction between the student's morals, their actual life, and Scripture. All of this has implications for both the teacher's role and the task of teaching. For the teacher …

- Teaching for content mastery but not to the exclusion of affective affirmation and behavioral change. We are teaching students and the Bible – not just the Bible to students.

- Move beyond the content. Include "why." For the teacher, this is more than a matter of instructional method but a personal requirement. We first have to ask ourselves "why" before bringing others along for the journey.

- Teachers as mentors. Our influence on students has to extend beyond the classroom door. We are not only instructors with lectures and lessons but also with discussions and examples.

- Be sensitive to moral levels. Teachers cannot assume that all of their students are on an equal par morally. Hence, teachers must listen to students so as to ascertain their level of moral formation and aid them in advancing.

Dissonance and the previous model of instruction provide numerous implications for the task of teaching—as listed below:

- Utilize biblical instruction, precedent, and examples in moral discussion.

- Avoid providing simple answers to moral dilemmas.

- Clarify and analyze moral issues.

- Intentionally aim for not just cognitive but affective and behavioral learning objectives.

- Reflect critically on moral reasoning (sources of authority, line of reason, base issue).

- Become transparent with students, sharing with them your moral processing and issues – without damaging your personal example.

- Teach beyond the classroom but with a debriefing/classroom, e.g., cross-cultural experiences.

- "Scripture Saturation,"[66] i.e., early church model of teaching for reflection – almost *lectio divina.*

- Site biblical, historical, personal, and practical examples of moral solutions.

- Distinguish facts, opinions, and judgments on moral issues.

- Develop moral principles, reflecting Christian beliefs and commitments.

- Character studies; but go beyond the typical "good-bad" paradigm, e.g., Abraham is portrayed as "good" vs. Lot being "bad." The Genesis narrative of Abraham's life also shows periods of moral failure and Lot being morally strong.

- Consider consequences and implications of moral choices.

- Use lecture but mixed with other methods, e.g., case study.

Moral Formation and the Faith Community

The Church, as a community of faith, can provide an excellent context for the formation of morals. Through relationships, instruction, service, and worship, individuals can be presented a moral vision or image (such as that presented by Moran and Dykstra) so as to promote moral formation. As such, moral development theory has provided insights into the approach and practice of ministry within congregations.

"Do what you have learned and received and heard and *seen in me*, and the God of peace will be with you" (Philippians 4:9, emphasis added). Stonehouse comments that moral formation is fostered when the atmosphere is one of respect, belonging, justice, and openness.[67] Similarly, Downs speaks of the influence of involvement and participation in a just or moral community, such as the church or Christian institutions.[68] In these contexts, the previously mentioned moral relationships are formed and, hence, are critical for the formation of moral affect with oneself, others, church and society, and ultimately God.[69]

Downs also speaks of the value of "modeling morality," citing 1 Corinthians 15:33, "Do not be deceived: 'Bad company corrupts good morals.'"[70] Family, neighborhood, school, and church can all provide such relationships. Perhaps an extension of this factor is that of moral exemplars that serve as models for not only behavior but also moral reasoning and moral affect. In so doing, the church can be an aid to parents and other caregivers in moral formation as a means of additional and supportive nurture.[71] Historically, providing moral biographies has been a consistent approach to moral education in the church and Christian school—with a wide diversity of individuals as models from the Old and New Testaments as well as the history of the church. If the church is to be a moral voice in the world, it must be a moral community itself. It should set an example for the world as a people who espouse a life that is pleasing to God. To accomplish this, the church must engage in the process of moral formation.

Reflection Questions

1. What makes morality (and moral formation) Christian?

2. What is your opinion of the four approaches to moral development? Which is most amenable to you?

3. How do you assess Kohlberg (and Gilligan)? Friend or foe? Why? What is the value of the cognitive and/or affective approach to moral development?

4. How might the work of the Holy Spirit operate in the process of moral formation?

5. How can you use the Bible more effectively in moral formation for yourself? Students? Congregants?

6. Where in your congregation do you use indoctrination? Values clarification? Developmental moral education? If any of these are not used, what may be the effects (pro or con) on the moral formation of the congregation?

ENDNOTES

[1] I have previously published two chapters on the subject of moral development: "Education and Moral Development," *Christian Ethics: The Issues of Life and Death,* Larry Choinard, David Fiensy, and George Pickens, eds. (Joplin, Missouri: Parma Press, 2004), 29-50 and with Alvin W. Kuest, "Moral Development," *Introduction to Christian Education,* Michael Anthony, ed. (Grand Rapids: Baker Book House, 2001), 73-82 – as well as presented a paper at the annual ETS meeting on the subject.

[2] Cf. Bonnidell Clouse, *Teaching for Moral Growth* (Downer's Grove, Illinois: Victor/ Bridgepoint, 1993) for an excellent survey and Christian perspective on these four views.

[3] Cf. Estep and Kuest, "Moral Development," 73-82.

[4] Jean Piaget, *The Moral Judgement of the Child* (New York: Free Press, 1965), 13.

[5] Cf. Ronald Duska and Mariellen Whelan, *Moral Development: A Guide to Piaget and Kohlberg* (New York: Paulist Press, 1975), 8-11.

[6] Lawrence Kohlberg and P. Turiel, "Moral Development and Moral Education," *Psychology and Educational Practice,* G. Lesser, ed. (Scott Foreman, 1971), 415.

[7] Kohlberg and Turiel, "Moral Development and Moral Education," 415.

[8] Lawrence Kohlberg and Clark Power, "Moral Development, Religious Thinking, and the Question of a Seventh Stage," *Zygon,* 16 (3): 203-59. Cf. Peter Feldmeier, *The Developing Christian: Spiritual Growth through the Life Cycle* (New York: Paulist Press, 2007), 45.

[9] John Michael Murphy and Carol Gilligan, "Moral Development in Late Adolescence and Adulthood: A Critique and Reconstruction of Kohlberg's Theory," *Human Development,* 23: 77-104.

[10] Carol Gilligan, *In a Different Voice* (Cambridge, Massachusetts: Harvard University Press, 1982), 42.

[11] Feldmeier, The Developing Christian, 48.

[12] Dennis H. Dirks, "Moral Development in Christian Higher Education." *Journal of Psychology and Theology,* 16 (4): 324-6.

[13] Bonnidell Clouse, "Moral Development and Justice," *Journal of Psychology and Christianity,* 10 (4): 293-9.

[14] Joel Brondos, "Sanctification and Moral Development." *Concordia Journal,* 17 (4): 419-39.

[15] Brondos, "Sanctification and Moral Development," 437-8.

[16] Samuel F. Rowan, "Testing Validity: Moral Development and Biblical Faith," *Moral Development Foundations* (New York: Abingdon Press, 1983), 111-37.

[17] Nels F. S. Ferré, *A Theology for Christian Education* (Philadelphia: Westminster Press, 1967), 146.

[18] Dirks, "Moral Development in Christian Higher Education," 326.

[19] Perry Downs, *Teaching for Spiritual Growth* (Grand Rapids: Zondervan Publishing House, 1994), 103-5.

[20] Ronald Duska and Mariellen Whelan, *Moral Development: A Guide to Piaget and Kohlberg* (New York: Paulist Press, 1975), 99.

[21] Dan Motet, "Kohlberg's Theory of Moral Development and the Christian Faith," *Psychology and Theology,* 6 (1): 18.

[22] R. G. Shepherds, "Biblical Progression as Moral Development: The Analogy and Its Implications," *Journal of Psychology and Theology*, 22 (3): 182-96.

[23] Timothy S. Gibson, "Proposed Levels of Christian Spiritual Formation," *Journal of Psychology and Theology*, 32 (4): 295-304.

[24] Bonndell Clouse, "Jesus' Law of Love and Kohlberg's Stages of Moral Reasoning," *Journal of Psychology and Christianity,* 9 (3): 12. Cf. also Clouse, *Teaching for Moral Growth*, 384.

[25] Clouse, "Jesus' Law of Love and Kohlberg's Stages of Moral Reasoning," 12-3.

[26] Catherine Stonehouse, "The Power of Kohlberg," *Nurture That Is Christian*, John Dettonni and James Wilhoit, eds. (Wheaton, Illinois: Victor Books, 1995), 71.

[27] Dirks, "Moral Development in Christian Higher Education," 326.

[28] Mary Frances Callan, "Feeling, Reasoning, and Acting: An Integrated Approach to Moral Education," *Readings in Moral Education*, Peter Scharf, ed. (Minneapolis: Winston Press, 1978), 199 [198-209].

[29] Paul Vitz, "The Kohlberg Phenomenon," *Pastoral Renewal,* 7 (8): 64-5.

[30] Cf. James Michael Lee, "Christian Religious Education and Moral Development," *Moral Development, Moral Education, and Kohlberg,* Brenda Munsey, ed. (Birmingham, Alabama: Religious Education Press, 1980), 333-6.

[31] Iris V. Cully, *Christian Child Development* (San Francisco: Harper and Row, 1979), 86.

[32] Lawrence Kohlberg, "Moral Education Reappraised," *The Humanist,* 3 (Nov/Dec): 14, 15 [13-5].

[33] Cf. Catherine Stonehouse, "Moral Development," *Evangelical Dictionary of Christian Education* (Grand Rapids: Baker Book House, 2002), 484-8.

[34] Perry Downs, "Promoting Moral Growth and Development," *Street Children* (Monrovia, California: MARC, 1997), 66.

[35] Robert M. Cooper, "Moral Formation in the Parish Church," *Anglican Theological Review* 69 (3): 283.

[36] David R. Krathwohl, Benjamin S. Bloom, and Bertram B. Masic, *Taxonomy of Educational Objectives: Handbook 2 – Affective Domain* (White Plains, New York: Longman, 1964), 180 [emphasis added].

[37] Krathwohl, Bloom, and Masic, *Taxonomy of Educational Objectives*, 180.

[38] Stonehouse, "Moral Development," 488.

[39] Donald Joy, *Moral Development* (New York: Abingdon Press, 1983), 23.

[40] Joy, *Moral Development*, 23, 33.

[41] Joy, *Moral Development*, 16.

[42] Joy, *Moral Development*, 20.

[43] Joy, *Moral Development*, 33-4.

[44] Adapted from Donald Joy, *Moral Development*, 24.

[45] Joy, *Moral Development*, 21.

[46] Gabriel Moran, *Religious Education Development: Images for the Future* (Minneapolis: Winston Press, 1983), 93.

[47] Moran, *Religious Education Development*, 87-105.

[48] Craig R. Dykstra, *Vision and Character: A Christian Educator's Alternative to Kohlberg* (New York: Paulist Press, 1981), 34.

[49] Dykstra, *Vision and Character*, 79-80.

[50] Clouse, *Teaching for Moral Growth*, 49.

[51] Joy, *Moral Development*, 25.

[52] Ted Ward (1989), *Values Begin at Home* (Wheaton, Illinois: Victor Books, 1989), 108.

[53] Ward, *Values Begin at Home*, 108-9.

[54] Ward, *Values Begin at Home*, 89-92.

[55] This illustration was first published in Estep, "Education and Moral Development," 41.

[56] Samuel F. Rowan, "Testing Validity: Moral Development and Biblical Faith," *Moral Development Foundations*, Donald Joy, ed. (New York: Abingdon Press, 1983), 111-37.

[57] Joel Brondos (1991), "Sanctification and Moral Development," *Concordia Journal* (October): 219-439.

[58] Downs, *Teaching for Spiritual Growth*, 95.

[59] Allen Verhey, "Able to Instruct One Another: The Church as a Community of Moral Discourse" in Mark Husbands and Daniel J. Treier, eds., *The Community of the Word:Toward an Evangelical Ecclesiology* (Downer's Grove, Illinois: IVP, 2005), 146-70.

[60] Peter Scharf, "Indoctrination, Values Clarification, and Developmental Moral Education as Educational Responses to Conflict and Change in Contemporary Society," *Readings in Moral Education* (Minneapolis, Minnesota: Winston Press, 1978), 18-35.

[61] Kohlberg, "Moral Education Reappraised."

[62] Cf. M. Daniel, R. Marroll, and Jacqueline E. Lapsley, eds. (2007), *Character Ethics and the Old Testament: Moral Dimensions of Scripture* (Louisville, Kentucky: Westminster / John Knox Press) and Robert L. Brawley, ed. (2007), *Character Ethics and the New Testament: Moral Dimensions of Scripture* (Louisville, Kentucky: Westminster / John Knox Press).

[63] Nels F. S. Ferré (1954), *Christian Faith and Higher Education* (New York: Harper and Brothers), 80.

[64] Adapted from Scharf, "Indoctrination, Values Clarification, and Developmental Moral Education," 34.

[65] Based on Ronald W. Johnson, Robert J. Kelly, and Barbara A. LeBlanc, "Motivational Basis of Dissonance: Adversive Consequences or Inconsistency," *Personality and Social Psychology Bulletin*, 21 (8): 850-5.

[66] Patrick Henry Reardon (2003), "Scripture Saturation," *Christian History*, 80: 30-4.

[67] Catherine M. Stonehouse, *Patterns of Moral Development* (Eugene, Oregon: Wipf and Stock, 2000), 67-85.

[68] Downs, "Moral Growth and Development," 75-6.

[69] Tom Wallace, "Values and Spirituality: Enhancing Character Development and Teaching/Learning Processes for a New Millennium," *Journal of Christian Education* (43.1): 44.

[70] Downs, "Moral Growth and Development," 75.

[71] Cf. Donald B. Rogers, "Christian Formation: The Neglected Mandate," *Religious Education*, 96 (3): 427-40.

CHAPTER 6

FAITH DEVELOPMENT
AND CHRISTIAN
FORMATION

By Timothy Paul Jones and Michael S. Wilder

Faith grows, or at least, it should. The apostles once implored their Lord, "Increase our faith" (Luke 17:5)—and no wonder. According to the teachings that the apostles had heard from the lips of Jesus, it was possible for faith to blossom from an almost imperceptible speck—"the size of a mustard seed"—into an earthshaking force (Matthew 17:20; Luke 17:6). The apostles had listened as Jesus praised "great faith" and then as He rebuked His followers for their "little faith" (Matthew 6:30; 8:10,26; 14:31; 15:28; 16:8; Luke 7:9; 12:28). Evidently, when Jesus returned from the heavens to Earth, faith would be one aspect of what He would be looking for: ". . . when the Son of Man comes," Jesus asked, "will he find that faith on the earth?" (Luke 18:8). Jesus wanted faith to be present when He returned to Earth, and He expected this faith to have grown.

From the perspective of the inspired authors of the New Testament writings, growth in faith was both desired (2 Corinthians 10:15; Ephesians 4:13-14; 2 Thessalonians 1:3) and expected (Hebrews 5:11-6:2). If an individual's faith failed to grow, the validity of that person's faith was doubtful (Hebrews 10:39). In the decades following the Savior's death and resurrection, the faith of Jesus multiplied—not only by increasing within believers as they received apostolic instruction (1 Thessalonians 3:2,10) but also by spreading from one person to another (Acts 6:7; 2 Timothy 1:5).

Exploring Faith Development

A dilemma emerges at this point though. Despite the fact that growth in faith is praised throughout the New Testament, Scripture provides no explicit step-by-step sequence for this growth. How, then, is it possible to assess whether or how an individual's faith is developing in a healthy way? Is it conceivable to describe faith development in a series of styles or stages? And, for that matter, what *is* faith?

Near the end of the book of Hebrews, one inspired author does provide a brief definition of faith. Yet it is a definition that seems to complicate as much as it elucidates: "Now faith is the reality of what is hoped for, the proof of what is not seen" (Hebrews 11:1).[1] Tellingly, what follows this definition is not a sequence of developmental stages but a series of stories—the narratives of past prototypes of faithfulness, recounted in rapid succession. So the question remains, "How does faith grow?" The goal of this chapter will be to explore that critical query.

Dominant Perspectives on Faith Development

In the opening years of the twenty-first century, the theory that James W. Fowler first posited in the 1970s continues to dominate discussions of faith development. As such, much of this chapter will focus on Fowler's theory. At the same time, other developmental models—both from modern theorists and from historic Christian reflection—will provide additional frameworks for the discussion.

Fritz Oser and Paul Gmünder, John Westerhoff, James Loder, and Heinz Streib have offered modern alternatives and correctives to Fowlerian stage-development. In the end, while recognizing the validity of much of this research, we will question whether the reality that these theorists have described as "faith" is actually faith at all. In wrestling with this question, we will examine closely how Scripture and orthodox Christian theologians have described faith development throughout the centuries. After exploring historical perspectives on faith development, we will posit a model for Christian formation and relate this model to the process of Christian sanctification.

"Seeking to Understand Faith": The Gap in Evangelical Theological Reflection

In the eleventh century AD, Anselm of Canterbury summarized the task of the Christian theologian in the dictum that remains a touchstone for theological reflection still today: "Faith seeking understanding" (*fides quaerens intellectum*).[2] Anselm's adage defined the theologian's central task as the process of comprehending more deeply and articulating more clearly the truths that the Christian already believes.

While recognizing the importance of *fides quaerens intellectum,* we suggest that another task is equally vital for Christian formation and discipleship. Taking a turn from Anselm's adage, we describe this task as *quaerens intellegere fidem* ("seeking to understand faith"). Anselm's task of *fides quaerens intellectum* portrays the prescriptive process that clarifies—based on divine revelation—how Christians ought to understand the God in whom they believe. The task that we have termed *quaerens intellegere fidem* is a descriptive process that seeks to comprehend the underlying structures of faith as well as examining how these structures shape individuals' behaviors, perspectives, and ideals.

Despite the equivalent significance of these two tasks, evangelical theologians and educators have tended to place far more emphasis on *fides quaerens intellectum* than on *quaerens intellegere fidem.* Empirical studies from evangelical publishers describe significant factors in maturing faith.[3] Popular guides to the spiritual disciplines highlight effective means and methods for development as disciples of Jesus Christ.[4] Systematic theological texts spill much ink when it comes to the logical positioning of faith within the *ordo salutis* ("order of salvation") and to aspects of authentic faith.[5] Yet little space is expended in these worthwhile texts to explicate the structures that describe *how* faith grows throughout the Christian's life.

In one first-rate evangelical theology text, for example, the sole presentation of developmental structures in the Christian life is a three-stage process of (1) conversion, (2) growth in holiness, and (3) ultimate perfection in holiness.[6] The entire Christian life from conversion to consummation is summarized in the single category of "growth in holiness"! Although such a structure may well be accurate, it is not particularly helpful for the purpose of assessing Christian maturity or of guiding individuals toward deeper faithfulness to Jesus Christ.

James Loder

In *The Transforming Moment*, James Loder did not attempt to describe developmental stages of faith or religiosity. Instead, he described how conversion—or what he called a "convictional experience"—occurs. According to Loder, a convictional experience begins with (1) a point of *conflict* in which individuals recognize their current categories are inadequate. This is followed by (2) a *pause*, a time when individuals reflect on their options. At the point of (3) *insight*, some symbol or inner realization unlocks a new level of understanding. This insight is followed by (4) *repatterning* of individuals' inner commitments. (5) Ultimately, *transformed* individuals confirm their transformation through public declaration or testimony.

Theories of Faith Development

Perhaps because of the relative neglect of the developmental structures of faith among evangelicals, the principal theories of faith development have emerged—not from evangelical scholarship—but from liberal Protestantism. At the dawn of the twenty-first century, the predominant paradigm for faith-development studies remains the stage theory that Methodist theologian James W. Fowler first formulated in the 1960s and 1970s.[7]

James W. Fowler laid the foundations for his developmental theory at Harvard Divinity School in the 1960s "in the context of the bitterly dividing struggle in the United States over the Vietnam War."[8] During those years, Fowler developed a course for Master of Divinity students titled "Theology as the Symbolization of Experience." The writings of Paul Tillich and H. Richard Niebuhr provided Fowler's primary theological frameworks, which he integrated with the developmentalist perspectives of Erik Erikson and Robert Bellah. The research of Wilfred Cantwell Smith, professor of comparative religions at Harvard, molded Fowler's definition of faith.

Another influence soon engaged Fowler's attention and helped to shape his perspectives on faith. Lawrence Kohlberg, a professor in the Harvard Graduate School of Education, formulated a stage-development theory to describe how perceptions and practices of morality evolved throughout the lifespan.[9] Deeply influenced by Kohlberg's methods and stages, Fowler gathered a team of graduate students in the fields of theology and developmental psychology. Over a period of three years, Fowler and his students conducted 359 interviews, exploring what they perceived to be individuals' "faith development." Working from his earlier theoretical research and from these interviews, James W. Fowler constructed a stage-theory to describe how faith grows.

The stage-theory that Fowler developed served as the foundation for his 1981 book *Stages of Faith: The Psychology of Human Development and the Search for Meaning*—a text that, in 2005, had reached its fortieth printing.[10] Since the initial publication of *Stages of Faith*, dozens of doctoral dissertations and no fewer than 300 academic articles have explored Fowler's stage-theory.[11]

The Foundations of Fowler's Definition of "Faith"

Fundamental to Fowler's stage-theory is his definition of "faith." James W. Fowler sought a perspective on faith that transcended any specific content or beliefs. A few years before Fowler formulated his faith-development theory, moral theorist Lawrence Kohlberg had claimed that a universalized principle of justice could provide the necessary foundations for a moral-development theory.[12] Fowler sought a similar sort of universalized "content-empty" principle to undergird his theory of faith development.[13] The universal foundational principle for Fowler's theory became the individual's or the group's way of responding to transcendent value and power.[14] In keeping with this principle, Fowler defined faith as a "person's or group's way of responding to transcendent value and power as perceived and grasped through forms of the cumulative tradition."[15]

The potential for the phenomenon that Fowler has defined as "faith" results neither from divine action nor primarily from any human choice. The propensity for faith is a part of every human being's genetic code.[16] It is "a generic human phenomenon" and "an apparently genetic consequence of the universal burden of finding or making meaning."[17]

Although influenced by the theological perspectives of H. Richard Niebuhr and Paul Tillich, Fowler excluded content from the essential nature of faith, arising primarily from his reliance on the research of W. C. Smith, professor of comparative religion at Harvard. In *Stages of Faith,* James W. Fowler explicitly acknowledged his dependence on Smith's research, pointing out how "for nearly two decades [W. C. Smith] has devoted himself to . . . the task of researching and interpreting the contribution each of the central world religious traditions makes to our understanding of faith."[18]

In *The Meaning and End of Religion* (1963) and *Faith and Belief: The Difference Between Them* (1979), W. C. Smith had argued that, in the premodern world, to *believe* or to *have faith* did not imply the acceptance of specific content as true. Instead, these terms meant to regard another person with "a certain ultimate loyalty" and to set one's heart on a relationship with that person.[19] The very idea that faith might require the acceptance of specific content would have been alien to premodern people. Thus, the terms translated "faith," "belief," and "believe" in the Judeo-Christian Scriptures and premodern creeds could not—Smith claimed—connote assent to any specific claims about God at the times when these documents were written.[20]

In his developmental theory, Fowler followed Smith's foundational assumptions about the nature of faith. For Fowler, the terms translated "faith," "belief," and "believe" in the Hebrew and Christian Scriptures and in the writings of early Christians denoted personal allegiance ("I believe [have faith] in") but never assent to specific assertions about God ("I believe [have faith] that"). Faith was personal loyalty that required no intellectual assent to any specific concepts or propositions.[21] According to Fowler, "for the ancient Jew or Christian to have said, 'I believe there is a God,' or 'I believe God exists,' would have been a strange circumlocution. The being or existence of God was taken for granted."[22] Whether a person accepted specific claims as true was never "a matter of final human destiny" in the minds of early Christians.[23]

Neither Smith nor Fowler denied the presence or the necessity of truth within the reality to which they referred as "faith." Faith is, Smith claimed, "answerable to transcendent reality and truth."[24] Their "transcendent reality and truth" does not, however, entail assent to any specific beliefs. It is, instead, allegiance to truth as a transcendent principle, a perspective that Fowler echoed in his definition of faith as a way of responding "to transcendent value and power."[25] By defining truth as a transcendent principle devoid of content, W. C. Smith was able to assert:

> There is no reason, in the modem world, why in principle an intelligent and informed Jew or Muslim and an intelligent and informed Christian, and indeed an intelligent and informed and sensitive atheistic humanist . . . should have different beliefs. Yet also there is no reason why they should not continue to live in terms of their differing symbols.[26]

Following this line of thinking, James W. Fowler argued for a "cultural-linguistic" perspective on faith. Such a perspective treats doctrines not as declarations of truth but as "grammatical rules" that govern the language of a particular set of religious convictions.[27] Heard from this perspective, when a Christian declares "Jesus is LORD," the Christian's statement represents an ontologically true affirmation of the need to be committed to a reality that is greater than oneself—spoken within the grammatical rules of Christianity. When Muslims declare there is no God but Allah, they speak the same ontological truth in the grammar of their particular faith. According to Fowler, "despite the myriad variants of religions and beliefs," there is a universal "unity and recognizability" that points to an identical phenomenon of faith within every religion.[28]

Treated cultural-linguistically, faith functions as a *mode of knowing* that requires *no assent to specific knowledge*.[29] This content-empty pattern develops, according to James W. Fowler, within a covenantal triad that involves three entities: self, other persons, and shared centers of value and power (see figure 6.1). The "shared centers of value and power" represent unifying sagas and shared statements that point a community or an individual toward that which is transcendent and ultimately meaningful.[30] Although the cultural-linguistic expressions of these sagas and statements differ from one religion to another, the underlying realities—Fowler and others contend—remain the same.

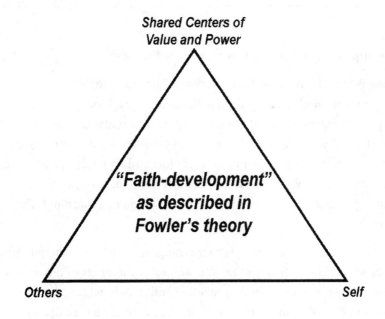

Figure 6.1: Fowler's Covenantal Triad

Fritz Oser and Paul Gmünder

The research of Oser and Gmünder has led to a "European school" of cognitive-psychological religious stage theory.[31] This theory focuses on "religious judgment"—that is, on the nature and structure of religious thinking, especially as it relates to persons' relations to that which is "Ultimate." The five stages of religious judgment specifically address how persons attempt to regulate or to control their relationship to the transcendent realm. Significant similarities exist between Oser's and Gmünder's stages of religious judgment and Fowler's stages of faith—even though the two theories developed independently (see figure 6.3).

Development according to Fowler's Stages[32]

James W. Fowler proposed one "prestage" of infantile faith development—followed by six full-fledged stages. From Fowler's perspective, when an infant cries and a parent provides comfort or nourishment, foundations for future faith grow within that child. Simply by being available and responding lovingly to a child's needs, parents and other caregivers help the preverbal child to cultivate a sense of mutuality—that is, the capacity to trust and to interact meaningfully with others.

Stage 1: Intuitive-Projective. Each morning, Caitlyn's mother and father gather her and her infant brother Wes for a few moments of prayer before Dad heads out the door. Three-year-old Caitlyn only understands a few phrases in each morning's prayer. Still, she is vividly aware that this process is an important part of her family's day. Right now, the precise implications of phrases like "thank You, Jesus" and "our Father in heaven" remain vague in Caitlyn's developing brain. Yet these phrases serve as important verbal signposts that will gain meaning as she grows.

According to Fowler, young children like Caitlyn are experiencing intuitive-projective patterns of faith development. Between the ages of three and seven, children intuitively assimilate the visible faith of their parents. They describe God in vague, nonhuman images and treat religious symbols as having power in themselves. Children in this stage are not yet capable of perceiving others' perspectives. Through symbols and imagery, intuitive-projective children respond emotionally to specific expressions of faith—even though they do not yet understand the knowledge behind these expressions. As they mature, children reflect more rationally on these early perceptions.

Stage 2: Mythic-Literal. Informed by a well-intended minister that she could "ask Jesus into her heart," nine-year-old Amy Jo turned her eyes toward her own chest. "But *how*," Amy Jo asked after a few moments of silent reflection, "does He get in *there*?" In Fowlerian terms, Amy Jo's development was struggling with what Fowler termed "mythic-literalism." She accepted symbolic language and analogies, but these symbols failed to function as intended within her mental framework.

Around seven years of age, children begin to perceive their world in the patterns that Jean Piaget identified as "concrete-operational." With the dawning of concrete operations, children begin to distinguish between what is real and what is fantastic. The resulting internal disequilibrium drives the child toward mythic-literal faith development. In the minds of mythic-literal children, the collective "myths" or "sagas" of their families or religious groups become central. Mythic-literal children view these sagas literally. While perceiving God as a personal being, the mythic-literal individual typically attempts to relate to transcendent reality through divine laws or intermediaries. In this stage, cause-and-effect sequences and logical reasoning become important tools for understanding life. The individual tends to operate according to an ethic of *do ut des* (Latin, "I-give so-that you-will-give"), believing that right actions will result in tangible rewards. According to Fowler, some adults never progress past the mythic-literal stage.

Stage 3: Synthetic-Conventional. A couple of years ago, I [Timothy] and my family visited a traditional church that sang from hardback hymnals instead of lyrics projected on a colorful screen. The pastor wore a dark robe and spoke from behind a pulpit instead of meandering around the stage in jeans and an untucked shirt—as I did when I preached. Theologically, this church was identical to our home church, but the practices seemed very different to our eleven-year-old daughter Hannah. So different, in fact, that Hannah whispered to me as our family headed to the parking lot after the service, "Are these people really Christians?" At that point in her life, Hannah's understanding of Christian faith was closely tied to the conventions and practices of the particular church where I served as pastor. She could not conceive that people with such divergent worship practices could possibly be Christians at all. In Fowlerian terms, Hannah was exhibiting early signs of synthetic-conventional development.

Persons in the synthetic-conventional stage deal with life's increasing complexity by conforming to the conventions of a particular group. During this stage, individuals begin to develop the capacity to distinguish their group's beliefs from the beliefs of others. The perspectives of their group—or of a significant leader within the group—mold the individual's beliefs and values. The individual perceives these beliefs and values as having a logical internal structure and consistency. Synthetic-conventional perspectives frequently characterize adolescents. In some cases, adults whose values are strongly peer-influenced never progress past the synthetic-conventional stage.

Stage 4: Individuative-Reflective. A Roman Catholic college student recounted an argument with her mother that marked a time of questioning in the student's life: "My mother felt that the [bread in Holy Communion] was actually the body of Christ. I said it didn't matter if it was really changed and thought of it more as a reenactment of the event."[33] The student retained some semblances of her earlier religious commitments, but she had reworked these commitments to fit her rationalized worldview.

In terms of Fowler's theory, this student's rationalized remolding of previous commitments signals individuative-reflective development.

In the individuative-reflective stage, the focus turns toward responsibility for one's commitments and beliefs. The individual—now operating in a fully formal operational mode—reflects on familiar assumptions, reconsidering and even rejecting prior beliefs and practices. New beliefs and newly reconsidered past beliefs are reworked into an individualized system that is perceived as cohesive and coherent. Symbols are important only inasmuch as they convey meanings that are helpful within this system.

While affirming much of Fowler's research, Sharon Daloz Parks—a former student of Fowler's—contended in her book *The Critical Years* that the fourth Fowlerian stage was inadequate. Parks identified a distinct and separate stage of development near the beginning of Fowler's individuative-reflective stage.[34] She referred to this proposed stage as "the critical years."

These years are critical, from Parks' perspective, not only because of their *critical importance* but also because emerging adults in this stage engage in *critical analyses* of previous perspectives. The critical years represent a period of probing questions and commitments that shift, depending on the student's context. Whereas synthetic-conventional adolescents seek self-definition through identification with meaningful groups, emerging adults in the critical years seek resolution of the fragmented commitments of a "divided self"—a self whose commitments change from group to group. Among college students, this resolution most often occurs as students interact with faculty and staff in environments that intentionally cultivate mentoring relationships. The resulting resolution is what enables the young adult to develop fully into Fowler's individuative-reflective stage. Eventually, this stage may lead to the "desert of criticism"—to dissatisfaction with rationalistic approaches to sacred rituals and symbols.[35] This dissatisfaction opens the individual to the broader possibilities of the paradoxical-consolidative approach to life.

Stage 5: Paradoxical-Consolidative (Conjunctive). Seldom reached before the age of 30, the paradoxical-consolidative stage requires recognition of the integrity of positions other than one's own. The conjunctive adult nurtures an identity that transcends race, class, or ideological boundaries. This identity consolidates traditional perspectives with the individual's doubts and with others' beliefs to form a broad and meaningful worldview—a worldview that is "balanced, . . . inclusive, . . . both/and."[36] Fowler has suggested that the paradoxical-consolidative stage "requires that one know suffering and loss, responsibility and failure, and the grief that is an inevitable part of having made irrevocable commitments of life and energy."[37]

The paradoxical-consolidative stage spawns new appreciation of religious sagas, rituals, and symbols—signs of faith that may have become the victims of rationalistic reductionism in the critical years or in the individuative-reflective stage. Persons in this stage understand religious sagas, rituals, and symbols as important yet inadequate signposts that point to an indescribable ultimate reality. This new awareness of transcendence leads the individual out of the "desert of criticism" and may blossom into a "second naïveté" in which the conjunctive adult reintegrates many meaningful elements that were discarded in previous stages.[38]

Stage 6: Universalizing. "After long study and experience," Mohandas Gandhi once declared,

> I have come to the conclusion that all religions are true; all religions have some error in them; [and] all religions are almost as dear to me as my own Hinduism. . . . My own veneration for other faiths is the same as that for my own faith; therefore no thought of conversion is possible.[39]

From the perspective of Fowlerian stage-development, such words—coupled with the life of the one who spoke them—exemplify the supreme stage of spiritual growth.

Having moved beyond paradoxes and polarities, persons in the universalizing stage root their lives in oneness with all people. Ultimate reality has replaced the self as the central reference point for life. This renewed vision of life frees persons in this stage to expend themselves for the sake of universal justice and love. From Fowler's perspective, the lives of such individuals as Mohandas Gandhi, Mother Teresa, and Martin Luther King, Jr. epitomize the universalizing stage of faith development. Fowler has regarded this stage as exceedingly rare. In his original sample of 359 interviewees, the team of researchers identified only one individual in the universalizing stage.

Transitioning from Stage to Stage. Fowler has presented his stages as universal, invariant, and hierarchical.[40] In other words, every person's development follows these stages, and it is desirable for persons to progress upward.[41] Biological maturation and life experiences are, according to Fowler, necessary for movement through the stages. Life experiences and biological growth alone, however, are never sufficient to move the individual from one stage to the next.[42]

How, then, do persons make the shift from stage to stage? Growth from one stage to another requires cognitive and relational transitions in no fewer than seven aspects of life. Shifts occur in the individual's (1) form of logic,[43] (2) social perspective-taking,[44] (3) form of moral judgment,[45] (4) perceptions of the exclusivity of social boundaries, (5) locus of authority, (6) form of world coherence, and (7) perceived function of symbols. From Fowler's perspective, the patterns associated with these seven aspects provide sufficient attitudinal and axiological markers for researchers to assess the maturity of an individual's faith.

Criticisms of Fowlerian Stage Development

James W. Fowler's stages provide not only a *theory* but also a *model*; they purport to portray not only *what is* but also *what ought to be*.[46] He intends his theory to "shape our teaching."[47] Put another way, Fowler's stages provide a map for people's lives,[48] and maps both describe and prescribe.

Maps not only depict particular destinations; maps also tell travelers how to traverse the terrain to arrive at the desired destination.

The question then becomes, "Is Fowler's map accurate?" Over the past three decades, more than a few ministers and scholars have questioned whether Fowler's cartography accurately depicts the terrain of faith development. Most of the critics have found fault with Fowler's stages in one or more of the following three areas: (1) Was Fowler's original sample sufficient to provide foundations for a universal model for faith development? (2) Given that faith seems to unfold within a complex and continuing life narrative, is it even possible for a traditional stage-development theory to describe faith development accurately? (3) From a biblical and theological perspective, is the reality to which Fowler referred as "faith" actually faith at all?

A Universal Model for Faith Development? Criticisms of Fowler's Methodology. James W. Fowler and his researchers drew their initial sampling of 359 interviewees from areas in and around academic communities in North America. Interviewees were selected purposively rather than randomly, and researchers collected no information about the subjects' educational backgrounds. Given these sampling irregularities and gaps in the data, it is unclear whether Fowler's sample accurately represented any larger population.

Other factors also suggest that Fowler's sample might not have represented the larger population: Despite the claim that faith development tends to advance with age, especially in the less mature stages, later studies have not consistently replicated this proposed relationship.[49] Although Fowler's findings have been replicated among nontheistic Jews, studies conducted with native Hawaiian and Korean populations replicated many aspects of Fowler's findings but also revealed significant gaps and cultural biases.[50] Paula Drewek's research among Bah'ai populations in Canada and India revealed particular culturally-rooted problems with the third and fourth Fowlerian stages.[51] Additionally, although Fowlerian stage assessments based on the interviews remained similar from one rater to another, it is unclear whether these assessments correlated consistently or significantly with any external measures.[52]

Perhaps the most pressing problem with Fowler's claim to have developed a universal stage-theory is the correlation between social class and Fowlerian stage-development. In studies conducted in the decades following the release of *Stages of Faith*, Fowlerian stage-development has related positively to educational level,[53] occupational level, job complexity, and income level.[54] Citizens in urban areas rate higher than rural folk,[55] and women tend to cluster in stages 3 and 5 while men have been found more frequently in stages 2 and 4.[56] All of this suggests the possibility of biases within Fowler's model. If such biases do exist, they would challenge the claim that Fowler has formulated a universal paradigm that transcends gender, class, culture, and religious tradition.

In Fowler's favor, factor analyses have suggested that his stages *do* constitute a structural whole that describes some actual dimension of human development.[57] Nevertheless, much of the data that undergirds Fowler's developmental sequences remains more heuristic than definitive—sufficient to allow for the proposal of a theory but perhaps inadequate to sustain such an all-encompassing developmental model.[58]

Stages or Styles? Criticisms of Fowler's Appropriation of Cognitive-Structural Developmental Theories. "It cannot be overlooked," European developmental theorist Heinz Streib has pointed out, "that the cognitive-structural theories of development, in their traditional shape of structural, hierarchical, sequential, and irreversible logic of development, are due to an all-too-optimistic interpretation of the project of modernity."[59] Streib specifically critiques James W. Fowler's theory in this regard.

According to Streib, Fowler's stages center almost exclusively on *cognitive decentration*—on constructive expansion of the individual's responsiveness to perspectives beyond his or her own. By centering on decentration, Fowlerian stage-development stumbles over itself by placing the "cart" of cognitive competencies in front the "horse" of personal biography and life history.[60] Wanting to work toward a view that is not so centered in individual cognitive competencies, Heinz Streib has urged theorists of religious development to shift their focus from decentration to phenomenology, from the development of cognitive competencies to the relationship of the individual's life-narrative to that which is perceived as transcendent or "Other."[61] In the process, Streib broadens the central phenomenon of his model from Fowler's content-empty "faith" to the ongoing appropriation of religion within the individual's life-narrative.[62]

In his resulting corrective to Fowler's cognitive-structural system, Streib suggests that spiritual formation transpires along the lines of five "religious styles."[63] With this corrective, Heinz Streib seems to have moved religious development from a "soft developmental theory" of the sort attempted by Fowler to a "functional model"—more akin to Erik Erikson's theory of psychosocial development (see figure 2.1).

Streib's five religious styles are very similar to five of Fowler's stages— beginning with Fowler's intuitive-projective stage (stage 1) and continuing consecutively through the conjunctive stage (stage 5)—with a couple of crucial distinctions: (1) In the first place, Streib's styles focus on the individual's expanding life-story and relationships instead of the individual's changing perceptions of meaning. (2) More importantly, although certain religious styles are likely to be more dominant during particular stages of life, all of Streib's styles are theoretically present throughout an individual's life (see figure 6.2). "The stages of faith," Streib contends, "are not confined to a certain age; there is more permeability and flexibility."[64] The Bielefeld-Based Cross-Cultural Study of Religious Deconversion has corroborated several facets of Streib's proposal—not only in Europe but also in North America. (See figure 6.3 for descriptions of each of Streib's styles.)

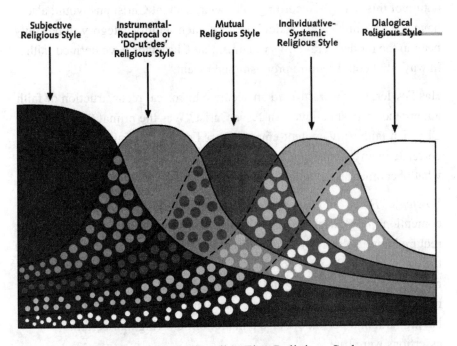

Figure 6.2: Heinz Streib's Five Religious Styles

Biblical and Theological Insights on Faith Development

The most strident criticisms of Fowlerian stage development have come from scholars who find deficiencies in Fowler's "content-empty" understanding of faith.[65] The concept of content-empty faith is unavoidably problematic for Christians who emphasize the regulative authority of Holy Scripture and who, because of this high view of Scripture, understand faith to require assent to specific content.

Definitions of "Faith" among the Developmental Theorists

Working from the historical reconstruction proposed by W. C. Smith, Fowler defined "faith" as personal allegiance to transcendent reality while excluding the necessity of assent to specific propositions regarding the nature of this reality. According to Fowler, ancient Christians would also have placed "faith" and "belief" in this content-empty category. It has only been in the modern era, Fowler claims, that Christians have defined faith in ways that could require propositional assent.[66]

Has Fowler, however, offered an accurate historical reconstruction of faith among the earliest believers in Jesus Christ? Was the primal form of Christian faith truly content-empty? Does Fowler's definition of "faith" correlate in any significant way with Christian faith development? If not, what phenomenon does Fowler's developmental theory actually describe?

Fowler's "Faith" in Historical and Theological Perspective. It is our contention that Fowler's claims about "faith" among the earliest Christians require highly selective readings of the Scriptures and of the theologians of the early church. A survey of the functions of *pisteuein* (Greek, "to believe" or "to have faith") and related terms in the New Testament reveals that the faith of the earliest Christians was not only a matter of having faith *in* a person but also a matter of believing *that* certain assertions were true.

It *is* true that, among the earliest Christians, "faith" did imply personal allegiance that resulted in a transformed life. Christian faith is, in fact, inseparable from such transformation. John the Baptist launched his ministry of proclamation with this charge: "Repent and believe in the good news!" (Mark 1:15). Jesus placed obedience and belief in synonymous parallelism (John 3:36). To have "faith in our LORD Jesus" was, for Paul, to "repentance toward God" (Acts 20:21; see also Romans 1:5,10:16, 16:26). For the author of Revelation, obeying God's commandments" is inseparable from remaining "faith in Jesus" (Revelation 14:12).

At the same time, such texts as Hebrews 11:3 make it clear that the life of faith also requires propositional assent to specific content: "By faith we know that the ages were created by God's Word, so that what is seen was not made out of things that are apparent." In other biblical texts, faith requires believers to recognize that God exists, that God raised Jesus from the dead, and that Jesus is the Savior (Romans 10:9; 1 Thessalonians 4:14; Hebrews 11:1-6; James 2:19; 1 John 5:1-5). In Paul's letter to the Romans, faith requires not only heartfelt submission to Christ's Lordship but also assent to the historical fact of his Resurrection (Romans 10:6-11).[67] Throughout the earliest decades of Christianity, "faith" implied both *propositional assent* and *personal allegiance.* If an individual abandons either aspect, the result is considered to be something other than authentic faith (see, e.g., 1 John 4:3,15; 5:1-5; 2 John 1:7).

Even in the Septuagint—the pre-Christian Greek translation of the Hebrew Scriptures that served as the first Bible for many early Christians—terms translated "belief," "believe," and "faith" repeatedly implied assent to specific historical and ontological assertions (see, e.g., Genesis 45:26; Exodus 4:5,8-9; 1 Kings 10:7; Job 9:16). This understanding of faith may also be found in the writings of the church fathers. In a crucial passage from his catechetical writings, Cyril of Jerusalem—the very theologian from whom W. C. Smith claimed to have derived primary proof for his historical misconstruction—clarified what he meant when he used the term "faith":

> The term "faith" is one word, yet it has two meanings: One kind of faith concerns doctrine. It involves the soul's rising to and *accepting some particular point* and it is profitable for the soul. ... For if you will *have faith that Jesus Christ is the Lord and that God raised him from the dead,* you will be saved and will be transported into paradise by the same one who brought the thief into paradise. ... The other kind of faith, ... given by the Holy Spirit as a special favor, is *not only doctrinal* but it also produces effects beyond any human capacity. ... Whenever anyone speaks in faith, having faith that it will come to pass, without doubting in his heart, he receives that grace. ... Since all cannot read the Scriptures, ... so that the soul may not perish because of ignorance, we pass on all of the doctrine of faith in a few lines. ... Be careful, brothers! Hold tightly to the things—handed down that you now receive![68]

The function of the terms translated "faith" in this particular passage suggests that this church father's definition of faith specifically required assent to objective claims.[69] This understanding of "faith" is also present in Latin theologians' use of the word *credere* (Latin, "to believe" or "to have faith"). For Cyprian of Carthage, for example, to believe in [*credere in*] God was to believe that [*credere quod*] God had appointed the church's leaders.[70] Writing in North Africa in the fifth century, Augustine of Hippo identified faith as "thinking with assent" regarding truths that God had revealed in Jesus Christ and in Scripture.[71]

This perspective persisted among the medieval theologians. Peter the Lombard's *Sententiae,* written in the twelfth century, includes one of the first developmental models to describe how Christian faith grows. Peter the Lombard's four-fold model strongly influenced Scholastic perspectives on the nature and function of faith. For Peter and other Scholastic theologians, (1) faith begins as "implicit faith" (*fides implicita*)—an innate sense of trust in a higher source of knowledge.[72] (2) Faith then grows to include assent to the historic reality of God, revealing Himself in Jesus Christ ("historical faith" or *fides historica*). Although not fully constitutive of Christian faith, this act of assent provided a necessary foundation for Christian faith. *Fides historica* gives way to (3) personal allegiance or "explicit faith" (*fides explicita*). Ideally, *fides explicita* grows into (4) *fides formata caritate* ("faith formed by love"). In *fides formata caritate*, the believer believes not because of blessings that he or she may receive but out of sheer love.[73]

The sixteenth-century Reformers, such as John Calvin and Martin Luther, did not wholeheartedly embrace the Scholastic perspective on faith. Early Protestant theologians contended that, prior to the point of *fides explicita*, no authentic faith could be found in anyone's heart.[74] Until an individual explicitly trusted in Jesus Christ, his or her assent was merely "notional" and could not lead to eternal life.[75] Calvin defined Christian faith in terms of "firm and certain knowledge of divine benevolence toward us"; prior to such certainty, authentic faith does not exist.[76] This point of difference should not, however, overshadow a crucial point of agreement: The Scholastics and the Reformers alike understood Christian faith to require assent to specific objective assertions about God.

From the first century forward, Christian faith entailed personal allegiance to an unfathomable transcendent reality. Yet this faith also referred to transcendent reality by a certain name, required that this reality be linked to specific redemptive acts in human history, and called believers to embrace particular assertions about the essential nature of this reality. The difficulty with Smith's and Fowler's understanding of faith is their apparent assumption that the primacy of personal allegiance somehow excludes the necessity of propositional assent to specific content. Given the clear function of the terms translated "faith" in the New Testament and throughout the church's history, Fowler's claim that the phenomenon of faith among premodern Christians was "a mode of knowing" that required no specific assent appears to be misguided at best.[77]

Fowler's "Faith" and Christian Maturity. According to Fowler, every religious tradition describes faith in ways that ultimately exemplify "the same phenomenon."[78] Fowler simultaneously insists that maturation within his model "implies no lack of commitment to one's own truth tradition."[79] If these claims are true, development, according to Fowler's stages, ought to correlate strongly and positively with increasing maturity in any religious tradition. Even within the conservative-evangelical Christian tradition, increasing growth in Christian faithfulness should relate positively to increasing maturity, according to Fowler's stages.

Research has not, however, substantiated this supposition. In a 2003 study, a sampling of evangelical Christians was grouped according to Fowlerian stage development and then evaluated using a standardized instrument— the "Shepherd Scale"—to assess Christian faith maturity.[80] A significant relationship was observed between Christian faith maturity and Fowlerian stage development—but not in the direction that one might expect! Participants, who showed evidence of a mature Christian faith, were slightly *less likely* to exhibit advanced development, according to Fowler's stages.

What these data suggest is that, though Fowler and his researchers may have measured some actual developmental pattern, Fowler's model may have failed to describe faith in any sense that evangelical Christians could identify as faith. Despite Fowler's insistence on "the unity and recognizability" of an identical phenomenon of faith in every truth tradition,[81] research simply does not seem to bear out such claims. At least within the evangelical tradition, the phenomenon of Christian faith differs radically from the phenomenon that Fowler has identified as faith.

John Westerhoff III

A professor of Christian nurture at Duke University Divinity School, Westerhoff described faith development in terms of four "styles." He compared these styles to rings of a tree trunk. A tree is still a tree—regardless of how many rings may be found in its trunk; however, as a tree matures, more rings are evident. Likewise, faith is "transmitted, sustained, and expanded through our interactions with other faithing selves in a community of faith."[82] Westerhoff's styles of faith, moving from the core outward, are (1) experienced faith, (2) affiliative faith, (3) searching faith, and (4) owned faith.

Rejection, Adaptation, or Redefined Appropriation?

How then should evangelical educators respond to faith-development theories such as that of James W. Fowler? The simplest paths of response are *rejection* or *adaptation*. Each path is, however, problematic. On the one hand, to reject these theories completely is to refuse to deal adequately with the fact that such theorists as Fowler seem to have measured some real phenomenon. On the other hand, to adapt a universalized "faith," such as that of Fowler, to coincide with Christian faith is to fail to recognize the radical variance that separates these disparate definitions of faith.[83]

A third path is also possible though—the path of *redefined appropriation.* Here is what we mean by "redefined appropriation." Although the dominant faith-development theories have failed to define faith in any way that is admissible from an evangelical Christian perspective, these theories may describe some reality that significantly impacts Christian formation. Put another way, Fowler and others have described *something.* Although this "something" appears not to be Christian faith, the phenomenon may still have some relevance for processes of Christian discipleship.[84]

Pursuing this third pathway, we offer three specific proposals for interacting with the dominant social-scientific models of faith development. (1) In the first place, it is crucial to point out that *significant commonality exists among the developmental theories that attempt to depict religious or faith development.* Despite their differences, the theories proposed by James W. Fowler, Fritz Oser and Paul Gmünder, Heinz Streib, John Westerhoff III, and others share a strikingly similar set of patterns and transitions. This commonality is not surprising: In John Westerhoff's book *Will Our Children Have Faith?,* published prior to Fowler's *Stages of Faith,* Westerhoff explicitly notes his dependence on Fowler's burgeoning theory.[85] Oser and Gmünder, as well as Fowler, drew heavily from Kohlberg's moral-development theory, while Streib's five religious styles rework Fowler's stages.[86]

What are the common elements in these developmental paradigms? Each model or theory begins with the individual's *subjective assimilation* of patterns of meaning-making in their families and other close social relations. As this phase draws to a close, children discover rules and patterns of life that, when followed, lead to positive outcomes in their particular contexts. In this phase of *instrumental reciprocity,* the natural tendency is to keep the rules and to follow certain rituals to avoid consequences and to receive rewards. *Social conventionality* emerges when the individual begins to develop his or her values according to the expectations of a meaningful group. Eventually, individuals realize that inconsistencies exist—even within their selected group. Some individuals move from group to group, still deriving their values and identities from groups. Others, however, embark on a process of *individuative systemization,* developing a personalized worldview to deal with life's increasing complexity. Some individuals move from this point to *dialogical consolidation.* These persons may retain an individuated worldview, but they reconcile this worldview with a newfound capacity to enter into appreciative dialogue with dissimilar groups, perspectives, and worldviews.

	Styles of Faith (John Westerhoff)	Stages of Faith (James W. Fowler with Sharon Daloz Parks)	Stages of Religious Judgment (Fritz Oser and Paul Gmünder)	Religious Styles (Heinz Streib)
Subjective Assimilation	**Experienced Faith:** A child "first learns Christ not as a theological affirmation but as an affective experience."[87]	*Intuitive-Projective Faith:* Prior to the age of seven, children intuitively and affectively respond to the experience of their parents' faith.	*Religious Heteronomy:* Until age eight or so, children feel themselves to be passive respondents to The Ultimate.	*Subjective:* Children develop initial religious perceptions through experiences with their primary caregivers.
Instrumental Reciprocity	*Affiliative Faith:* Individual affiliates with the faith community first through following rules and rituals ...	*Mythic-Literal Faith:* Persons relate to transcendent reality through rituals and laws—with emphasis on cause-and-effect sequences.	*Do ut Des:* That which is Ultimate can be influenced through obedience, rituals, and conformity to the conventions of a particular community.	*Do ut Des:* "Good" is what authority wants —especially obedience to rituals and commands; "bad" is what results in punishment.

	Styles of Faith (John Westerhoff)	Stages of Faith (James W. Fowler with Sharon Daloz Parks)	Stages of Religious Judgment (Fritz Oser and Paul Gmünder)	Religious Styles (Heinz Streib)
Social Conven-tionality	... then through relationships within the community.	***Synthetic-Conventional Faith:*** Persons deal with life's increasing complexity by conforming to the conventions of a particular group.		***Mutual:*** Persons seek the unquestioned security of a social or religious group.
Indivi-duative System-ization	**Searching Faith:** "In order to move from an understanding of faith that belongs to the community to an understanding of faith that is our own, we need to doubt and question that faith."[88]	**The Critical Years:** Emerging adults may question past beliefs and seek resolution in relationships with persons who help them to develop a coherent worldview. **Individuative-Reflective:** New beliefs and newly reconsidered past beliefs are reworked into an individualized system that is perceived as consistent.	**Ego Autonomy and One-Sided Responsibility**: Individuals begin to perceive themselves as the ones personally responsible for life and for their beliefs about that which is perceived as Ultimate.	***Individuative Systemic:*** Persons reflect critically on religious matters and become able to give reasons for their individual beliefs or skepticisms.

	Styles of Faith (John Westerhoff)	Stages of Faith (James W. Fowler with Sharon Daloz Parks)	Stages of Religious Judgment (Fritz Oser and Paul Gmünder)	Religious Styles (Heinz Streib)
Dialogical Consoli- dation	**Owned Faith:** Mature faith is when individuals hold strongly to their faith and to the faith community while respecting others' dissimilar expressions of faith.	**Paradoxical- Consolidative:** Persons in this stage understand faith community, sagas, rituals, and symbols as important, yet inadequate, signposts that point to an ultimate reality that stands beyond all human description. *Universalizing:* Persons expend themselves for others, living in oneness with all people and with Being itself. (Evidence for actual existence of this stage may be inadequate.)	**Mediated Autonomy:** Social engagement with faith community and with dissimilar others become primary religious expression. **Unconditional Religiosity:** Individuals become able to think paradoxically, perceiving sacredness in all of life.	**Dialogical:** No longer predominantly concerned with defending their religious identity, persons embrace and learn from religious orientations other than their own.

Figure 6.3: Points of Commonality in Social-Scientific Theories of Religious and Faith Development

(2) Recognizing significant shared elements among these theories, we further suggest that *the dominant theories of religious development have described an actual phenomenon that constitutes some single structural whole.*

To be sure, several aspects of these theories lack sufficient supporting data. Neither Fowler's nor Oser's data, for example, can unambiguously substantiate their proposed progression past the point of social conventionality.[89] The research underlying Fowler's universalizing stage specifically lacks sufficient support. Furthermore, several aspects of each theory also must be challenged on theological grounds—the assumption, for example, that advanced development should result in a pluralistic perspective on other belief-systems. Furthermore, it should be recognized that some developmental structures may stem from human depravity and self-centeredness rather than the goodness of creation or the grace of redemption. As such, developing discipleship processes around these developmental structures may not always lead to Christ-centered maturity.

At the same time, despite disparate samples and methods, these theories do present us with common elements that overlap in ways that support the supposition that all of them describe some similar phenomenon. It already has been demonstrated that this phenomenon is probably not Christian faith. If this shared phenomenon is *not* faith, however, *what is it*? How does it impact Christian faith development?

(3) Our proposal is that *what the social-scientific theorists have described as "faith development" relates more closely to the biblical concept of wisdom.* Biblically, wisdom begins with "the fear of the LORD" (Job 28:28; Psalm 111:10; Proverbs 1:7; 15:33; Isaiah 33:6)—that is to say, with the awe-inspiring awareness that there is an orderliness and an immensity around us that is not easily comprehended or perceived. This awareness compels not only the believer but also the pagan to pursue some semblance of morality and to seek some greater meaning behind the events of life.[90] Viewed in biblical perspective, these pursuits cultivate wisdom—that is to say, the reasoned search for universal patterns in natural and social contexts that enables individuals to develop habits and attitudes that enable the accomplishment of certain goals. Or, to put our definition of wisdom in somewhat simpler terms, these pursuits lead to "intellectual understanding expressing itself in sensible living."[91]

According to the inspired biblical authors, wisdom was a *universal phenomenon* available both within and beyond the believing community

(Genesis 41:8; Exodus 7:11; Isaiah 19:11; Ezekiel 28:1-17; Daniel 2:12-18, 4:6-18; Acts 7:22)—embedded by God not only in Scripture but also in nature (Psalm 104:24; Proverbs 8:1,22; Jeremiah 8:9). Wisdom was a *developmental phenomenon.* Wisdom began in the child with the cause-and-effect reciprocity of parental discipline (Proverbs 29:15-17), matured with age (Job 12:12, 15:8-10; Luke 2:40, 52; cf. function of "wisdom" in *Sirach* 6.18, 34; 25.4-5); and operated at its highest level when individuals made ethical decisions based not on rigid rules but on overarching principles (1 Kings 3:16-28). Individuals could use wisdom *positively* (Ecclesiastes 7:25; Proverbs 3:19-20) or *negatively* (Exodus 1:10; 2 Samuel 13:3). Perhaps most important, wisdom entailed *an expanding quest to find meaning in life's events* (Ecclesiastes 7:25, 8:16; cf. function of "wisdom" in 4 *Maccabees* 1.16).[92]

Nearly all of these elements also may be located in the social-scientific theories of "faith" and "religious judgment." The developmental phenomenon that these theories describe constitutes a "universal human concern" and "a consequence ... of the universal burden of finding or making meaning" in which the individual moves beyond cause-and-effect ethics and embraces a "principled higher law" in search of "order, unity, and coherence."[93] One key question to elicit persons' perceptions of this phenomenon in Fowler's faith-development interview has been: "When and where do you experience wonder, awe, or ecstasy?"[94] Viewed together, these elements coalesce to depict a reality very similar to the biblical phenomenon of "wisdom."

To be sure, some developmental theorists seem to have misconstrued many aspects of wisdom. For Fowler and others, the endpoint of development is cultural-linguistic pluralism. In the Judeo-Christian Scriptures, the ultimate goal and specific content of wisdom is Jesus Christ (1 Corinthians 1:21-30, Colossians 2:2-3).[95] Nevertheless, it appears these theorists—like the unbelieving sages from whom Moses gleaned knowledge during his years in Pharaoh's palace (Acts 7:22)—have seen and systematized elements of an authentic phenomenon, one that the inspired authors of Scripture described thousands of years earlier.

Some aspects of these theorists' research may be usable in evangelical explorations of human development and formation in wisdom. The patterns that these developmental theorists have described are *not,* however, faith development in any biblical sense. Their "faith" is a distinct phenomenon—distinguishable from Christian faith not only in its developmental patterns but also in its essential nature.

A Christian Approach to Faith Development

What then might a uniquely Christian model of faith development look like? Before presenting a specific model, we suggest three specific criteria that ought to characterize a Christian approach to faith development. (1) Such an approach should be *centered in content that is both particular and personal.* The substance of Christian faith is not a universal experience that is shared by all people; the goal and substance of Christian faith is Jesus Christ (Hebrews 12:2). As such, a Christian approach to faith development ought to be centered in the particular person of Jesus Christ—as He is recognized through Holy Scripture and revealed through the Holy Spirit. (2) Christian faith development should be understood as *inseparable from the theological construct of sanctification.* (3) Given that Christian faith is rooted in God's covenant—not merely with individuals but with a community, *a Christian approach to faith development should reflect the crucial role of the faith community.*

Content and Christian Faith

As presented in the New Testament, Christian faith requires patterns of active and personal allegiance (Hebrews 11:7-30; James 2:17,26; 1 John 3:2-3). Faith also, however, requires that believers assent to specific content that is rooted in God's consummate self-revelation in Jesus Christ (see, e.g., Romans 10:9; 1 Thessalonians 4:14; Hebrews 11:1-6; James

2:19; 1 John 5:1-5). Far from being "content-empty," the faith of the earliest Christians was nothing less than *life-defining allegiance to Jesus— as recognized through Holy Scripture and as revealed through the Holy Spirit—that resulted in increasing confidence in God's decisive action on their behalf in Jesus Christ and in increasing conformity to the character of Jesus Christ.* Such faith results immediately in justification and eventually in sanctification (Romans 5:1-2; 6:8-23; 10:9-10). When content is removed from faith, however, the result is not Christian faith at all. It is instead a relativistic recognition of transcendence—devoid of any foundation beyond the fleeting experience of the individual (see figure 6.4). Such substitutes for authentic faith endow penultimate realities with ultimate value and, thus, constitute idolatry.

"FAITH" AS RELATIVISTIC RECOGNITION OF TRANSCENDENCE	FAITH IN BIBLICAL PERSPECTIVE
Propositional assent to specific truths about transcendent reality: **No** Personal allegiance to reality beyond myself: **Yes**	Propositional assent to specific truths about transcendent reality (Gospel truths): **Yes** Personal allegiance to reality beyond myself (Jesus Christ): **Yes**
"FAITH" AS SELF-CONFIDENCE	"FAITH" AS REDUCTIONISTIC ACCEPTANCE OF FACTS
Propositional assent to specific truths about transcendent reality: **No** Personal allegiance to reality beyond myself: **No**	Propositional assent to specific truths about transcendent reality: **Yes** Personal allegiance to reality beyond myself: **No**

Figure 6.4: Taxonomy of Perspectives on "Faith"[96]

Sanctification and Christian Faith Development

Often the doctrine of sanctification is viewed as a category for theologians; while faith development is perceived as the domain of Christian educators. In truth, the two categories should be seen as inextricable. Sanctification is *the process of being set apart for God's purposes and restored to the image of God by means of the Holy Spirit's gracious work in the believer's life from regeneration through glorification* (Romans 8:29-30; 2 Corinthians 3:18; Ephesians 4:20-24; Colossians 3:10). Faith development is one aspect of this transformative process and an integral component throughout the Spirit's sanctifying work. Jesus Himself declared it is by faith that believers experience sanctification (Acts 26:18). Through faith, the sanctifying Spirit is received (Galatians 3:2, 14). As such, an accurate and a useful model of Christian faith development ought to take into full account the Holy Spirit's work of sanctification.

Sanctification is both an event that God accomplishes when an individual becomes a believer (1 Corinthians 6:11; Hebrews 10:10) and a transformative process that persists throughout the believer's earthly life (Romans 6:19-23; Hebrews 10:14). Sanctification requires assent to specific truth (John 17:17) and is ultimately rooted in the character of Jesus Christ (1 Corinthians 1:30). Although sanctification begins with the divine work of regeneration, sanctification also requires progressive human effort on the believer's part. The process of sanctification will remain incomplete until the believer's glorification in eternity (Romans 6:22) when faith becomes sight.

Faith Development and the Faith Community

Faith in Jesus Christ results from an individual's response to God's grace. At the same time, the life of faith—as presented throughout the New Testament—is experienced in a community of faith. The church is, after all, "the household of faith" (Galatians 6:10) wherein Christians strive together for their shared commitment (Philippians 1:27). Faith is held in "common" with other believers (Titus 1:4) to be "delivered" from one generation of believers to the next (Jude 1:3). Through faith, believers encourage one another (Romans 1:12). The idea of a solitary believer in Jesus Christ—someone who pursues sanctification and Christian formation in isolation from other believers—is utterly foreign to the New Testament.

From the perspective of the Christian Scriptures, I cannot follow Jesus alone—anymore than I can get married alone. To have faith in Jesus Christ is to be enmeshed in a particular community of fellow travelers on the journey of faith.

Jesus did not call isolated individuals to follow Him. He called a group of disciples. He gathered a crowd. ... Privacy is not a Christian category. We are saved from our privacy by being made part of a people who can tell us what we should do with our money, with our genitals, with our lives. We have been made part of a good company, a wonderful adventure, so that we no longer need "mine."[97]

This is not a light commitment of the Christian. It will demand such things as loving others sacrificially, maintaining a servant attitude, not coveting, controlling emotions, bearing others' burdens, giving generously, confronting graciously, and admitting sin. It means applying scriptural truths in difficult situations, allowing iron to sharpen iron as our lives intertwine with one another.

Implications for Christian Formation

A Christian approach to faith development should be—we have suggested—centered in specific content, clearly connected to sanctification, and cultivated in the faith community. Our dynamic model for Christian faith (figure 6.5) depicts one possibility for such a paradigm of faith development. In our model, spiritual growth is not the result of movement through a static series of stages in which the individual discards one perspective and progresses to another. Growth begins with and is driven by personal allegiance to God as Father, Son, and Holy Spirit—coupled with assent to specific truths about God's self-revelation in Jesus

Christ as revealed in Holy Scripture. This two-sided coin of allegiance and assent is what the Scholastics identified as *fides explicita.* The believer does not leave behind his or her initial faith in the process of sanctification. This faith remains a fixed and permanent core throughout faith development.

In our model, there is a "tree-ring" effect in which a dynamic interaction occurs among the believer's faith in God; the means of growth in faith through love of others, love for God, and suffering; and the shaping of one's identity in Christ. The growth of a tree entails the addition of layers or rings in response both to inward and outward stimuli. So is the case in Christian faith development. Formed in the context of the faith community (*fides ecclesiam formata*), faith leads to authentic fellowship as believers embrace God's work among His people—despite their frailties and failures (Ephesians 4:1-6; 2 Thessalonians 1:3). Formed by love (*fides caritate formata*), faith leads to a life of gratitude as believers learn to delight in God—not because of the gifts that God may give but simply because of who God is (Ephesians 3:17-21; 1 Timothy 1:5; Habakkuk 2-3). Faith is also formed through suffering (*fides cruciatu formata*) and, through these momentary afflictions, becomes increasingly steadfast and complete (Acts 14:22; James 1:2-6; 1 Peter 1:6-7).

These formative episodes do not occur sequentially in a believer's life. Furthermore, simply because faith has been formed once in a particular area does not mean the individual has somehow solved that developmental dilemma once and for all. "God's school is, after all, not like most," one pastor has noted. "It's not regimented, age-adjusted, fixed in its curricula. The classroom is life itself; the curriculum, all of life's demands and interruptions and tedium, its surprises and disappointments."[98] This class and curriculum may be messy and unpredictable at times; they do, however, have a definite goal. With each formative episode and event, the believer becomes more aware of and hopeful for faith in its fullness (*fides plenus,* figure 6.5) when "until we all reach unity in the faith and in the knowledge of God's Son, [growing] into a mature man with a stature measured by Christ's fullness" (Ephesians 4:13).

The hope for faith in its fullness provides a unifying goal for faith development. Of course, this "oneness of faith and authentic knowledge" are not likely to be experienced in their fullness on this side of eternity. Yet, even here and even now, believers are gifted with momentary glimmers of this glorious hope wherein faith is fulfilled. It is a hope for that eternal moment when all value and identity are found in Jesus Christ when "we will be like Him, because we will see Him as He is" (1 John 3:2).

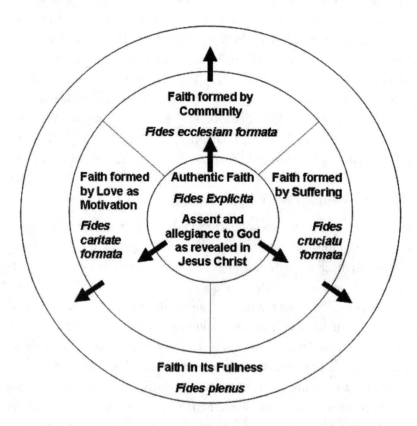

Figure 6.5: Dynamic Model for Christian Faith Development[99]

Pastoral and Educational Implications

Throughout this chapter, we have emphasized the twofold nature of faith: Christian faith is both *personal allegiance* and *propositional assent.* Christian faith requires both a theological core that continually deepens and a lifestyle of faithfulness that develops and grows. Yet, in practice, these two sides of a single coin often seem to be pitted against each other in the growth and spread of Christian faith. For example, one leader in a prominent Protestant denomination recently declared, "The victories of faith … did not happen because men and women loved doctrine. They happened because they loved Jesus."[100] But this presents a false dichotomy. In distinction to such divided thinking, what we have contended in this chapter is that growth in personal allegiance to Jesus is inseparable from ever-deepening devotion to sound doctrine. If someone adores Jesus but ignores doctrine, that individual often ends up loving his or her spiritual experiences rather than the sovereign God who intersected history in the flesh of Jesus Christ. Conversely, if someone's devotion to doctrine trumps devotion to Jesus, that person's faith becomes a lifeless system of logic rather than what it is intended to be—a living belief and a mystery, a lifestyle yet "a history, new every morning."[101]

Christian faith requires both personal allegiance to Jesus and devotion to the truth about Jesus—as revealed through the Holy Spirit and recorded in Holy Scripture. But what significance does this have for our day-to-day ministries of discipleship and leadership? Quite a lot—as it turns out. In the earliest Christian communities, to be committed to Jesus was to be devoted to "the apostles' teaching" (Greek, *didache*) (Acts 2:42). The apostle John tested his readers' faith—not only on relational and moral bases but also on doctrinal and confessional bases (1 John 4:1-3).[102] According to the apostle Paul, freedom from sin and obedience from the heart are inseparable from deepening commitment to doctrinal instruction (Romans 6:17-18). Contemporary research seems to confirm the crucial importance of doctrinal devotion coupled with personal allegiance. In a recent study of 80,000 congregants in 200 evangelical churches, the researchers identified two spiritual catalysts that were significant throughout the process of spiritual growth.[103] These two catalysts were *the primacy of Christ in the believer's daily life* and *the individual's commitment to the authority of Scripture*—interestingly, one a point of personal allegiance and the other assent to a doctrinal assertion.

Also significant for pastoral and educational ministry is the place of suffering and community in Christian faith development. Frequently, structural-developmental models have ignored or downplayed the role of painful failures and interpersonal fellowship. In our dynamic model of Christian faith—as in the Christian Scriptures, suffering and community play crucial roles. Viewed in terms of these two dynamics, every tribulation provides an opportunity for the believer to experience greater fullness of faith, and the community of faith provides a primary context for the cultivation of growing faith.

Conclusion

"Faith is believing what you know ain't so," the schoolboy declared in a novel published under the name Mark Twain.[104] A few decades later, journalist H. L. Mencken echoed these same sentiments, defining faith as "an illogical belief in the occurrence of the improbable."[105] Viewed in this way, faith is the hope of a fool, an irrational longing for some state of being that does not exist in reality. For a Christian, however, faith falls into a category that is far from irrational yearning. Christian faith is an ever-developing phenomenon that is both rational and experiential, confessional and experimental, propositional and personal, objective and subjective, human and divine.

This chapter has said much about faith, and we hope what we have described is useful in your ministry. The final word about faith is not to be found in these pages though. The final word about faith is not, in fact, to be found in any human sentence at all because this Word is not a proposition but a Person: "Jesus, the source and perfecter of our faith, who for the joy that lay before Him endured a cross and despised the shame, and has sat down at the right hand of God's throne" (Hebrews 12:2). It is with Him that all true faith begins, and it is in Him that our faith will one day find both its foundation and its perfection.

Reflection Questions

1. G. K. Chesterton, a Christian writer in the early twentieth century, once said, "Real development is not leaving things behind as on a road but drawing life from them as with a root."[106] Do you agree with Chesterton? How is this perspective seemingly reflected in the developmental theories proposed by Heinz Streib and John Westerhoff III? How about James W. Fowler's theory?

2. Which model of development in this chapter most accurately reflects the perspectives found in Holy Scripture? After answering this question, use your scriptural knowledge as well as the information presented in this chapter to develop your own model of Christian faith development. Include the primary faith-forming events of your life in your model.

3. How will you, as a minister, structure the discipleship processes in your church to develop propositional assent and personal allegiance in congregants' lives? Sketch out a discipleship process or sequence that will deepen both allegiance and assent in the lives of growing believers.

4. How do hard developmental models differ from soft, functional, and cultural-age models? Into which of these categories does Christian faith development fit best? Why?

5. The authors of this chapter have defined faith as *life-defining allegiance to Jesus—as recognized through Holy Scripture and as revealed through the Holy Spirit—that resulted in increasing*

confidence in God's decisive action on their behalf in Jesus Christ and in increasing conformity to the character of Jesus Christ. What would you change in this definition?

6. How does Christian faith development relate to sanctification? Which is the broader category—sanctification or faith development? Is Christian faith development an aspect of sanctification, or is sanctification an expression of formation in Christian faith?

ENDNOTES

[1] Unless otherwise indicated, all Greek and Latin texts are translated by Timothy Paul Jones from primary source materials.

[2] Anselm seems to have developed this clause from the Latin Vulgate rendering of Isaiah 7:9. Anselm clarified his intentions with these words, which allude to Augustine of Hippo *Sermo* 43:7-9: "Non tento, Domine, penetrare altitudinem tuam, quia nullatenus comparo illi intellectum meum; sed desidero aliquatenus intelligere veritatem tuam, quam credit et amat cor meum. Neque enim quaero intelligere ut credam, sed credo ut intelligam. Nam et hoc credo: quia 'nisi credidero, non intelligam'" ("I do not endeavor, Lord, to penetrate Your heights, because I cannot even compare my intellect with that; but I do desire somehow to understand Your truth—the truth that my heart has believed and loved. I do not seek to understand that I may believe; I believe in order that I may come to understand. For this also I believe—that unless I believed, I should not understand.") (*Proslogion,* "Prooemium" and "Excitatio mentis ad contemplandum Deum"). For the text of Anselm's *Proslogion,* see <http://www.thelatinlibrary.com/anselmproslogion.html>; for Augustine's *Sermo* 43, see <http://www.augustinus.it/latino/>.

[3] See, e.g., Brad Waggoner, *The Shape of Faith to Come* (Nashville, Tennessee: Broadman & Holman, 2008).

[4] See, e.g., Dallas Willard, *The Great Omission* (New York: HarperSanFrancisco, 2006).

[5] See, e.g., Millard Erickson, *Christian Theology,* 2d ed. (Grand Rapids, Michigan: Wm. B. Eerdmans, 1998) 218, 946-54; Wayne Grudem, *Systematic Theology.* Rev. ed. (Leicester, United Kingdom: InterVarsity Press, 2000) 669-70, 709-20; Louis Berkhof, *Systematic Theology.* One vol. ed. (Grand Rapids: Wm. B. Eerdmans, 1996) 415-22; Charles Hodge, *Systematic Theology* (http://books.google.com) 3:3b:3; 3:5c. The classical *ordo salutis* includes such concepts as foreknowledge, predestination, election, regeneration, evangelism, faith, justification, conversion, repentance, sanctification, perseverance, and glorification. The precise order of these elements differs, depending on particular theological commitments.

[6] Grudem, 748-51.

[7] For a survey of studies related to Fowler's theory, see Heinz Streib, "Faith Development Research at Twenty Years," in *Developing a Public Faith,* Richard Osmer and Friedrich Schweitzer, eds. (St. Louis: Chalice, 2003) 15-42.

[8] James W. Fowler and Mary Lynn Dell, "Stages of Faith from Infancy through Adolescence," in *The Handbook of Spiritual Development in Childhood and Adolescence,* Eugene Roehlkepartain, et al., eds. (Thousand Oaks, California: SAGE, 2005), 35.

[9] Lawrence Kohlberg, "The Claim to Moral Adequacy of a Highest Stage of Moral Judgment," *Journal of Philosophy* 70 (1973): 630–46.

[10] Fowler and Dell, 36.

[11] See, e.g., Heinz Streib, "Faith Development Research Revisited," *International Journal for the Psychology of Religion* 15 (2001): 99-121; Heinz Streib, "Faith Development Research at Twenty Years," *Developing a Public Faith,* R. R. Osmer and F. Schweitzer, eds. (St. Louis: Chalice, 2003) 15-42.

[12] Lawrence Kohlberg, From Is to Ought: How to Commit the Naturalistic Fallacy and Get Away with It in the Study of Moral Development (New York: Academic Press, 1971).

[13] James W. Fowler, "Faith Development Theory and Postmodern Challenges," *International Journal for the Psychology of Religion* 11 (July 2001): 164.

[14] James W. Fowler, "Stages of Faith and the Adult Life Cycle," *Faith Development in the Adult Life Cycle,* Kenneth Stokes, ed. (New York: Sadlier, 1982), 202; James W. Fowler, *Weaving the New Creation* (San Francisco: Harper, 2002) 100-2.

15 James W. Fowler, *Stages of Faith: The Psychology of Human Development and the Quest for Meaning* (New York: Harper, 1981), 9; James W. Fowler, "Faith/Belief," *Dictionary of Pastoral Care and Counseling,* Rodney J. Hunter, ed. (Nashville: Abingdon, 1990), 394.

[16] Fowler, *Stages of Faith*, 303.

[17] Italics in original, Fowler, *Stages of Faith,* xiii, 5, 33; James W. Fowler and Antoine Vergote, *Toward Moral and Religious Maturity* (Morristown, New Jersey: Silver Burdett, 1980), 52; see also W. C. Smith, *Faith and Belief: The Difference Between Them* rev. ed. (Princeton: Princeton University, 1998), 129; see also James W. Fowler, "Stages of Faith: Reflections on a Decade of Dialogue," *Christian Education Journal* 13, 1(1992): 18; James W. Fowler, "Faith and the Structuring of Meaning," *Faith Development and Fowler,* Craig Dykstra and Sharon Daloz Parks, eds. (Birmingham, Alabama: Religious Education Press, 1986), 16.

[18] Fowler, *Stages of Faith,* 9. See also Frederick Downing, "Toward the Second Naivete," *Perspectives in Religious Studies* 12, 1(1985): 40-1, 47; Fowler, *Weaving the New Creation,* 16.

[19] Smith, *Faith and Belief,* 5-6, 108.

[20] Smith, *Faith and Belief,* 247; see also Fowler, *Stages of Faith,* 11-2.

[21] Smith, *Faith and Belief,* 71-91; see also Fowler, *Stages of Faith,* 12.

[22] Fowler, *Stages of Faith,* 12; but cf. Hebrews 11:6 where the biblical author uses precisely the terminology to which Fowler refers as a "strange circumlocution."

[23] Smith, *Faith and Belief,* 159.

[24] Smith, *Faith and Belief,* 125.

[25] Smith, *Faith and Belief,* 167-8; cf. Fowler, *Stages of Faith,* 9; Fowler, "Faith/Belief," 394.

[26] Smith, *Faith and Belief,* 171.

[27] Fowler, "Faith/Belief," 396; Fowler, "Stages of Faith: Reflections on a Decade of Dialogue," 22; George Lindbeck, *The Nature of Doctrine* (Philadelphia: Westminster, 1984) 32-41, 63-9. Lindbeck contrasts this approach to "cognitive-propositionalism" on one hand and "experiential-expressivism" on the other.

[28] Fowler, *Stages of Faith,* 14-5.

[29] Fowler, *Stages of Faith,* 11; James W. Fowler, "Faith, Liberation, and Human Development," *Christian Perspectives on Faith Development,* Jeff Astley and Leslie Francis, eds. (Grand Rapids: Eerdmans, 1992), 11; see also Perry Downs, "The Power of Fowler," *Nurture That Is Christian,* Jim Wilhoit and John Dettoni, eds. (Grand Rapids: Baker, 1995) 76; James W. Fowler, "Dialogue Toward a Future in Faith-Development

Studies," in *Faith Development and Fowler*, 278; Richard Niebuhr, "On the Nature of Faith," in *Religious Experience and Truth,* Sidney Hook, ed. (New York: New York University, 1961), 93-102.

[30] See Dykstra and Parks, 1986, 16-17; Fowler, *Stages of Faith*, 16-18.

[31] Fritz Oser and Paul Gmünder, *Religious Judgment,* trans. H. F. Hahn (Birmingham, Alabama: Religious Education Press, 1991).

[32] This section draws from various texts, including Perry Bassett, "Faith Development and Mid-Life Transition" (Ph.D. diss., Baylor University, 1985) 21-3; F. L. Downing, "The Dangerous Journey Home," in *Perspectives in Religious Studies* 25 (1998): 261; Fowler, *Stages of Faith*; James W. Fowler, "Faith Development Research," in *Dictionary of Pastoral Care and Counseling,* Rodney Hunter, ed. (Nashville: Abingdon, 1990), 399-401; Fowler, *Weaving the New Creation*, 18; Robert W. Pazmiño, *Foundational Issues in Christian Education.* 2d ed. (Grand Rapids: Baker Book House, 1997), 208-9; and, David Rose, "An Instrument to Measure Four of James Fowler's Stages of Faith Development (Ph.D. diss., California School of Professional Psychology, 1991), 95-7.

[33] Dan McAdams, *The Stories We Live By* (New York: Guilford, 1997), 183.

[34] Sharon Daloz Parks, *The Critical Years* (New York: Harper, 1986). Steve Garber furthers this vision of Christian higher education in his book *The Fabric of Faithfulness: Weaving Together Belief and Behavior* (Downers Grove, Illinois: InterVarsity Press, 2007). See also Stanley Hauerwas, *A Community of Character* (South Bend, Indiana: University of Notre Dame Press, 1981).

[35] Dan Stiver, *Theology after Ricoeur* (Louisville, Kentucky: Westminster John Knox, 2001), 64-5, 138-45.

[36] Jeff Astley and Leslie Francis, "Introduction" in *Christian Perspectives on Faith Development* (Grand Rapids: Wm. B. Eerdmans, 1992), viii.

[37] James W. Fowler, et al., *Life-Maps* (Waco, Texas: Word, 1978), 81.

[38] Paul Ricoeur, *The Symbolism of Evil* (New York: Harper, 1967 rpt. 1986), 352-4; Paul Ricoeur, *Figuring the Sacred* (Minneapolis, Minnesota: Augsburg Fortress, 1995), 2-6.

[39] Mohandas K. Gandhi, *All Men Are Brothers* (Paris: UNESCO, 1958), 60.

[40] James W. Fowler, "Faith Development Theory and Postmodern Challenges" *International Journal for the Psychology of Religion* 11, 3 (July 2001): 167; James W. Fowler, "Faith and the Structuring of Meaning," *Faith Development and Fowler,* Craig Dykstra and Sharon Parks, eds. (Birmingham, Alabama: Religious Education, 1986), 26.

[41] For Fowler's stages as "norming" indicators of the adequacy of a person's spiritual development, see especially Fowler, *Stages of Faith*, 293; James W. Fowler, "Stage Six and the Kingdom of God," *Religious Education* 75, 3 (May-June 1980): 231-48.

[42] Fowler, Weaving the New Creation, 17.

[43] For Fowler's derivation of this aspect from Jean Piaget, see Jeff Astley and William Kay, "Piaget and Fowler" in *Religion in Education* vol. 2, Jeff Astley and William Kay, eds. (Leominster, United Kingdom: Gracewing, 1998), 162-5.

[44] R. L. Selman, *The Growth of Interpersonal Understanding* (London, UK: Academic, 1980).

[45] Lawrence Kohlberg, *The Psychology of Moral Development* (San Francisco: Harper, 1984).

[46] James W. White, *Intergenerational Religious Education* (Birmingham, Alabama: Religious Education Press, 1988), 119; cf. H. G. Koenig, *Aging and God* (New York: Haworth, 1994), 93. James W. Fowler, *Faith Development and Pastoral Care* (Nashville: Abingdon, 1987), 57, 80.

[47] Gloria Durka, "Reflections on a Gift to Religious Educators," *Religious Education Journal* 99, 4(2004): 424.

[48] See, e.g., one of James W. Fowler's earlier works, *Life-Maps* (Waco, Texas: Word, 1978).

[49] James W. White, "Faith Stages Affiliation and Gender" (Ph.D. diss., Boston University, 1985); Timothy Paul Jones, "An Analysis of the Relationship Between Fowlerian Stage Development and Self-Assessed Maturity in Christian Faithfulness among Evangelical Christians" (Ed.D./Ph.D. diss., The Southern Baptist Theological Seminary, 2003), 78-9; Rose, 22-3, 111.

[50] Randall Furushima, "Faith Development Theory" (Ph.D. diss., Columbia University, 1982); Soon Keun Lee, "Fowler's Faith-Development Interview Questions in a Korean Context" (Ph.D. diss., Trinity International University, 1999). The results of J. Snarey's study of nontheistic kibbutz leaders did replicate many of Fowler's results. "Faith Development, Moral Development, and Non-Theistic Judaism," *Handbook of Moral Development and Behavior: Research,* vol. 2, W. Kurtines and J. Gerwitz, eds. [Hillsdale, New Jersey: Erlbaum, 1991]).

[51] Paula Drewek, "Cross-Cultural Testing of James W. Fowler's Model of Faith Development among Bahá'ís" (Ph.D. diss., Ottawa University, 1996); Furushima, "Faith Development Theory."

[52] In *Stages of Faith,* Fowler claimed to have achieved 85 percent inter-rater reliability; however, it remains unclear whether these internal relationships correlated strongly or significantly with any measure beyond his own interview. For discussion, see H. G. Koenig, *Aging and God,* 101-2; J. Chirban, "Intrinsic and Extrinsic Motivation and Stages of Faith (Ph.D. diss., Harvard Divinity School, 1981).

[53] S. Dreidger, "Relationships among Faith Development, Ego Development, and Religious Orientation in HIV+ Individuals" in *Dissertation Abstracts International B* 58, 12 (1998): 6842.

[54] Snarey, "Faith Development, Moral Development, and Non-Theistic Judaism."

[55] Snarey, "Faith Development, Moral Development, and Non-Theistic Judaism"; see also R. Timpe, "Faith Development Scale," *Measures of Religiosity,* P. Hill and R. Hood, eds. (Birmingham, Alabama: Religious Education Press, 1999).

[56] Jones, "An Analysis of the Relationship," 74-7.

[57] Snarey, "Faith Development, Moral Development, and Non-Theistic Judaism," 288-92; Jones, "An Analysis of the Relationship," 111-3.

[58] *Faith Development and Fowler,* Craig Dykstra and Sharon Daloz Parks, eds. (Birmingham, Alabama: Religious Education Press, 1986) 190; F. C. Power, "Hard *versus*

Soft Stages of Religious Development," *Stages of Faith and Religious Development,* James W. Fowler, K. E. Nipkow, and F. Schweitzer, eds. (London: SCM, 1991).

[59] Heinz Streib, "Faith Development Theory Revisited," *The International Journal for the Psychology of Religion* 11, 3 (2001): 155.

[60] Streib, "Faith Development Theory Revisited," 144. Speaking from a feminist perspective, Nancy Devor has similarly criticized Fowler's theory for being so rooted in individual cognitive competencies that it ignores relational values and development. See Nancy Devor, "Toward a Relational Voice of Faith" (Ph.D. diss., Boston University 1989); see also A. R. Vanden Heuvel, "Faith Development and Family Interaction" (Ph.D. diss., Union for Experimenting Colleges, 1985) 22-3; Robert Wuthnow, "A Sociological Perspective on Faith Development," *Faith Development in the Adult Life Cycle,* Kenneth Stokes, ed. (New York: Sadlier, 1982), 222; Nicola Slee, *Women's Faith Development* (Burlington, Vermont: Ashgate, 2004), 164-8; Stephen Parker, "Measuring Faith Development," *Journal of Psychology and Theology* 34, 4 (2006): 341.

[61] Streib, "Faith Development Theory Revisited," 144.

[62] Streib, "Faith Development Theory Revisited," 149.

[63] Streib's styles have much in common with Gil Noam's phases of the self. See Gil G. Noam, "The Theory of Biography and Transformation," *Cognitive development and child psychotherapy,* S. R. Shirk, ed. (New York: Plenum, 1988) 273-317; Gil G. Noam, "Beyond Freud and Piaget," *The Moral Domain,* T. Wren, ed. (Cambridge, Massachusetts: MIT Press, 1990), 360-99.

[64] Heinz Streib, "Extending Our Vision of Developmental Growth and Engaging in Empirical Scrutiny," *Religious Education* 99, 4 (Fall 2004): 432-3.

[65] For the phrase "content-empty," see James W. Fowler, "Faith-Development Theory and Postmodern Challenges" in *International Journal for the Psychology of Religion* 11, 3 (July 2001), 164.

[66] Fowler, *Stages of Faith,* 12.

[67] Thomas Schreiner, *Romans* (Grand Rapids: Baker, 1998), 560.

[68] Translated from Cyril of Jerusalem, "Cyrilli Archepiscopi Hierosolymitani Opera Quae Existant, Catechesis V, De Fide et Symbolo" in *Patrilogiae Cursus Completus, Series Graeca,* 5.10-13. Italics added.

[69] Classical Greek authors, including Homer, Plato, and Xenophon, employed *pisteuein* and its cognates to describe the trustworthiness of the statements in a treaty. Later Greek authors, such as Plutarch and Plotinus, used *pisteuein* when discussing the existence or nonexistence of the pagan deities. Again, *pisteuein* implied assent to specific claims. See Carroll Stuhlmueller, "The Biblical View of Faith: A Catholic Perspective" in *Handbook of Faith,* James Michael Lee, ed. (Birmingham, Alabama: Religious Education, 1990), 105.

[70] Cyprian of Carthage, "Epistle 68," in *The Ante-Nicene Fathers,* Alexander Roberts, ed. (Wheaton, Illinois: Christian Classics Ethereal Library, n.d.), CD-ROM.

[71] "Quamquam et ipsum credere, nihil aliud est, quam cum assensione cogitare" (Augustine of Hippo, *De Praedestinatione Sanctorum,* [2] 5: <http://www.augustinus.it/latino/>).

[72] Alexander McKelway, "Theology of Faith: A Protestant Perspective," *Handbook of Faith,* J. M. Lee, ed. (Birmingham, Alabama: Religious Education, 1990), 170.

[73] Peter [the] Lombard, *Sententiarum libri quatuor, P. Lombardi magistri sententiarum* in *Patrologiae cursus completus, series latina*, J. P. Migne, ed. (Paris: Lutetiae Parisiorum) 3:23. See also Timothy Paul Jones, "An Analysis of the Relationship," 2, 14-5, 149-55.

[74] See John Calvin, *Institutio Christianae religionis* in *Ioannis Calvini opera selecta*, Peter Barth, Wilhelm Niesel, and Donna Scheuner, eds. (Munich: Christliche Kaiser, 1926) 3:2:3; Karl Barth, *Die kirchliche Dogmatik*, vol. 4, *Die Lehre von der Versöhnung* (Zollikon: Verlag der Evangelischen Buchhandlung, 1957) 4:63:1; Karl Barth, *Evangelical Theology*, trans. Grover Foley (New York: Holt, Rinehart, and Wilson, 1963), 98.

[75] Alexander McKelway, "The Logic of Faith," *Toward the Future of Reformed Theology*, David Willis, et al., eds. (Grand Rapids: Eerdmans, 1999), 211-2. For discussion in the context of the New Testament, see Thomas Schreiner, *New Testament Theology* (Grand Rapids: Baker, 2008), 616.

[76] Calvin, *Institutio*, 3:2:7.

[77] Fowler, *Stages of Faith*, 10-5.

[78] Fowler, *Stages of Faith*, 14.

[79] Fowler, *Stages of Faith*, 186.

[80] Jones, "An Analysis of the Relationship," 98-106.

[81] Fowler, *Stages of Faith*, 14-5.

[82] John Westerhoff III, *Will Our Children Have Faith?* rev. and exp. ed. (Harrisburg, Pennsylvania: Morehouse, 2000), 88-91.

[83] Perry Downs, for example, suggests that Fowler's stages may be adapted to coincide with an evangelical vision of faith (Perry Downs, "The Power of Fowler," *Nurture That Is Christian*, Jim Wilhoit and John Dettoni, eds. [Grand Rapids, Michigan: Baker, 1995], 84).

84 Others also have pursued this path: Derek Webster, for example, admits Fowlerian stage-development as an actual phenomenon. However, he identifies Fowler's phenomenon not as faith but as the process of "how the self constructs its meanings" (Derek Webster, "James Fowler's Theory of Faith Development," *Christian Perspectives on Faith Development*, 83; see also J. Harry Fernhout, "Where Is Faith?," *Faith Development and Fowler*, Craig Dykstra and Sharon Daloz Parks, eds. [Birmingham, Alabama: Religious Education Press, 1986], 70).

[85] Westerhoff, *Will Our Children Have Faith?* rev. and exp. ed., 86-8.

[86] Fowler and Dell, "Stages of Faith from Infancy through Adolescence," 43; Heinz Streib, "Faith Development Theory Revisited," *The International Journal for the Psychology of Religion* 11, 3 (2001): 150-5.

[87] Westerhoff, *Will Our Children Have Faith?* rev. and exp. ed., 92.

[88] Westerhoff, *Will Our Children Have Faith?* rev. and exp. ed., 96.

[89] It is possible this is because their individuative and dialogical stages are actually alternative endpoints rather than hierarchically ordered developmental steps. See C. D. Batson, P. Schoenrade, and W. L. Ventis, *Religion and the Individual: A Social Psychological Perspective* (New York: Oxford University Press, 1993).

[90] R. N. Whybray, *Wisdom in Proverbs* (London, United Kingdom: SCM, 1965), 93-6. Throughout Scripture, wisdom is said to begin with "the fear of the Lord" (Job 28:28; Psalm 111:10; Proverbs 1:7, 9:10, 15:33; Isaiah 33:6). Scripture also affirms that some

wisdom is present and available beyond the believing community. (Exodus 1:10, 7:11; Acts 7:22) Therefore, some measure of "the fear of the Lord" must be present and available – even among persons who do not clearly recognize the true God.

[91] John Goldingay, *Psalms: Volume 3: Psalms 90-150* (Grand Rapids, Michigan: Baker, 2008), 306.

[92] James L. Crenshaw, *Old Testament Wisdom* (Louisville, Kentucky: Westminster John Knox, 1981, 1998), 190-206; Gerhard von Rad, *Wisdom in Israel* (London, United Kingdom: SCM, 1972), 148.

[93] See Fowler, *Stages of Faith*, xiii, 5, 24, 33, 92-3, 245; Fowler 1992b, 18; Fowler and Vergote, *Toward Moral and Religious Maturity*, 52; Smith, *Faith and Belief*, 129.

[94] Fowler, *Stages of Faith*, back cover.

[95] In the 2003 study cited earlier (Jones, "An Analysis of the Relationship"), Christian faith maturity and Fowlerian stage development diverged as individuals exhibited greater maturity, according to Fowler's stages. It is possible this divergence is due to the dissimilarity of the endpoints in Christian faith development and Fowlerian stage development.

[96] Timothy Paul Jones, Lectures for 45250 Family Ministry through the Lifespan, 2008-9.

[97] William Willimon and Stanley Hauerwas, *Lord, Teach Us* (Nashville: Abingdon 1996), 28-29, 77, 108.

[98] Mark Buchanan, "Schedule, Interrupted," <http://www.christianitytoday.com>.

[99] Timothy Paul Jones, Lectures for 45250 Family Ministry through the Lifespan, 2008-9.

[100] Morris Chapman, "The Southern Baptist Convention and Great Commission Resurgence," SBC Executive Committee Presidential Report, June 23, 2009.

[101] Karl Barth, *Evangelical Theology*, trans. Grover Foley (New York: Holt, Rinehart, and Wilson, 1963), 103.

[102] For discussion of "tests" presented in 1 John, see Daniel Akin, *1, 2, 3 John* (Nashville, Tennessee: Broadman & Holman, 2001), 28-32, 171-2.

[103] Greg Hawkins and Cally Parkinson, *Follow Me* (South Barrington, Illinois: Willow Creek Resources, 2008).

[104] Mark Twain, "Pudd'nhead Wilson's New Calendar," *Following the Equator*: <http://www.gutenberg.org/ebooks/2895>

[105] H. L. Mencken, "The Believer," *Prejudices: Third Series*: <http://books.google.com>.

[106] G. K. Chesterton, *The Victorian Age in Literature* reprint edition (Charleston, South Carolina: BiblioBazaar, 2008), 13.

CHAPTER 7

ADULT DEVELOPMENT AND CHRISTIAN FORMATION

By Gregory C. Carlson

"When does a child become an adult, and does an adult still have the capacity to grow spiritually?" The questions came during a Bible study as this phrase had caught the young woman's attention: "…When I became a man, I put aside childish things" (1 Corinthians 13:11). "What makes you think male children *ever* become adult?" I humorously answered. Her question, however, was a good one and raises significant issues! What is adult development, and how does it relate to Christian formation? Are there understandable patterns to adult development? What prompts or guides spiritual growth during the adult years? Do adults "stabilize" in their spiritual development because they have "put away childish things"? In light of what we are learning about adult development, are there more effective ways for the church to reach, edify, and equip adults and families?

Adult development is "the study of the growth and maturing process of adults and can focus on such areas as moral, social, mental, physical, or faith development."[1] These various aspects of adult development all have some relationship to the endeavor of Christian education. Theological integration with adult development theory can provide fresh ways of looking at how to minister to adults in the evangelical church. This chapter seeks to unpack some of the theories, approaches, and contexts to provide deeper understanding for the Christian educator.

In this chapter, we will review theories that specifically focus on the adult period of life. This first section will focus on theories of adult development and learning. The second section will then address biblical and theoretical insights into adulthood. Then the third and the rest of the chapter will address how adult development relates to Christian formation and what implications that has for the ministry of the church.

Theories of Adult Development and Learning

Current developmental theory *of* adults instructs and clarifies our spiritual formation efforts *with* adults. What can we learn from social science to assist us in our faith ministry in discipling adults toward Christian maturity?

The following is a survey of developmental theory that specifically relate to adulthood. It is a representative list—although certainly not an exhaustive one. We will endeavor to describe the theory, relate it to our model of Christian education purposes, and give several implications for ministry for each of the models/theories described.

The Phases of Adult Life

Is adult life predictable? Numerous scenarios have been proposed regarding the typical life pattern or phases in adulthood, e.g., marriage, parenthood, empty nest, retirement. However, one should be cognizant of the fact that these phrases are more culturally driven than the result of study on actual human development.

Roger Gould brought developmental theory to light in adult study. He outlined a course of individual phases which follow an orderly progression throughout the adult lifespan. He particularly focused upon the social developmental aspect of an adult's life. One of his first books[2] has been instrumental in use by several subsequent authors. For this reason, we will describe only his pioneer work and mention this accomplishment: Adult understanding of the various stages of development is not only perceivable but also valuable to educators.

Daniel Levinson (1920-94) researched and wrote about the framework which seems to map the development of all adults.[3] He outlines a concept called "life structure" and defines it as:

> The underlying pattern or design of a person's life at any given time. The life structure of a man, I found, evolves through a

211

sequence of alternating periods, each lasting some five to seven years. A period of building and maintaining a life structure is followed by a transitional period in which we terminate the existing structure and move toward a new one that will fully emerge in the ensuing structure building-maintaining period.[4]

Each of the three key "transitions" is noted in the list below. While each period can be disrupted, the building/maintaining tension only increases as age inevitably forces movement toward the next life stage. In understanding these life-structure stages, one can assume—for men and women—these stages to emerge:

Early Adult Transition (Ages 17-22)

Entry Life Structure for Early Adulthood (Ages 22-28)

Age 30 Transition (Ages 28-33)

Culminating Life Structure for Early Adulthood (Ages 33-40)

Midlife Transition (Ages 40-45)

Early Life Structure for Middle Adulthood (Ages 45-50)

Age 50 Transition (Ages 50-55)

Culminating Life Structure for Middle Adulthood (Ages 55-60)

Late Adult Transition (Ages 60-65)

Era of Late Adulthood (Ages 60-?)[5]

Levinson's work has influenced other stage theorists. Author Gail Sheehy has popularized the idea of transitions in her book *Passages: Predictable Crises of Adult Life.*[6] Former divinity school professor Charles M. Sell also brought a strong evangelical perspective to the discussion with his book *Transitions Through Adult Life.*[7] For example, Sell describes the transitional power of young adults: "Inner forces combine with new social roles. Young adults seem to face the world in a way that is distinct from their adolescent days. It is not that they were unexposed to world conditions during their teenage years. The difference is that their perception has changed."[8]

Learning in Adulthood

Adults learn differently than children. Learning in childhood is designated by the term *pedagogy*; but in adult life, two dominant approaches to adult learning have arisen: andragogy and transformational learning. This section will focus on the two leading theorists in the field: Malcolm Knowles and Jack Mezirow.

Malcolm Knowles (1913-97) was the major promoter of a dominant theory of adult education called *andragogy* (Gk. *andra*—mankind, Gk. *logos*—study or doctrine). The five tenets of andragogy formed the basis of practice and theoretical development in the late twentieth century.[9] First, Knowles proposed that adult learners are self-directed. "It is the normal aspect of the process of maturation for a person to move from dependency toward increasing self-directedness . . . . Adults have a deep psychological need to be generally self-directing, although they may be dependent in particular temporary situations."[10]

Second, adult learners have significant experience. When we continue to minimize the past learning of adults, we exclude a resource for their maturation. "As people grow and develop, they accumulate an increasing reservoir of experience that becomes an increasingly rich resource for learning—for themselves and others."[11]

Third, the adult learner is ready to learn when he/she experiences a need. Knowles states the various stages of development are "points of readiness to learn."[12] Certainly, stages of development are not the only "needs" that adults sense, but they are significant in education.

Fourth, adult learners are oriented toward an experiential life-base. In andragogy, the shift in education is from the process of teaching to the realization of learning. Usually, this emphasis occurs when specific needs are addressed—not in a linear, fragmented way but in a systems approach of problem solving, planning, managing, or evaluating.

Finally, the adult learner is motivated internally more than externally. Knowles has in mind the concept of a "competent person—one who is able to apply knowledge to solve a variety of life problems."[13]

Jack Mezirow is the main figure associated with transformational learning—also known as transformative learning and perspective transformation. He endeavored "to help the individual become a more autonomous thinker by learning to negotiate his or her own values, meanings, and purposes rather than to uncritically act on those of others."[14] In his theory, he suggests that adults learn as they undergo a change of mind that leads toward personal and ultimately social change. Hence, learning is represented as a change of perspective. He wrote, "Rather than [adults] merely adapting to changing circumstances by more diligently applying old ways of knowing, they discover a need to acquire new perspectives in order to gain a more complete understanding of changing events and a higher degree of control over their lives."[15] Transformational learning theory is centered on three dominant themes: (1) Critical reflection of assumptions, i.e., one does not challenge their current assumptions; the need for change is never recognized; and hence, learning begins with challenging one's current perspective. (2) Awareness of frames of reference, i.e., the point at which the need for change is acknowledged. (3) Participate in rational discourse, i.e., we "attempt to understand—to learn—what is valid in the assertions made by others and attempt to achieve consensual validation for our own assertions."[16] These three elements combine to form the basis for transformational learning.

The process of transformational learning moves the adult learner through these three elements. It is presented by a 10-step process—with the three previously identified elements readily recognized within the proposed learning process:

1. A disorienting dilemma.

2. Self-examination with feelings of guilt or shame, anger or fear.

3. A critical assessment of personally internalized role assumptions and a sense of alienation from traditional social expectations (of epistemic, sociocultural, or psychic assumptions and distortions).

4. Relating one's discontent to similar experiences of others or to public issues, recognizing that one's problem is shared and not exclusively a private matter.

5. Exploring options for new ways of acting (new roles, relationships, and actions).

6. Planning a course of action.

7. Acquiring knowledge and skills for implementing one's plans.

8. Building competence and self-confidence in new roles.

9. Provisional efforts to try new roles and to assess feedback.

10. A reintegration into society on the basis of conditions dictated by the new perspective.[17]

While criticisms of this theory have been leveled by both non-Christian and Christian respondents, others find some of its tenets correspond with the Christian faith. Shawn Lindsay identifies four such corresponding points: Adult learning and development call for: (1) change in frames of reference (John 3:18; Romans 12:1; Philippians 4:8); (2) emancipation as a meta-theme (Romans 6:6-11; 14-23); (3) participation in community (Ephesians 4:1ff); and (4) necessity of action (James 1:19-25; 2:14-26).[18]

Summary of Adult Development and Learning Principles

Adults continue to learn. Adults progress and interact, either formally or informally, throughout their lifetime. They may focus that learning in schooling or adult education, or it may show up in participation in self-directed or church-guided studies. The internal desire to learn and the external "learning projects"[19] certainly give cause for Christian educators to be involved in *adult* learning.

Adults learn in stages, phases, or cycles. When we have a "one-size-fits-all" mentality to adult Christian education, we miss some of the richness of spiritual formation in our people. Robert Havinghurst describes the normal process of learning during age-related stages as "developmental tasks." Churches are well served to custom-fit their educational endeavors to meet the challenges of each of these stages. They can do this by:

1. *Age-related Studies.* Looking at the various ages to see what particular stresses and need areas emerge. Simple survey via questionnaires could be used. More effective is the idea of a pastor having a "focus group" where he gathers adults from the various age stages and asks questions. He then lists the areas which he believes emerge from the discussions. Following this, the spiritual leadership pray and determine what studies and sermon series may be most appropriate to address the needs of the congregation.

2. *Role-related Education.* Here is an area where there is biblical precedent (see the area under "Instruction" below). The various developmental tasks could be sorted according to the learner's age, or electives could be offered which would cross age-spans. Older mentors teaching younger seems the most effective ministry activity, but peers also can learn much from each other.

3. *Problem-solving Courses.* Examples of this type of education are the studies focusing on financial management or the small-group

series addressing topics such as divorce recovery, children of divorce, sexual addiction, abuse recovery, blended family sessions, marriage enrichment, premarital preparation, parenting classes, step-parenting, college selection, application and choosing, and other areas. A young single adult group we led had a feature which created several small-group studies. Every Thursday evening (the night of our large-group gathering called Thursday Nite Live), we would feature a member of the leadership team giving practical advice. We had presentations and interactive sessions on everything from flossing teeth and the maintenance of cars to instructions on Bible study, journaling, or how to spend a day fasting and praying.

4. *Combinations of Educational Offerings.* Overlap with the three ways mentioned above can fit into a sound structure. In a small church pastored by us, we had electives with consistent selections to allow choices during the church quarters/semesters. For example, congregations could focus more intently on consistency in our classes during Sunday morning Bible study and allowed small groups to address specific needs. Small groups needed a place to land and launch to have a consistent strategy of education. The key may be a consistent strategy—for educating as you do and educating for a reason—to conform our people to the image of Christ (Romans 8:29).

Adults desire interactive learning. While many adults will *say* they like the old ways best, they *learn* more if education is interactive, problem-oriented, and creative. Noninvolvement, pointless instruction (a mentor describes it as "being so heavenly-minded they are of no earthly good"),[20] and boring teaching do not create maximum life-change. One adult teacher in a church described it this way: "Pastor, my job description as a Sunday school teacher of adults is to *comfort* the *afflicted . . .* and to *afflict* the *comforted!*"

Adults can handle mutuality. Mutuality may be described as a joint sharing of responsibility for learning. Disengaged learners are the discouragement of many a teacher. Sometimes this reluctance for involvement stems from too much teacher control, no mutual goal-setting, evaluation, or sharing of experience. Adults then become dependent on an authority "to tell them what to do" and stop examining the Scriptures daily to see if what the teacher said is true (cf. Acts 17:11).

The field of adult development is still in search of adequate theory. University of Georgia assistant professor Laura L. Bierema argues that the entire specialty field of Human Resource Development (HRD) within adult development can be enhanced by further research, deeper thinking about theories of HRD, and gaining knowledge through practice.[21] If this is true of business applications of the adult development field, it certainly is equally meaningful to church education.

Biblical/Theological Insights on Adult Development

The Bible seems to use the physical understanding of development to help us understand what happens to any age of person spiritually. Adult development underpinnings then assist in clarifying, organizing, and promoting spiritual growth. Follow the biblical progression (figure 7.1):

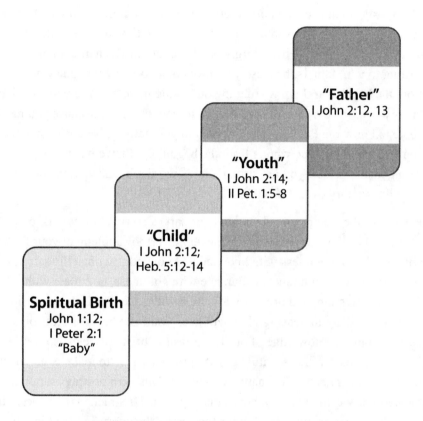

Figure 7.1: Biblical Progression toward Adulthood

One starts with a spiritual "birth"—"Do not be amazed that I told you that you must be born again" (John 3:7). Too often, we involve ourselves in nurture and spiritual formation before a spiritual birth has happened. Evangelism must be emphasized in any spiritual formation process. Then growth occurs. Peter seems to indicate that growth proceeds from the "baby" phase of life in Christ to the mature. "Like newborn infants, desire the unadulterated spiritual milk, so that you may grow by it in [your] salvation" (1 Peter 2:2).

The apostle John uses the normal growth phases of child, youth, and parent to encourage his readers to mature. "I am writing to you, little children, because your sins have been forgiven on account of His name. I am writing to you, fathers, because you have come to know the One who is from the beginning. I am writing to you, young men, because you have had victory over the evil one. I have written to you, children, because you have come to know the Father. I have written to you, fathers, because you have come to know the One who is from the beginning. I have written to you, young men, because you are strong, God's word remains in you, and you have had victory over the evil one" (1 John 2:12-14).

Peter describes the process by which our part of spiritual growth is to happen. "For this very reason, make every effort to supplement your faith with goodness, goodness with knowledge, knowledge with self-control, self-control with endurance, endurance with godliness, godliness with brotherly affection, and brotherly affection with love. For if these qualities are yours and are increasing, they will keep you from being useless or unfruitful in the knowledge of our LORD Jesus Christ" (2 Peter 1:5-8). What is our part in this spiritual growth process? It is "to make every effort to add" what is needed for maturity to occur. This verb portrays supplying the necessary elements for a lavish display as R. H. Strachan describes: "In Attic drama, (it) is one who defrays the cost of the chorus, at the bidding of the State, as an act of citizenship. It was a duty that prompted to lavishness in execution."[22]

Paul describes the two different stages of physical life and uses it to demonstrate maturity in the spiritual life. "When I was a child, I spoke like a child, I thought like a child, I reasoned like a child. When I became a man, I put aside childish things" (1 Corinthians 13:11). The writer of the book of Hebrews chastises his readers for not moving on toward maturity. "For although by this time you ought to be teachers, you need someone to teach you again the basic principles of God's revelation. You need milk, not solid food. Now everyone who lives on milk is inexperienced with the message about righteousness, because he is an infant. But solid food is for the mature—for those whose senses have been trained to distinguish between good and evil" (Hebrews 5:12-14).

Is There a Definition of Adulthood?

Frequently, those involved in ministering to children are posed with the question of a child's age of accountability, meaning the age at which a child becomes responsible for their actions. Scripture does indeed seem to indicate that, before a certain age, an individual is not cognizant of their actions; but at some point, they are indeed responsible for the implications of their actions. Perhaps in the context of this chapter, the mirror image is of interest. When does the child become responsible, entering adulthood?

> "For before the boy knows to reject what is bad and choose what is good " (Isaiah 7:16).

> "Your corpses will fall in this wilderness — all of you who were registered [in the census], the entire number of you 20 years old or more — because you have complained about Me" (Numbers 14:29).

> "Your little children who you said would be plunder, your sons whom don't know good from evil, will enter there. I will give them the land, and they will take possession of it" (Deuteronomy 1:39).

The New Testament echoes this principle (Romans 14:12; James 4:17). The general principle seems to be that adulthood entails the ability to personally affirm and assume responsibility for one's spiritual and moral life. However, these passages are insufficient to establish a definitive age of adulthood from Scripture.

A Christian Approach to Adult Development

Four questions are a helpful framework to incorporate and shape the process of spiritual development. First, *biblical definitions*—What does a "mature" person look like? What is the profile of a mature believer? I have found too often that pastors and church leaders have very little idea of what they would like to achieve in the lives of adults within their congregations. A vague "members of the church and witnesses for Christ" answer is sometimes given; but the study of Scripture, reflection of written intent, tempering of practice, and give-and-take of discussion rarely occur. Hence, we rarely have a workable profile for church leaders to use; e.g., develop a profile of a mature believer by looking to the summative passages Paul wrote to describe qualifications of leadership—passages such as 1 Timothy 3 and Titus 1 or a respected contemporary resource.

Second, *personal evaluation*—How do I compare to that kind of person? While this may be a very personal question, it also is a matter of corporate ministry. Paul urged both Timothy and Titus to appoint leaders who exhibited worthy characteristics. Paul warned Corinthian believers: "Test yourselves [to see] if you are in the faith. Examine yourselves. Or do you not recognize for yourselves that Jesus Christ is in you? — unless you fail the test" (2 Corinthians 13:5).

Third, *spiritual disciplines*—How does one develop into a person like that? Ephesians 4 gives a practical outline of how this development should happen. Leaders equip. (Ephesians 4:11-12) Followers of Christ involve themselves in two parallel activities—works of service and edification (Ephesians 4:12). Unity and maturity are the results (Ephesians 4:13). Error and hindered development are avoided (Ephesians 4:14). The process is summarized:

> But speaking the truth in love, let us grow in every way into Him who is the head — Christ. From Him the whole body, fitted and knit together by every supporting ligament, promotes the growth of the body for building up itself in love by the proper working of each individual part (Ephesians 4:15-16).

What does this process look like today? It looks like the activities of the church, where personal and corporate disciplines are employed to accomplish the purposes of instruction, fellowship, and service. Service can be described as having the threefold expression of worship (upward to God in reasonable service—Romans 12:1); building up the body of Christ (Ephesians 4:12-16); and evangelism (outward to reach those who are yet to believe—John 17:20). We then emphasize that practical church actions can enhance the environment of adults in their development of faith. Personal spiritual disciplines show much promise for the adult in their development. Corporate spiritual disciplines are not to be neglected.

Finally, *ministry design*—What is my plan in ministering with people like that?

The Christian educator would be well-served to have a ministry design which focuses on the three essentials of discipleship as we have proposed them in this chapter. A balance of "Instruction . . . Fellowship . . . Service" seems to provide the best environment for spiritual formation. Having these essentials of discipleship as the grid of decision-making gives the Christian educator a foundation of biblical truth, a structure of balanced effort, and an implementation of comprehensive fulfillment of what it means to be like Christ.

Implications for Christian Formation

Confusion in spiritual formation sometimes exists because we do not make a distinction between the *process* of spiritual formation and the *transformation* of becoming a new person in Christ. Professor Emeritus of Systematic Theology from Dallas Theological Seminary Robert Lightner makes three contrasts between regeneration and spiritual formation:

1. Regeneration describes a work completely carried out by God, whereas spiritual formation requires the believer's cooperation with God.

2. Regeneration is instantaneous and complete, while spiritual formation is progressive and incomplete.

3. Regeneration is a gift from God; and spiritual formation results, in part, from obedience and faithfulness to Him.[23]

Adult development and spiritual formation also can be glimpsed in the life of Christ. He reached the age of maturity—twelve. He asked His earthly parents, " Didn't you know that I had to be in my Father's house?" (Luke 2:49). But then, for nearly 18 years, he lived in submission and obedience to them. The writer of the book of Hebrews summarizes, "Though [He was God's] Son, He learned obedience through what He suffered" (Hebrews 5:8). Even our Lord had a developmental growth in physical, social, mental, and spiritual obedience to His heavenly Father. There are several implications for this:

1. We must go back to a strong, integrated underpinning of Scripture in our education in the church. We should develop a "maturity profile" and progressive steps of growth in spiritual formation which are congruent with Scripture.

2. Church leaders must be courageous enough to look at the way things really are in the lives of the followers of Christ who are in their charge. They should compare their lifestyle to that which is described in the Bible. Then take on the role of prophetically addressing these lacks (and successes—see Jesus' message to the churches in Revelation 2 and 3).

3. Adults are dynamic. We should employ the same creativity and interactivity with which we address children's and youth ministries.

4. Ministry design should minimize running the "machinery" of the church to maximize the growth of individual members in instruction, fellowship, and service.

5. Perhaps the most obvious, and yet unstated, implication for Christian formation is an ongoing, lifelong process. Adult

development does not cease; and hence, the potential for ongoing growth in Christ is not limited by age.

Pastoral and Educational Implications

Criticism toward this dominant theory of adult development shows the need for a comprehensive theory which integrates biblical input and broadens to church practice. For example, two of the leading contemporary adult educators Sharan B. Merriam and Rosemary S. Caffarella state: "Considering that andragogy has been the primary model of adult learning for nearly thirty years, relatively little empirical work has been done to test the validity of its assumptions or its usefulness in predicting adult learning behavior."[24] However, in looking at the comparison to a biblical teaching model[25] and the wide acceptance in the applied fields of human resource development and adult education, it is surprising that more attention has not been given to andragogy. Special emphasis could be placed upon these issues in religious education. Below are some observations as applied to Christian educational practice.

First, we sometimes minimize the educational capability of learners. Rarely do we teach with any of Paul's passion in Romans 15:14 as he describes his Roman learners: "My brothers, I myself am convinced about you that you also are full of goodness, filled with all knowledge, and able to instruct one another."

Second, we have very little mutuality in setting goals for learning; and we discount the learning experiences from the past history of adults. Perhaps this is why small groups have had such an impact upon the spiritual formation of some church members. "The best discipleship is group discipleship. . . . People who are discipled in the context of a small group experience benefit from the wisdom and discernment of many group members, are able to use their gifts in a safe and encouraging setting, can have needs met and prayed for by several brothers and sisters in Christ, and can be encouraged toward team ministry." [26]

Third, we can improve the educational settings for Christian education (not just small groups functioning but overall) by functioning according to the keys as proposed by Harley Atkinson, small-group analyst and Christian education professor: "The Christian educator must take precautions to insure the small-group participants know exactly what is to be accomplished by clearly stating the topic or problem or thoroughly describing the task. . . . It is critical to understand the importance of what the groups are accomplishing in a broader context. . . . Students must be prepared for small-group activities in two ways . . . a certain amount of substantive content . . . and group dynamics and small-group behavior. . . . The Christian educator must know when to bring the small-group discussions to closure."[27]

Fourth, we need to provide education where our teaching is more than telling but involvement. "A major element in transformation of ideas, of attitudes, of behavior patterns is the personal interactive involvement of the one being transformed."[28] Finally, we must focus on internal life change rather than just external behavior change. Two Scriptures come to mind: Paul's description of people in the last days who have a "form of godliness" but deny the power of true faith and Isaiah's portrayal of the nation that "'Because these people approach Me with their mouths to honor Me with lip service — yet their hearts are far from Me, and their worship [consists of] man-made rules learned [by rote] " (Isaiah 29:13).

Biblical Approach to Adult Development

What biblical insights can we gain for the threefold essentials of discipleship we have been describing?

First, instruction—The striking assertion that Paul makes for the proper functioning of relationships in Titus 2 establishes these principles of adult development. Specifically, adults are to be "taught," and behavior is in focus as a natural part of "sound doctrine." The *didaskalia* (teaching) was to relate to "sound living." "But you must speak what is consistent with sound teaching" (Titus 2:1). Stages of adult development are implied and expected to fulfill specific roles. Note the roles that are described by the New Testament in the following section on fellowship.

Second, fellowship—The adult development described in the Bible focuses strongly on "roles of relationships." These roles not only are shaped by adult development (e.g., working); but individuals also are shaped by the role, e.g., marriage.

Older/Younger Framed by Family Analogy. The Pastoral Epistles certainly have much to contribute to the idea of the social-side of adult development. Paul exhorts Timothy, "Do not rebuke an older man, but exhort him as a father, younger men as brothers, older women as mothers, and with all propriety, the younger women as sisters" (1 Timothy 5:1-2). Relationships with older men and women should be handled with esteem and respect. Young men and women should be treated with collegiality and purity.

Marriage as a Key Adult Development Role. One of the most troubled institutions of adult behavior today may be that of marriage. Placing honor upon the specific roles of husband and wife is reinforced by the writer of Hebrews: "Marriage must be respected by all, and the marriage bed kept undefiled, because God will judge immoral people and adulterers" (Hebrews 13:4). Notice the retribution which is to accompany violations of this social arrangement. The Ephesian church was exhorted to have a husband love and cherish his wife. The wife should respect and submit to her husband (Ephesians 5:22-33).

Work Relationships to Glorify Christ. Christians often act as though the opportunity to work is a result of the fall of mankind into sin, but the work which one does is also a place where fellowship or love relationships can come to glorify God. "Slaves, obey your human masters in everything; don't work only while being watched, in order to please men, but [work] wholeheartedly, fearing the Lord. Whatever you do, do it enthusiastically, as something done for the Lord and not for men, knowing that you will receive the reward of an inheritance from the Lord—you serve the Lord

Christ" (Colossians 3:22-24). Professor and pastor Dallas Willard says of the original design of creation:

> But in light of the immensity of the task, God also gave humankind another very important ability—the ability to live in right relationships to God and to other human beings. Only in those relationships—in the communication needed to keep those relationships healthy and thriving—could everything be found that was required to succeed at the work assigned.[29]

Government Interactivity and Submission Impacts Adult Development. Paul appeals to the high law of love in his writing to the Roman Christians: "Pay your obligations to everyone: taxes to those you owe taxes, tolls to those you owe tolls, respect to those you owe respect, and honor to those you owe honor. Do not owe anyone anything, except to love one another, for the one who loves another has fulfilled the law" (Romans 13:7-8). As such, the spirituals development of an adult must include an awareness of the governing authorities in the community in which they live.

Third, service—When we describe this essential to the adult development of spiritual maturity, what are we talking about? Fruitfulness! Our service to the Lord is an overflow of our connectedness to the life of Christ and results in good works. The "fruit" or works of the Christian could be listed as:

- The life submitted to Lordship produces righteous living (Luke 6:43-44).

- Believers draw their fruitfulness from the Vine of Christ (John 15:5).

- Fruitfulness is dependent upon asking according to the Father's will (John 15:16).

- Contributions for the poor are an example of fruit (Romans 15:26-28).

- The fruit of the Spirit is a part of the service of the believer in Christ (Galatians 5:22-23).

- Goodness, righteousness, and truth are fruits of a follower of Christ (Ephesians 5:9).

- New believers in Christ are fruit (Colossians 1:6).

- Every good work can be a summary of the fruitfulness of service: "…so that you may walk worthy of the LORD, fully pleasing [to Him], bearing fruit in every good work and growing in the knowledge of God" (Colossians 1:10).

Specific Recommendations

First, develop a portrait of how your congregation describes a mature believer. Rarely does a church leader or ministry group have a profile or summary of what they expect from their people. Church leaders, such as Reggie McNeal, challenge each of us:

> The quality of leadership we need for the renewal of the North American church requires that we have people who are operating from a well-thought-out approach; so they will know why they are doing what they are doing, not just copying someone else's cool idea. . . . I want to get you in a position to hear from God by helping to create for you a new mental landscape as you listen and look for Him.[30]

Second, provide a way of evaluating your Christian formation. For example, Lifeway's Spiritual Growth Assessment Process[31] is a tool which measures spiritual growth and gives opportunity for church leadership to counsel and advise members—as does the Christian Life Profile.[32] Normal shepherding skills are enhanced by such tools which assist in evaluating individuals. However, we also need to evaluate total church programs, a ministry audit. Every ministry must have a current purpose; every purpose must have ministry strategies; and we have very little resource to do other than that.

Third, facilitate participation in broad-based Christian education. It would appear that the adult developmental literature would be an ally in spiritual formation ministry. Two fields of endeavor highlight this potential— spiritual disciplines and informal learning practices. Much attention has been given to the implementation of personal spiritual disciplines. Corporate spiritual disciplines also can be taught, experienced, and promoted. Educator and publisher Kenneth Boa provides insight about disciplined spirituality:

> Discipline should work in concert with dependence since grace is not opposed to effort but to earning. The multiple benefits of the time-tested disciplines of the faith contribute to spiritual formation in the same way that training prepares us for skillful endeavor.[33]

Another aspect which may show promise for Christian education is to adapt informal learning practices to apply them to church education. English proposes three strategies to foster the spiritual development of adults: *Mentoring* is the personal and professional assistance that one adult (the mentor) provides to another, less experienced adult (the mentee); *Self-Directed Learning*, and *Engaging in Dialogue*, i.e., the interpersonal connections and interchanges among people that encourage and promote their spiritual development.[34]

Finally, what is my plan in ministering with people like that? *Ministry Design.*

Any ministry program, which focuses only upon one aspect of discipleship, will produce diminished growth for the people impacted by that ministry. Are not some churches proud of the full notebooks of sermon notes and the extensive personal libraries or online blogs of their leaders? But how have the ideas in the minds of the learners impacted the lives of those same disciples? Have not all attended meetings where the emphasis was upon "fellowship" and went home longing to know if there was any difference between the event we just attended and a class reunion? Where is the supernatural, world-changing, life-transforming power of God? Observing the tired lives of committed servants makes one wonder if we are really accomplishing the gains of spiritual growth or just exhausting our most willing members. Where is the overflowing power of God, filling and empowering the ministry of the servant-leaders in our congregations?

Adult development has enjoyed a corresponding interdependence with adult education. As such, much profit may be gained from heeding adult and continuing education practices for the ministry design of Christian education. Researcher and adult education specialist Jane Vella proposes twelve principles which seem applicable to the design of ministry in Christian education for adults:

Needs assessment: participation of the learners in naming what is to be learned.

Safety in the environment and the process. We create a context for learning that can be made safe.

Sound relationships between teacher and learner and among learners.

Sequence of content and reinforcement.

Praxis: action with reflection or learning by doing.

Respect for learners as decision makers.

Ideas, feelings, and actions: cognitive, affective, and psychomotor aspects of learning.

Immediacy of the learning.

Clear roles and role development.

Teamwork and the use of small groups.

Engagement of the learners in what they are learning.

Accountability: How do they know they know?[35]

Conclusion

Teach? Adhere to the principles of how God has designed adults to develop. Certainly, we will include more interactivity and attention to learning styles. Be able to discern the *needs* of adults as they develop—both in the *stages* of normal chronological growth and the *phases* of dealing with what life brings and God designs. Also included for the master teacher would be the ability to set mutual goals. Being mindful of the instructional, fellowship, and service needs of those you teach is essential for producing disciples of Christ. Teach with creativity and interest to those the Lord has allowed you to shepherd.

Lead? Be aware of how adults develop. Do not be afraid of sharing responsibility to assess needs, set goals, and implement programs. Move from the understanding of thinking, reasoning, and acting—as if we believe our followers are children—to allow them to be adults. Be wise to counsel and exhort according to adult development roles, and growth will be the hallmark of the future Christian education pacesetter. Leaders should know their maturity profile, be able to assess needs according to it, and implement personal and corporate activities to increase ministry effectiveness.

Plan? The neglected area of planning for corporate programming within ministries is a grave concern. The overly fragmented programming of some ministries has created an environment where we do not program at all and increase the brokenness of the fabric of church life. The highly structured control of some church leaders produces either rebellious followers or unthinking clones. Vitality in biblically-based, courageously-risking, wisely-understanding ministry endeavors is as greatly needed today as perhaps at any time in history.

Reflection Questions

1. Which of the essential areas of discipleship described—instruction, fellowship, and service—is the strongest educationally in your church? Your personal life?

2. What insight from adult development experts could you apply to your present ministry?

3. Which model of adult development do you feel has the greatest application to your ministry?

4. Where are you in the progression of the four questions of spiritual formation?

5. What does a mature person look like?

6. How do I compare . . . etc.?

7. Would you have to do the most work if given the opportunity to revise your adult education program?

8. What passages of Scripture were the most significant to me in the content of this chapter?

ENDNOTES

[1] Gregory C. Carlson, "Adult Development," *Evangelical Dictionary of Christian Education,* edited by Michael J. Anthony (Grand Rapids: Baker Academic, 2001), 31.

[2] Roger Gould, *Transformations: Growth and Change in Adult Life* (New York: Simon & Schuster, 1978).

[3] Daniel J. Levinson, *The Seasons of a Man's Life* (New York: Knopf, 1978).

[4] Daniel J. Levinson, *The Seasons of a Woman's Life* (New York: Ballantine, 1996), 6.

[5] Levinson, *The Seasons of a Woman's Life.*, 18.

[6] Gail Sheehy, *Passages: Predictable Crises of Adult Life* (New York: Ballantine, 1974, 2006).

[7] Charles M. Sell, *Transitions Through Adult Life* (Grand Rapids: Zondervan, 1991).

[8] Sell, *Transitions Through Adult Life,* 29.

[9] Malcolm Knowles. *The Adult Learner: A Neglected Species* (Houston: Gulf Publishing Company, 1973) and *The Modern Practice of Adult Education: From Pedagogy to Andragogy* (Chicago: Association Press/Follett Publishing Co., 1980).

[10] Knowles, *The Modern Practice of Adult Education,* 44.

[11] Ibid.

[12] Malcolm S. Knowles, "Gearing Up for the Eighties," *Training and Development Journal,* 32(7): 12.

[13] Malcolm S. Knowles, "The Professional Organization as a Learning Community," *Training and Development Journal,* 33(5): 36.

[14] Jack Mezirow, "Transformative Learning: Theory to Practice," *New Directions for Adult and Continuing Education,* (74): 11.

[15] Jack Mezirow, *Transformative Dimensions of Adult Learning* (San Francisco: Jossey-Bass, 1991), 3.

[16] Jack Mezirow, "Concept and Action in Adult Education," *Adult Education Quarterly,* 35(3): 142-143. Cf. Mezirow, "Transformative Learning," 9

[17] See Jack Mezirow, "A Critical Theory of Adult Learning and Education," *Adult Education,* 32(1): 7; Mezirow, *Transformative Dimensions of Adult Learning,* 167-168; or Jack Mezirow, "Learning to Think Like an Adult," *Learning as Transformation* (San Francisco: Jossey-Bass, 2000), 22 for slightly varying forms of this list.

[18] Shawn Lindsay, "Preparing to Teach Adults," unpublished Master of Arts Thesis (2005), Lincoln Christian Seminary (Lincoln, Illinois), 80-4.

[19] Allen Tough, *The Adult's Learning Projects: A Fresh Approach to Theory and Practice in Adult Learning* (San Diego: University Associates, Inc., 1979), 1.

[20] Harold Carlson, conversation with his son, October 1996.

[21] Laura L. Bierema, "Moving Beyond Performance Paradigms in Human Resource Development," in *Handbook of Adult and Continuing Education,* Arthur L. Wilson and Elisabeth R. Hayes, eds., (San Francisco: Jossey-Bass, 2000), 287-9.

[22] R. H. Strachan, "The Second Epistle General of Peter," *The Expositor's Greek Testament*, W. Robertson Nicoll, ed., (Grand Rapids: Wm. B. Eerdmans Publishing Company, 1980), Vol. 5, 126.

[23] Robert P. Lightner, "Salvation and Spiritual Formation," *The Christian Educator's Handbook on Spiritual Formation*, Kenneth O. Gangel and James C. Wilhoit, eds., (Grand Rapids: Baker Books, 1994), 41-3.

[24] Sharan B. Merriam and Rosemary S. Caffarella, *Learning in Adulthood, a Comprehensive Guide, 2nd ed.* (San Francisco: Jossey-Bass Publishers, 1999), 276.

[25] Gregory C. Carlson, *Andragogy and the Apostle Paul.* Unpublished doctoral dissertation, University of Nebraska, Lincoln, December 1987.

[26] Bill Donahue, *Leading LIfe-Changing Small Groups* (Grand Rapids: Zondervan Publishing House, 1996), 15.

[27] Harley Atkinson, *The Power of Small Groups in Christian Education* (Nappanaee, IN: Evangel Publishing House, 2002), 132–33.

[28] Julie A. Gorman, *Community That Is Christian: A Handbook on Small Groups* (Grand Rapids: Baker Books, 2002), 98.

[29] Dallas Willard, *The Spirit of the Disciplines* (San Francisco: Harper Collins, 1988), 49-50.

[30] Reggie McNeal, *The Present Future: Six Tough Questions for the Church* (San Francisco: Jossey-Bass, 2003), xix.

[31] Available at www.lifeway.com/discipleship.

[32] Randy Franzee, *The Christian Life Profile Assessment Tool Workbook* (Grand Rapids: Zondervan Publishing House, 1998, 2005).

[33] Kenneth Boa, *Conformed to His Image: Biblical and Practical Approaches to Spiritual Formation* (Grand Rapids: Zondervan Publishing House, 2001), 75.

[34] English, "Spiritual Dimensions of Informal Learning," 30-6.

[35] Jane Vella, *Learning To Listen; Learning To Teach* (San Francisco: Jossey-Bass, 2002), 4.

CHAPTER 8

SPIRITUAL FORMATION AND CHRISTIAN FORMATION

By Mark A. Maddix

The language of "spiritual" and "spirituality" has become increasingly common in our world. People are interested in spirituality and metaphysical realities. They have a hunger and thirst for something beyond themselves.

In 2005, *Newsweek's* article, "In Search of the Spiritual," gave a glowing glimpse of spirituality in America. The article claimed that "Americans are looking for personal, ecstatic experiences of God." The article also showed that, even though people are interested in spirituality, they are not necessarily interested in a particular religious orientation.

The growth in spirituality is evident in the diversity of religious expressions of faith in our culture. Christianity is no longer the predominant religion. However, people are separating their spirituality from religion. Institutional religion has become a negative phrase. Many seekers consider themselves "spiritual" but not religious.[1] The term is used in secular and sacred settings as a way to reflect the human hunger for the transcendent or to make meaning out of life.[2]

The spiritual thirst of our time has become a social phenomenon. People from all walks of life and many faiths are searching with renewed interest for a spiritual center. For some, spirituality is described as a relationship to whatever is most important in their lives; for others, it is the process of becoming positive and creative persons. These examples reflect the hunger for spirituality without a transcendent being, a secular spirituality.[3]

It would be a mistake to think that spirituality is only a Christian term or that its usage is merely the prerogative of the Church. The term, as reflected in our culture, is broadly understood. For example, one can talk about Jewish and Islamic spiritualities, agnostic and atheistic spiritualities. It is not surprising that, given the wide range of understanding of spirituality in the public area, it has become difficult to determine what people mean by the term *spirituality*.

The term *spirituality* is derived from the Latin *spiritus*, meaning "breath, life, spirit." Thus, in the broadest sense, *spirituality* has to do with the whole of our life which is grounded in ultimate reality, in the spirit, and attuned to the spiritual dimension of existence—that which both animates and transcends our bodily, physical selves.[4] To speak of something being spiritual assumes the existence of a transcendent reality –this spirit-filled dimension of life—and then argues further that we humans can and do experience this reality in our midst and that we are drawn to both name and respond to it. Spirituality is a fundamental dimension of human beings which suggests that humans, *homo sapiens,* are distinctly spiritual beings, *homo spiritualis*; that is, human beings are capable of receiving a call, an address from a transcendent "subject"—whether that subject is understood as God, nature, an undifferentiated unity, or as an esthetic experience.[5] Therefore, every discussion of spiritual matters presupposes divine activity in the form of grace. For Wesleyan theologians, the understanding of "prevenient grace" and for Calvinistic theologians of "common grace" provides a theological explanation of this phenomenon. Human beings do not have the human capacity to transcend God; only through the gift of God's grace can every person experience God.

The chapter begins with this important theological presupposition—that humans are spiritual beings with the capacity, by God's grace, to experience Him. The chapter discusses the meaning of spirituality and then moves toward developing a definition of Christian spiritual formation. Spiritual formation is viewed from a biblical perspective, including the role of Scripture in spiritual formation. Also, terms used to describe Christian formation, Christian education, and spiritual formation are discussed. The article focuses on the history of spirituality by distinguishing different aspects of spirituality and the classical movement of spiritual transformation. Finally, an exploration of current spiritual practices is explored. The chapter concludes with a brief discussion about the relationship of spiritual formation and developmental theory.

Toward a Definition of Spiritual Formation

What is distinct about Christian spirituality? What are the unique aspects of Christian spirituality as compared to a more general understanding of spirituality in our culture? In order to begin to answer these questions, a definition of spiritual formation will be explored. The word *spirituality* is derived from the Latin term *spiritualitas*. Like its cognates *spiritus and spiritualis, spiritualitas* is a suitable translation of the original Greek terms *pneuma* and *pneumatikos* which mean "spirit." Paul, in 1 Corinthians 2:15, maintains, "The spiritual person, however, can evaluate everything, yet he himself cannot be evaluated by anyone." The spiritual person, then, the *pneumatikos*, is under the leadership of the Holy Spirit; the carnal person is not.[6] Therefore, Christian spirituality refers to those who are living by the presence and power of God's Holy Spirit, the Third Person of the Triune God. Christian spirituality describes a particular way of responding to the Spirit of God—mediated to the world and ultimately known through Jesus Christ. Christian spirituality focuses on the progressive transformation of the human person into the likeness of Jesus Christ. It is the result of the cooperation of our whole lives with the power and presence of Christ's Spirit who is alive and working within the whole person—body and soul, thoughts and feelings, emotions and passions, hopes and fears and dreams.[7]

A definition of spiritual formation first begins with a focus on being "formed" and "transformed." The human person is being transformed into the "image and likeness of Christ." Spiritual formation is derived from Galatians 4:19 where St. Paul wrote, "My children, again I am in pains of childbirth for you until Christ is *formed* in you" (emphasis added). Paul uses the word *morphoo* (form) which is closely related to *metamorphoo* (transform). It refers to the essential nature, not mere outward form. Paul is praying the inward nature of the Galatian believers would become so like Christ that one could say that

Christ has been formed in them. They would be more human—not divine, not a Savior themselves; but they would have real Christlike character and behavior.[8] Thus, according to Galatians 4:19, spiritual formation can be defined as "the whole person in relationship with God, within the community of believers, growing in Christlikeness, reflected in a Spirit-directed, disciplined lifestyle, and demonstrated in redemptive action in our world."[9] Spiritual formation then is the outworking of the grace of God in the hearts and actions of human beings. Robert Mulholland says, "Spiritual formation is a process of being conformed to the image of Christ, a journey into becoming persons of compassion, persons who forgive, persons who care deeply for others and the world."[10] We cannot "conform ourselves" to the image of Christ, but God is the One who conforms and transforms us by the power of the Spirit. Dallas Willard states, "Spiritual formation, without regard to any specifically religious context or tradition, is the process by which the human spirit or will is given a definite 'form' or character."[11] Spiritual formation refers to the process of shaping our spirit and giving it a definite character. It means the formation of our spirit in conformity with the Spirit of Christ. Of course, it involves the Holy Spirit in action, but the focus of spiritual formation is the formation of our spirit.

Willard defines spiritual formation: "Spiritual formation in Christ is the process whereby the inmost being of the individual (the heart, will, or spirit) takes on the quality or character of Jesus Himself."[12] Also, Mulholland defines spiritual formation as "a process of being conformed to the image of Christ for the sake of others."[13] It is a process that happens to everyone. The most despicable—as well as the most admirable—of persons have had a spiritual formation. Their spirits or hearts have been formed. Spiritual formation is about pilgrims—Christians, being on a journey to become more Christian. The story of the Exodus illustrates this process. Just as the people of Israel were led out toward freedom, spiritual formation leads us out toward freedom in Christ. This leading out is not directionless but aims at the promised land of the kingdom of God. It aims at growth in grace toward Christian maturity.

The second aspect of spiritual formation focuses on our human participation and obedience to Jesus Christ. It is important to note it is not what we do that transforms us; but through our participation in the "means of grace," that we receive from God, we are changed. James Wilhoit defines spiritual formation by including both the human and divine aspect of spiritual formation. "Spiritual formation is the intentional communal process of growing in our relationship with God and becoming conformed to Christ through the power of the Holy Spirit."[14] Wilhoit's focus on "intentional processes" is a way to distinguish it from the broad sense in which spiritual formation refers to all cultural forces, activities, and experiences that shape people's spiritual lives.[15] For Wilhoit, spiritual formation is comprised of intentional and deliberate actions whereby a person is being transformed into the image of Christ. Historically, the Church has discovered that certain disciplines, devotional skills and practices, and acts of Christian service keep us in the presence of Christ where the Holy Spirit has an opportunity to go on transforming us.

Third, spiritual formation is a lifelong process that takes place in the context of community. Much of Western Christianity views salvation and spiritual formation as individualistic. In ancient biblical times—with a collectivist form of social organization, the overriding significance of the community was taken for granted.[16] However, today the Western church has become fragmented and individualistic, which makes spiritual formation more difficult. Christian faith is often practiced, being void of the community. The Christian life is best lived in community where worship, fellowship, small groups, and service are practiced. In this context, spiritual formation takes place in and through the community. Wilhoit's primary thesis of his book *Spiritual Formation as If the Church Mattered* supports the claims that spiritual formation is communal and takes place in the context of the life of the Church.[17]

The closest relationship between participation in Christian community and spiritual formation is because the Church, the Christian community, is the eschatological community. The community is eschatological because the promised age of the Spirit has arrived in the life, death, and resurrection of Jesus Christ and is present in the Church's continuation of His ministry.[18] This means this community represents the anticipation of the fullness of God's kingdom in the midst of history. The Church is a community that anticipates, proclaims, and celebrates this kingdom.[19]

Also, spiritual formation is a lifelong process. Many in the field of spiritual and faith formation use the metaphor of a journey to describe the life of faith.[20] Hagber and Guelich state, "A journey involves process, action, movement, change, experience, stops and starts, variety, humdrum, and surprises. Whereas a trip focuses on a destination, a journey has significance when seen as a whole."[21] Our journey of faith connotes the process and passages in our response to God's overture to us when we view our lives as wholes. Hagberg and Guelich—along with James Fowler—have developed stages of faith as a way to look at our faith journeys. For Fowler, these are predictable life stages; for Hagberg and Guelich, they develop phases from the life of faith as recorded in the history of the Church.[22] Just as a child grows through stages of physical development and growth, so do we grow spiritually. The idea of spiritual formation as a continuous process is counter to our instant-gratification society. The path to spiritual formation includes joy and success as well as struggle and disappointment. Much of the history of Christianity focuses on struggle and suffering—based on the suffering of Christ—as a necessary aspect of growth and maturity. Mulholland says, "Life itself is a process of spiritual development. The only choice we have is whether that growth moves us toward wholeness in Christ or toward an increasingly dehumanized and destructive mode of being."[23]

The Christian journey, therefore, is an intentional and a continual commitment to a lifelong process of growth toward wholeness in Christ. It is the process of growing "in every way into Him who is the head— Christ" (Ephesians 4:15) until we grow "into a mature man with a stature measured by Christ's fullness" (Ephesians 4:13). For this purpose, God is present and active in every moment of our lives.[24]

Fourth, spiritual formation includes the nurturing of self and relationship to others. We are created to be in relationship with God. This relationship is to be characterized by uniqueness, unity, and reciprocity. Similar to the interrelationships with the Triune God, humans are to experience simultaneous communion with God that does not jeopardize our uniqueness. In our union with the Triune God, our human particularity is not lost. God acts not as a dominating Other but as the One in whom "we live and move and exist" (Acts 17:28). Our relationship with God does not sacrifice our uniqueness; rather, it allows us to become more fully who God created us to be. Spiritual formation includes participation in caring for ourselves and nurturing our selves in light of the Triune God.

Balswick states, "Our understanding of God for human development begins in relationship with the divine and the human other. In mutually reciprocating relationships, we encounter the other and ourselves most fully."[25] It is our belief that God's intention for spiritual development is to be intertwined with the understanding and care of self, our relationship with God, and one another. When we live in this reality, we become more fully human and bear the image of the Triune God.

A definition of spiritual formation includes a focus on the inner transformation of the human person into the likeness of Jesus Christ. This transformation takes place as humans participate in avenues of God's grace such as worship, prayer, Bible study, communion, and acts of service. These intentional practices provide a "channel" for participation and communion with the Triune God. Finally, spiritual formation takes place as humans care for their "selves," relate to others in Christian community, and serve others.

Biblical Images of Christian Spiritual Formation

Spiritual formation is the primary task of the Church. People are formed and shaped in the context of Christian community as they encounter the Triune God in worship, fellowship, discipleship, and service. The very nature of the Church is reflected in the nature of God—*mission Dei* (mission of God). The mission of God for the Church is established in the Great Commission—Matthew 28:19, to "go, therefore, and make disciples of all nations . . . ." When the Church is faithful to her mission, lives are formed and transformed into the "image and likeness of Christ."

The Bible provides significant examples of the spiritual life. James Wilhoit summarizes these examples in three sets of images: nurture (agriculture, gardening, human growth, intimacy); the journey (race, battle, struggle); and death and resurrection (dying with Christ, being born again).[26]

First, Wilhoit begins with the image of Christian life and nurture. The image of Jesus as the True Vine (John 15) vividly communicates the spiritual truth we need to stay spiritually connected to Christ.[27] Wilhoit states, "We often misread this image as being just about 'me abiding in Jesus' when the actual image and language have a strong community focus; when the branches are connected to the vine, a marvelous crop of grapes is produced."[28] We live and have our being as we stay connected to the Source, Jesus Christ.

Second, Wilhoit provides the image of Christian life as journey and struggle.[29] Paul uses imagery of training and discipline in the Christian life (i.e., 1 Corinthians 9:24-27). The emphasis of the athletic race image is a call for Corinthian believers to adopt the singular focus of a trained athlete who follows Christ.[30] The most popular example of this image is Philippians 3:13-14 which depicts the image of "straining forward and pressing on toward the goal."[31] Also, the journey includes struggle against "reaching forward" and "pursuing the goal" (Ephesians 6:12). This battle imagery results in struggle and risk; it is necessary for growth and sanctification.

The third image developed by Wilhoit is the image of the Christian life and Resurrection.[32] Scripture is full of examples of the movement from death to life. Wilhoit states, "The death-rebirth pattern is an archetypal pattern present throughout the Bible. The pattern shows itself in the flood (Genesis 6-9) as God destroys the entire world... and then brings forth life on the earth out of the barrenness of destruction."[33] Other examples are the death and resurrection of Christ, the new birth as recorded in John 3:1-8, and the symbolism of baptism—being "buried" in Christ's death and raised again in new life (Romans 6:4).

According to Wilhoit, these three images of nurture, journey, and struggle and death/resurrection capture the essential aspects of spiritual formation.[34] Also, Willard argues that the primary image of spiritual formation is in the life of Jesus Christ. He states, "Christian spiritual formation is focused entirely on Jesus. Its goal is an obedience or a conformity to Christ that arises out of an inner transformation accomplished through purposeful interaction with the grace of God in Christ."[35] He builds his argument on Galatians 4:19, "until Christ is formed in you," and 2 Corinthians 3:6, "the Spirit produces life."[36] Willard's primary thesis is that the biblical imagery of spiritual formation is most reflected in being a follower, a disciple of Jesus Christ. For Willard, discipleship is central to spiritual formation and practice.

Spiritual Formation as Christian Formation

The term "spiritual formation" has different meanings to different faith traditions. Historically, the etymology of this term originates from the Roman Catholic theology which represents a post-Vatican II notion of spirituality. During this same time, the term began to gain popularity in Protestant circles. Since Vatican II, there has been an increased interest in spirituality by Catholics and Protestant congregations. However, Hughes Oliphant Old points out, "Calvinists have usually preferred the term 'piety' to the term 'spirituality.'"[37] Reformed theologians usually have spoken of the doctrine of the Christian life when they speak about what Roman Catholics call "spirituality theology."[38] The confusion reflected in Old's history makes it difficult to narrow the meaning of spiritual formation. Also, a review of various traditions within the field of Christian education reveals a plethora of terms such as spiritual development, spiritual growth, spiritual development, faith development, and Christian formation.

Spiritual formation as a discipline within Protestant Christianity—influenced by Roman Catholic spirituality—is a relatively new movement. Spirituality and spiritual formation—as a self-conscious movement in Protestantism—have arisen, in part, because of the inadequacy of Christian education to address the care of the souls. Christian education is influenced by modernism that is focused on transmitting cognition—especially when conveying the ancient truths of Scripture. Christian education has given considerable energy in didactically taught doctrines and beliefs. Most Christian educators believe the transmission of propositional truth and belief are central to the educational task—especially as they relate to theology and theological traditions. Also, Christian education is influenced by educational theory and method. Christian educators develop course objectives that must be measured and assessed for effective learning. A renewed focus of Christian education will include both transmissive aims as well as transformation.[39]

Also, society has been in a reactive shift from modernism with a focus on rationalism and objectivism to postmodernism with its great emphasis on subjectivity and connectivity.[40] Because of this shift in focus, the literature is moving toward the language of "Christian formation" to provide a more encompassing term to house Christian education and spiritual formation.

Distinguishing Different Spiritual Formation Traditions

In the history of spirituality, it has been helpful to delineate different types of spiritual traditions according to their distinctive elements and characteristics. Barbara Bowe provides two different types of spiritual traditions: the "apophatic" and the "kataphatic."[41] Bowe states the "apophatic spiritual traditions (from the Greek *apophasis* which means 'denial, negation') affirm the absolute unknowability of God and reject all conceptual attempts to name, symbolize, or speak about God in concrete images."[42] The apophatic way is the way to God through negation and abandonment of images, through darkness and surrender to the unknown. Bowe claims there are considerable biblical warrants for such a spiritual path, going back to the revelation of God to Moses on the holy mountain of Sinai/Horeb in Exodus 19 and 20.[43] There Yahweh spoke to Moses with the words, "I am going to come to you in a dense cloud" (Exodus 19:9). After Moses received the commandment, we learn that "the people remained at a distance, while Moses approached the thick darkness where God was" (Exodus 20:21). Moses' example of the "way of negation" provides an example of how the Church has focused on spirituality by "way of negation," which exhorts Christians to "leave behind everything" to follow God.

In contrast to the apophatic tradition, the history of spirituality is rich with examples from the kataphatic spiritual traditions (from Greek *kataphasis* which means "affirmation").[44] Bowe states, "These spiritual traditions affirm that God the Creator can be known, by way of analogy, through images, symbols, and concepts drawn from human experience in the created world."[45] At the heart of these traditions is the conviction that God is fundamentally a revealing God who seeks to make Himself known to the world. This spiritual way also has deep biblical foundations—especially in the Wisdom literature of both Testaments.[46] In these texts, those who seek God are invited to discern the divine presence within all of creation.

For Christian spirituality, God is made known through the revelation of His Son, Jesus Christ. Such texts as John 14:9, ". . . The one who has seen Me has seen the Father," and John 1:18, "No one has ever seen God. The One and Only Son—the One who is at the Father's side—He has revealed Him," ground the conviction that God can be experienced and known in and through Jesus the Christ. This kind of Christ-centered, kataphatic spirituality supports and undergirds Christian spirituality.[47]

Contemplative and Apostolic Spirituality

Another classic distinction in the history of spirituality is the difference between contemplative and apostolic dimensions of spirituality. The term "contemplative," according to Bowe, is "that transforming and unitive movement, in love, toward the mystery of God."[48] It involves a person's desire or longing for God—together with the realization that God lives in all created things. It implies the corresponding effort to make oneself aware of God's presence. Contemplative spirituality often has been linked with the mystical dimension of faith that sees the inner harmony of all things and denies any dualistic notion of life that opposes spirit and matter, the divine and human.[49] The Contemplatives have searched for God in solitude (hermetical tradition) and in communal settings (Monastic tradition). These Contemplatives have removed themselves from society to experience the presence of God. Examples include Meister Eckhardt (1260-1327), Julian of Norwich (1343-1415), Teresa of Avila, and John the Cross. One of the best-known Contemplatives is Thomas Merton (1915-68) who has written extensively about spirituality. These examples and others see the contemplative life as a way to be united with God and to recognize the unity of all life.

To contrast the contemplative life of separation from the world, Apostolic Spirituality focuses on an active way of discipleship in which believers participate in and further their saving mission.[50] At the heart of the apostolic tradition is living out the mission of Jesus Christ—to go and fulfill the Great Commission (Matthew 28:19-20). The apostolic tradition continues to grow through the example of the first apostles. They shared in Jesus' mission of teaching, healing, reconciling, and calling all people to His fullness of life. Much of Christian spirituality focuses on discipleship as central to Christian faith and practice. Christian disciples are urged to "take up the cross" and "follow" Jesus on a daily basis. Willard, in his book *The Great Omission,* argues that Christian discipleship is not an option. He states, "The disciple is one who, intent upon becoming Christlike and so dwelling in His 'faith and practice,' systematically and progressively rearranges his affairs to that end. By these decisions and actions, even today, one enrolls in Christ's training and becomes His pupil or disciple. There is no other way."[51]

Both the contemplative and apostolic spiritualities are ways of responding to God. They share a common core of reverencing the mysterious otherness of God and recognizing God's Spirit and presence at the heart of all life. Both embrace God's design and purpose for the life of the world—manifest in the ministry of Jesus Christ.[52] Some faith traditions—such as the Roman Catholic and Eastern Orthodox Churches and Anglican traditions—place a greater emphasis on the contemplative spirituality; while most Protestant denominations place a greater emphasis on apostolic spirituality. Both are necessary for effective spiritual growth and formation. Bowe states, "Just as completive spirituality is profoundly apostolic in its concern for and union with all that God loves, so too, apostolic spirituality discerns the mystery of God within the very heart of human engagement and contemplates the face of Christ in the faces of the brother and sister in need."[53] Therefore, authentic spirituality will include both contemplative and apostolic spirituality.

Six Historical Movements in the Church

Founder of Renovare, an ecumenical organization with a distinct Christian perspective, Richard Foster asserts that the history of the Church is marked by six movements or traditions. These movements describe how God's Spirit has moved upon individuals and groups with a particular mission.[54] The movements provide a pathway to understand how spiritual formation is viewed by different faith traditions. All of these movements have strengths and weaknesses. According to Foster, all are necessary for a balanced approach to spiritual formation. A summary of the movements given below are from *A Spiritual Formation Workbook* written by James Bryan Smith and Lynda Graybeal.

Movement: In the fourth and fifth centuries, men and women fled city life to found cloisters and monasteries where they emphasized the importance of solitude, meditation, and prayer. Antony of Egypt was the early leader of the "Desert Mothers and Fathers."[55] Foster argues that the contemplative movement reflects the life of Christ's devotion to God.[56] However, the weaknesses of those involved in the contemplative movement are they failed to be engaged in God's creative work in the world.

Holiness Movement: In the early eighteenth century, John Wesley and his friends formed a group called the "Holy Club," focusing on moral laxity and the need for Christians to overcome sinful habits. They developed a "method," and the Church took sin seriously. The purifying effects of Methodism were dramatic.[57] Foster argues that the holiness movement reflects the aspect of the life of Christ as being virtuous in thought, word, and action.[58] The weakness of this moralist approach is that the focus on sin and morality results in a neglect of compassion.[59]

Charismatic Movement: In the seventeenth century, the Church witnessed a new outbreak of the Holy Spirit in the lives of men and women called "Quakers" who were led by George Fox. The active presence of the Spirit in the lives of believers became the empowering principle behind scores of conversions. The active role of the Spirit was at the center of their worship; and He propelled them into evangelism, missions, and social concerns.[60] Foster argues that the charismatic movement reflects the life of Christ as being empowered by the Spirit.[61] The weakness of this movement is the neglect to proclaim the gospel.[62]

Social Justice Movement: In the late twelfth century, Francis of Assisi and a group of followers abandoned their former lives and went about caring for the sick, the poor, and the lame. Men and women followed

Francis's lead, forming the Franciscan and Poor Clare orders. Their impact on disease and poverty was remarkable.[63] Foster argues that the Social Justice Movement reflects the life of Christ and His compassion toward all people—especially the sick and needy.[64] The weakness of this movement is their inability to listen to God due to their focus on action.[65]

Evangelical Movement: In the sixteenth century, Martin Luther and others proclaimed the gospel of Jesus Christ after discovering its message anew in the Bible. The message of hope and victory was expressed by clergy and laity in sermons, mission efforts, and personal witnessing.[66] The evangelical movement reflects the life of Christ in its focus on the proclamation of the good news of the gospel.[67] The weakness is the lack of emphasis on the work of the Holy Spirit.[68]

Incarnational Movement: In the eighteenth century, Count Nicholas Ludwig von Zinzendorf allowed remnants of the persecuted Moravian Church to build the village of Herrnhut on his estate. Initially divided, the group became unified when they experienced a powerful outpouring of the Holy Spirit after Zinzendorf led them in daily Bible studies and in formulating the "Brotherly Agreement." The Moravians joyfully served God—praying, evangelizing, and helping others—in the midst of baking, weaving, and raising families. The Incarnational Movement reflects the life of Christ in bringing harmony between faith and work.[69] The weakness is their inability to revel in secret, harmful sins.[70]

In viewing these differential approaches to spirituality—along with Foster's six historical movements—Christians have a framework to measure and evaluate their own spirituality. A balanced approach to spiritual formation—coupled with the community of faith—helps us maintain equilibrium in our spiritual lives. Each approach reflects an important aspect of the life of faith and Christian practice. Our engagement in these approaches will help us grow in our relationship with Christ and ultimately help us reflect Christ's love more clearly to others.

Classical Spiritual Formation

One of the most popular models of spiritual transformation in the Christian tradition often is referred to as the "three ways" of purgation, illumination, and union.[71] By the thirteenth century, this threefold process was the overarching schema that shaped the Christian understanding of spiritual growth. It makes sense to attend to the testimony of those in the Christian tradition who focused their lives most intensely on the dynamics of spiritual transformation.

The "purgative" way is typically related to an experience of "awakening." One awakens into a new awareness that one's way of life is tending toward death. This openness of the seeker provides an opportunity to be "purged."[72] This painful experience is what some mystics and contemplatives refer to as the "dark night of the soul." Through this dark journey, one seeks for the promise of new being and opens to the experience of "illuminative" way. Here one experiences a new sense of joy and peace in God's presence. Also, during purgation, it may require that a person deal with the old aspects of his/her life that is inconsistent with God's will. It is here where the deliberate sins, or "willful transgressions of the known will of God," can be forgiven. Purgation also probes the unconscious sins and omissions of life. It is here where we begin to let the Spirit of God reveal to us aspects of our inner being that have been invisible to our view and have hindered us from growth toward spiritual maturity.

This illumination, the second stage, transforms people as they come to interpret the new world in light of the divine presence. They learn to depend on God rather than depend on their capacity. Illumination is the experience of total consecration to God in love. Rather than being in charge of my relationship with God, God is given control of the relationship.[73] Also, illumination is characterized by increasing social concerns—not out of obligation but out of a deep sense of God's love for others. During the process of illumination, a paradigm shift takes place in our motives. Rather than having a self-concern for our relationship with God, our motivation becomes a heart burning for the love of God.[74]

Then, the person is united with God. Historically, this "unitive way" refers to a process through which one comes into an experience of relational unity with the divine.[75] It is characterized as complete oneness with God in which we find ourselves caught up in adoration, praise, and a deep peace that passes all understanding. Shults and Sandage state, "The very meaning of 'experience' itself is transformed in this 'unity' of intimacy with God, which is sometimes described as an 'infusion' of the absolutely gracious gift of divine presence."[76]

The journey through the stages of purgation, illumination, and union provides a pattern of transformation necessary for spiritual growth and formation. This pattern provides a "guidance system" to keep the vehicle of our lives on the route toward wholeness in Christ. Often through patterns, God breaks in and upsets our lives in order for transformation and change to take place. Mulholland provides an example of this classical approach to transformation in figure 8.1 below. He includes the category of "awakening" in his pattern to show that the first step to transformation takes place through an encounter with the living God.

The Stages	Their Aspects
Awakening	Encounter with God
	Encounter with self
	Comfort
	Threat
Purgation	Renunciation of blatant sins
	Renunciation of willful disobedience
	Unconscious sins and omissions
	Deep-seated structures of being and behavior
	Coming to trust
Illumination	Total consecration to God in love
	God experienced within
	Integration of being
	Unceasing prayer
	Increasing social concern
Union	Abandonment to grace
	Prayer of quietness
	Dark night of the senses
	Full union/ecstatic union
	Dark night of the spirit

Figure 8.1: The Classical Christian Pilgrimage[77]

Scripture as Spiritual Formation

Christians believe the Bible is authoritative for Christian faith and practice. In reading the Bible, Christians find guidance, inspiration, and knowledge as to how to live out their faith. Christians believe that Scripture is God's specific revelation given through divine inspiration. Christians also believe the Bible to be central to spiritual formation. In reading the Bible, however, Christians have read the Bible primarily as an activity to master a body of information. The Bible is read as a way to instruct, teach, and give information. Mulholland states, "We are more often seeking some tidbits of information that will enhance our understanding of the Christian faith without challenging or confronting the way we live in the world."[78]

In recent centuries, the interpretive practices of biblical scholarship have tended to focus on those matters regarding "what the text meant" since these texts were written in and to particular historical contexts. However, these prevailing interpretive approaches to the Bible—characterized largely by historical concerns that seek for the given text's meaning as a historical, static entity—often have left the Church wondering what, if anything, the Bible might actually say to her in contemporary settings. That is, the historical focus of biblical interpretation often may leave the Church with an abundant feast of ways to read and understanding the biblical texts in their original communicative contexts involving author and audience but starving for a fresh message that engages the present. When this happens, our passionate affirmations regarding the Bible's authority often ring hollow.

However, there is a renewed interest in interpreting and reading Scripture as a means of transformation instead of information. Much more than informing us through the mastery of materials, supremely Scripture forms and transforms us.[79] The Bible was written primarily for the Church. Stephen Fowl writes, "Christian communities are formed, through word and sacrament, to read Scripture in light of their proper end in Christ."[80] The Church is the place where Christians are formed as they interpret Scripture in ways that enhance the goal of being like Christ. Thus, Scripture is less about information but more about formation and transformation. In the information approach to reading, we give assent, mental agreement, to abstract conceptualizations; but we do not get involved personally, intimately, openly, receptively in that which we read. During the Reformation, Luther and Calvin both warned against a merely historical reading of the text and consequently against a merely historical faith. Luther insisted on an internal—not only a formal—external reading, paying heed to the true subject matter rather than the mere word; so that one would find Christ at the center of the Bible.[81]

Historically, the task of biblical scholars has been to interpret Scripture from a historical context—"what the text meant"—since, after all, these texts were written in and to particular historical contexts and situations and were, therefore, inseparable from the myriad of historical contingencies associated with those original settings. In more recent decades, this concern for grounding the theological-interpretive task historically has served to correct many errors associated with what was identified in decades past as the "biblical theology" movement by giving careful attention both to the theological influences behind the text and to the theological aspects of the composition and rhetoric of the various books of the Bible, including both Testaments. The movement from a historical (text-centered) approach to interpretation to a narrative (reader-centered) approach to interpretation is built on the assumption that the inspired Scriptures can be interpreted within the context of Christian community. A person—regardless of his/her level of biblical expertise—can read the Bible and encounter God.

Formation reading includes opening ourselves up to the text. In reading the Bible; we seek to allow the text to become the intrusion of the Word of God into our lives, to address us, encounter us. We allow the text to inform us rather than inform the text. Formational reading allows the text to master us instead of us mastering the text. We come to the text with an openness to hear, receive, respond, and be a servant of the Word rather than a master of the text. Sandra Schneiders indicates that biblical spirituality is a transformative process of person and communal engagement with the biblical text. The nonspecialist can approach the text not merely as an historical record or even as a literary medium but as the Word of God.[82] Historical and critical analysis do not always lead to transformation. Rather, the subjectivity of the reader is always transformed by the Word of God, by the work of the Holy Spirit.

As they read the Bible for transformation and information, Christians will read the Bible with new excitement and energy. Formational reading will require the development of a new discipline. Preparation is necessary and will require time to "center down" (to use the Quaker phrase) to become still, relinquish, let go of your life in the presence of God.[83]

Lectio Divina: Experiencing God's Word

One approach to reading the Bible for transformation is the ancient practice of *lectio divina,* meaning "sacred reading" of Scripture. Its roots are with the Benedictines, a religious order founded by St. Benedict of Nursia in the sixth century. Traditionally, *lectio divina* is described as a process that includes a series of prayer dynamics. Together, they move the reader of Scripture to a deep level of engagement with the text and with the Spirit that enlivens the text. The dynamics include:

Silencio (silence): When approaching the Bible and/or prayer, the believer is engaged in open, receptive listening.

Lectio (reading): The text is read audibly, slowly, and deliberately to evoke imagination. Hearing the text reminds us of the spoken Word of God.

Meditation: To meditate is to think about or mentally "chew on" what you have read. We have an opportunity to relax and mull over what has been read.

Ortio (praying): Prayer includes talking to God as you would in a close relationship. Speak to God—preferably out loud, or write your prayer in a journal.

Contemplatio (contemplation): Stop and rest silently before God. Receive whatever the Spirit gives.

Compassio (compassion): The fruit of the contemplation of God is love—love of God and neighbor. Whatever insight, feeling, or commitment emerges from our time in Scripture is to be shared as grace with others.[84]

Spiritual Practices: A Means of Grace

Spiritual growth takes place through a variety of Christian practices. John Wesley, the founder of Methodism, called these practices the "means of grace." The term "means of grace" was a particular term used in Protestant and Roman Catholic circles to describe the specific channels through which God conveys grace to His people. In Wesley's sermon "The Means of Grace," he states, "By means of grace are outward signs, words, or actions ordained by God and appointed for this end to be ordinary channels whereby God might convey to men preventing, justifying, and sanctifying grace."[85] Wesley uses the word "means" with the word "ordinance," on occasion, as an indicator that this participation was expected by God.[86] While the means of grace themselves had no salvific worth, they were channels by which the Holy Spirit works in extraordinary ways. The means, like grace, were available to all—even to those who did not yet experience what Wesley calls "salvation."[87]

Wesley divided the "means of grace" into two divisions: Instituted means of grace and Prudential means of grace. The Instituted means of grace are practices ordained by Jesus Christ: prayer, searching the Scriptures, participating in the Lord's Supper (Eucharist), fasting, and Christian conferencing (small groups). These means of grace—particularly in their corporate expressions—mirror the intended and ongoing sacramental life of the Church.

The Prudential means of grace are practices ordained by the Church: doing all of the good you can and attending to the private and public worship of God. Wesley believed that a person should try to do all of the good they can by caring for the needs of the poor and by loving one's neighbor. He also recognized the importance of attending public worship on a regular basis. The Prudential means of grace were designed to meet the person at his/her point of need. Thus, they are adaptable to a person's particular historical situation or context. The means of grace have both individual and communal aspects necessary for spiritual formation and discipleship.

Wesley did not confine God's grace to just these practices. Because he understood grace to be God's loving, uncreated presence, he believed many other activities could be means of grace. Thus, grace is still active—

even among those who have no access to specific means like Christian baptism, the Eucharist, or the study of Scripture.

However, Wesley believed that, by participation in the instituted means of grace, a person can be made aware of God's pardoning and empowering presence on a regular basis. Wesley's therapeutic focus is evident in his invitation for his people to meditate regularly on the affirmation that Christ "sealed His love with sacraments of grace, to breed and nourish up in us the life of love."[88] Thus, all who need further empowering by God's grace should faithfully participate in the instituted means of grace.

The "means of grace" are one avenue for discussing the role spiritual disciplines or practices play in the process of spiritual formation. Willard says, "The activities constituting the disciplines have no value in themselves. The aim of substance of spiritual life is not fasting, prayer, hymn signing, frugal living, and so forth. Rather, it is the effective and full enjoyment of active love of God and humankind in all the daily rounds of normal existence where we are placed."[89] He goes on to add that spiritual disciplines do not make a person "spiritually superior" but create the conditions in which grace may flow more freely.

Inward, Outward, and Corporate Practices

Richard Foster, a Quaker, in his book *Celebration of Discipline,* provides a radical call to spiritual formation through participation in spiritual disciplines.[90] Foster and Willard argue that the primary means of spiritual formation are based on a disciplined life in the Spirit which includes obedience to Christ and faithful engagement in spiritual practices.[91] While spiritual practices, in themselves, do not form or shape us, they do provide avenues by which we can practice a life of obedience to Christ. Many Christians struggle with developing intentional personal and communal practices. In a culture that demands instant gratification, the need and desire allow for no time for engagement in spiritual practices. However, there are those—on the other side of the spectrum—who lose sight of the intent of spiritual disciplines by making them legalistic and strict requirements of the Christian faith. Mulholland provides a helpful caution, "For those for whom disciplines becomes a rigid structure of life that allows no room for divine serendipities or grace interruptions of the disciplines, they can lead to works righteousness."[92] Obviously, between the avoidance of disciplines and the imprisonment of disciplines is the holistic practice of balanced spiritual disciplines which become a means of God's grace to shape us in the image of Christ.[93]

Parker Palmer and Charles Foster suggest that spiritual formation requires "practice."[94] The repetition of an action—until its accomplishment achieves a high standard of performance—is a critical component to learning. Foster states, "Practice is central to the habits, attitudes, and sensibilities that become second nature to people who live in a community seeking to incarnate the wisdom and compassion of Christ."[95] Practice is central to the vitality of our personal faith and congregational worship. We cannot pray, sing, or recite creeds if we have not practiced them. "It is through practice," Foster argues, "that Christian are made and nurtured in the faith."[96] These practices or disciplines become second nature to us and provide significant meaning in our life of faith Therefore, through these ordinary disciplines or practices, we become transformed into the likeness of Christ Jesus.

Historically, spiritual disciplines or practices are divided into three areas: inward, outward, and corporate domains (figure 8.2). *The inward domain* focuses on the transformation and development of the inner aspects of the human person. They include prayer, Scripture reading, meditation, silence, fasting, and journaling. *The outward domain* focuses on the social and behavioral aspects of the spiritual formation. Spiritual practices include blessed subtraction (take away specific things in your life), solitude, and acts of mercy, physical exercise, rest/sabbatical, and tithing. *The corporate domain* helps persons participate in practices of accountability through community and worship. Spiritual practices include public confession of sins, participation in public worship, celebration, and accountability by a spiritual director or small group leader. When all three of these domains are being practiced, the person is being formed and shaped holistically.

Inward Domain	Outward Domain	Corporate Domain
This domain centers on the internal righteousness of the person and typically involves disciplines like meditation, prayer, fasting, and study.	This domain focuses on the person's call to discover the social implications of simplicity, submission, and service.	This domain helps people explore the disciplines of confession, worship, guidance, and celebration as members of a community of faith.
Spiritual Practices: Prayer Scripture Reading Meditation Silence Fasting Journaling	*Spiritual Practices:* Blessed Subtraction Solitude Acts of Mercy Exercise Rest/Sabbatical Tithing	*Spiritual Practices:* Confession Worship (Liturgy) Spiritual Direction Celebration

Figure 8.2: Domains of Spiritual Formation

Along with these more traditional spiritual formational practices, there is renewed interest in resurrecting ancient prayers and liturgies in the Church. The increased interest in Christian icons in worship, participation in weekly Eucharists—practicing the Labyrinth, experiencing the Stations of the Cross, and participating in the Ignatian *examen*—are examples of the renewed interest in Protestant circles to find new avenues of spiritual formation.[97] Another example is praying the "sign of the cross" or kneeling and genuflecting before participation in worship.[98] For many Protestants, these new forms of prayers, creeds, and aspects of worship may be new. However, they are giving a new generation of Christians a renewed sense of connection to the catholicity of the Church.

Spiritual Formation and Human Development

This chapter has focused primarily on the biblical, historical, and practical aspects of spiritual formation. However, it is important to see the role played by developmental theory in the process of spiritual formation. Ted Ward compared the process of spiritual formation to an ecological system of human development. He asserted that five empirical domains of human development—(a) physical, (b) intellectual, (c) emotional, (d) social, and (e) moral—serve as "input and output functions to and from the spiritual core."[99] Ward stated, "Ecology refers to the interdependence of each component in the creation with respect to each other component."[100] Each of these components is an interrelated system of development.

Ward uses the illustration of the human hand to identify the six dimensions that represents the human person (figure 8.3). These six dimensions give us some solid empirical information about the complex of factors that form who we are as complete persons.

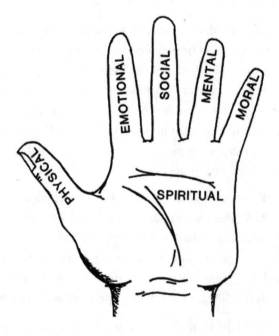

Figure 8.3. Six Aspects of the Human Person

The thumb on the hand represents the physical dimension with particular attention to the human body with all that it entails. The index finger represents the emotional dimension or affect. The middle finger represents social dimension and our ability to communicate and interact with others in a variety of social settings assuming a variety of social roles. The ring finger represents the intellectual dimension, or cognitive functions, that enable us to think. The little finger represents the moral dimension where matters of morality and ethics are entertained and considered. The palm of the hand represents the spiritual dimension that is made alive through a personal encounter with Jesus Christ. However, it is potentially present in every human being as a consequence of having been created in the image of God. The New Testament teaches us that this capacity, or creational human structure, is dead because of sin but is "quickened" or made alive through faith in Christ.[101]

The hand illustrates a holistic approach to spiritual formation. God works through our natural aspects or personalities to form us into the image of Christ. Spiritual formation includes the individual aspects of each person, but it is impossible to separate one aspect from the other. Within this model, we then are led to think about spiritual development as the central integrating dimension of human personhood—nested among other developmental capacities, all partaking of the same developmental patterns of growth. Roehlkepartain states:

> Although the evidence is incomplete, the editors hypothesize that spiritual development is a dimension of human life and experience as significant as cognitive development, emotional development, or social development. All of these dimensions of development are interrelated. It is the spiritual dimension that is most involved in a person's effort to integrate the many aspects of development.[102]

Spiritual formation is as significant as the other dimensions of human development, but it partakes of the same identical processes of maturational unfolding across the human lifespan. The fact that we place the spiritual dimension in the palm of the hand is purposeful. It cannot be separated from the rest of the hand and treated as though it was operating in a different universe with different laws of growth. The biblical methodology for teaching about spiritual development can lead us to no other conclusion since an understanding of how things grow in the spiritual realm always begins with an illustration of how things grow in the natural realm.[103] Most of the developmental systems theories identify the individual whole person in terms of the "biological, psychological, and behavioral characteristics"[104] or identify the various dimensions from the perspective of "biology, cognition, personality, and behavior."[105] Occasionally, a more elaborate list is offered that includes "biology, mental system, subconscious processes, values, norms, motives, and goals; self-structures and self-perceptions; and behavioral characteristics."[106] However one wishes to dissect the various dimensions of the whole person, they are all an attempt to view the individual person "as an integrated, complex, and dynamic totality."[107]

A holistic approach to spiritual formation that includes the natural aspects of the human person means that Christians cannot ignore or neglect any of the six aspects if he/she wants to be transformed into someone "with a stature measured by Christ's fullness" (Ephesians 4:13). If a person decides to stop growing intellectually, it impacts his/her spiritual formation. If a person decides against developing relationships within the body of Christ, he/she ceases to grow. Thus, the five aspects of the human person must be nurtured and developed in order for a person to grow toward spiritual maturity.

A holistic approach to spiritual formation mirrors "the whole measure of the fullness of Christ." In the New Testament, specific aspects of this wholeness are specified for purposes of analysis and emphasis. For instance, Paul calls upon the Christian community to "present your *bodies* as a living sacrifice" (Romans 12:1). On another occasion, he calls upon the Church to be "renewed in the spirit of your *minds*" (Ephesians 4:23). Jesus reminds us of the summary of the Old Testament law: "'Love the LORD your God with all your heart, with all your soul, with all your mind, and with all your strength.' The second is: 'Love your neighbor as yourself'" (Mark 12:30-31). This whole-person commitment is not an atomized dissection of the various ways in which we are to love God and neighbor.

When we nurture and give attention to these six aspects of the human person, we become closer to being fully human, being formed into the image and likeness of Christ. God works through the natural aspects of the human person in order for us to be spiritually formed and shaped. Often, approaches to spiritual formation negate the importance of the human aspects of spiritual formation. Effective spiritual formation requires the development of all aspects of the human person.

Conclusion

One aspect of Christian formation and development is the process of spiritual formation. The goals of both Christian formation and spiritual formation are the same: "to be shaped and formed into the image and likeness of Christ Jesus." Spiritual formation provides a distinct "niche" in the discussion on Christian formation—influenced by the history of Christianity, spirituality, and more recently the culture shift of postmodernity. Christian educators, pastors, and church leaders have a renewed sense of optimism about the impact spiritual formation has on their lives and the life of the Church. Through our participation in the classical spiritual disciplines of the Church, the inspirational reading of the Bible, and the community of faith, our lives are being continually formed and transformed. By the grace of the Triune God, by the work of the Holy Spirit, our inner being is continuing to be shaped into the image of Christ. As we become more like Christ, may we display His love and grace in service to God, others, and the world.

Reflection Questions

1. Define spiritual formation in your own words. What factors influenced your definition?

2. What is the difference between spiritual formation and Christian formation?

3. Place in order of your preference the six historical movements in spiritual formation described in this chapter: Contemplative, Holiness, Charismatic, Social Justice, Evangelical, and Incarnational. Why did you prioritize them in this way?

4. Which category of spiritual practice (inward, outward, corporate) do you most frequently practice? Why this one and not another?

5. Why might a children's pastor, youth pastor, and adult pastor have to address spiritual formation differently? (Hint: Remember human development.)

ENDNOTES

[1] Marjorie J. Thompson, *Soul Feast: An Invitation to the Christian Spiritual Life* (Louisville, Kentucky: Westminster John Knox Press, 1995), 2.

[2] James Fowler, Stages of Faith: *The Psychology of Human Development and the Quest for Meaning* (San Francisco: HarperOne, 1995).

[3] Dallas Willard, *Renovation of the Heart: Putting on the Character of Christ* (Colorado Springs, Colorado: Navpress, 2002), 19.

[4] Barbara E. Bowe, *Biblical Foundations of Spirituality: Touching a Finger to the Flame* (Lanham, Maryland: Rowman & Littlefield Publishers, 2003), 11.

[5] Collins, "What is Spirituality?," 80-1.

[6] Ibid., 81.

[7] Bowe, *Biblical Foundations of Spirituality*, 12.

[8] Wesley E. Tracy, et al., *The Upward Call: Spiritual Formation and Holy Living* (Kansas City: Beacon Hill Press, 1993), 9.

[9] Tracy, *The Upward Call*, 12.

[10] M. Robert Molholland, Jr., *Invitation to a Journey: A Road Map for Spiritual Formation* (Downers Grove, Illinois: InterVarsity, 1993), 25.

[11] Dallas Willard, *Renovation of the Heart: Putting on the Character of Christ* (Colorado Springs, Colorado: Navpress, 2002), 19.

[12] Dallas Willard, *The Great Omission: A Reclaiming; Jesus' Essential Teaching on Discipleship* (San Francisco: HarperSanFrancisco, 2006), 53.

[13] Molholland, *Invitation to a Journey*, 12.

[14] James C. Wilhoit, *Spiritual Formation as If the Church Mattered* (Grand Rapids: Baker Books, 2008), 23.

[15] Wilhoit, *Spiritual Formation as If the Church Mattered*, 23.

[16] Samuel M. Powell, *A Theology of Christian Spirituality* (Nashville: Abingdon, 2005), 36.

[17] Wilhoit, *Spiritual Formation as If the Church Mattered*, 23.

[18] Powell, *A Theology of Christian Spirituality*, 42.

[19] Ibid., 43.

[20] Fowler, *Stages of Faith*; Molholland, *Invitation to a Journey;* Janet O. Hagber and Robert A Guelich, 2nd ed., *The Critical Journey: Stages in the Life of Faith* (Salem, Wisconsin: Sheffield Publishing Company, 2005).

[21] Hagber and Guelich, *The Critical Journey*, 5.

[22] Ibid., 6.

[23] Molholland, *Invitation to a Journey*, 24.

[24] M. Robert Mulholland, Jr., *Shaped by the Word: The Power of Scripture in Spiritual Formation* (Nashville: Upper Room Books, 2001), 24.

[25] Ibid., 49.

[26] Wilhoit, *Spiritual Formation as If the Church Mattered*, 19.

[27] Ibid.

[28] Ibid., 19-20.

[29] Ibid., 20.

[30] Ibid.

[31] Ibid.

[32] Ibid., 22.

[33] Ibid.

[34] Ibid.

[35] Willard, *Renovation of the Heart*, 22.

[36] Ibid., 23.

[37] H. O. Old, "What Is Reformed Spirituality? Played Over Again Lightly," *Calvin Studies*, Vol. 7 (1994): 61-8.

[38] Willard, The Great Omission, 62.

[39] Paul Bramer. "Christian Formation: Tweaking the Paradigm," *Christian Education Journal*, 4:2 (2007): 356.

[40] Ibid.

[41] Bowe, *Biblical Foundations of Spirituality*, 16-8.

[42] Ibid., 16.

[43] Ibid.,, 16-7.

[44] Ibid.,, 17.

[45] Ibid.

[46] Ibid.

[47] Ibid.

[48] Ibid.

[49] Ibid., 18.

[50] Ibid.

[51] Willard, *The Great Omission*, 7.

[52] Bowe, *Biblical Foundations of Spirituality*, 18.

[53] Ibid., 19.

[54] James Smith and Lynda Graybeal, *A Spiritual Formation Workbook: Small-Group Resources for Nurturing Christian Growth* (Englewood, Colorado: Renovare, 1999), 26.

[55] Ibid., 27.

[56] Ibid., 28.

[57] Ibid., 27.

[58] Ibid., 28.

[59] Ibid., 29.

[60] Ibid., 28.

[61] Ibid.

[62] Ibid., 29.

[63] Ibid., 28.

[64] Ibid.

[65] Ibid., 29.

[66] Ibid., 28.

[67] Ibid.

[68] Ibid., 29.

[69] Ibid., 28.

[70] Ibid., 29.

[71] Roger Ray, *Christian Wisdom for Today: Three Classical Stages of Spirituality* (St. Louis, Missouri: Chalice, 1999).

[72] F. LeRon Schults and Steven J. Sandage, *Transforming Spirituality: Integrating Theology and Psychology* (Grand Rapids: Baker Books, 2006).

[73] Molholland, *Invitation to a Journey*, 94.

[74] Mulholland, *Shaped by the Word*, 97.

[75] Schults and Sandage, *Transforming Spirituality*, 27-8.

[76] Ibid., 27.

[77] Molholland, *Invitation to a Journey*, 81.

[78] Mulholland, *Shaped by the Word*, 52.

[79] Paul R. Stevens and Michael Green, *Living the Story: Biblical Spirituality for Everyday Christians* (Grand Rapids: Eerdmans, 2003), x.

[80] Stephen E. Fowl, "Further Thoughts on Theological Interpretation," in A. K. M. Adams, et.al., *Reading Scripture with the Church: Toward a Hermeneutic for Theological Interpretation* (Grand Rapids: BakerAcademic, 2006), 127.

[81] Hans W Frei, *The Eclipse of Biblical Narrative: A Study in Eighteenth and Nineteenth Century Hermeneutics* (New Haven, Connecticut: Yale University Press, 1974), 19.

[82] Sandra Schneiders, "Biblical Spirituality," *Intrepretation: A Journal of Bible and Theology* (2002): 136.

[83] Mulholland, *Shaped by the Word*, 60.

[84] Doug Hardy, "Lectio Divina: A Practice for Reconnecting to God's Word," *Preacher's Magazine: A Preaching Resource in the Wesleyan Tradition* (2009): 39-41.

[85] John Wesley, *The Works of John Wesley*, 3rd ed. (Peabody, New Jersey: Hendrickson Publishers, 1832, 1986), 187.

[86] Ibid., 185.

[87] Dean Blevins, "Worship: Formation and Discernment," *Wesley Theological Journal*, 33: 1 (Spring, 1998): 120-1.

[88] Randy L. Maddox, *Responsible Grace: John Wesley's Practical Theology* (Nashville: Abingdon Press, 1998), 200.

[89] Dallas Willard, *The Divine Conspiracy: Rediscovering Our Hidden Life in God* (San Francisco: Harper Collins, 1998), 137.

[90] Foster, *Celebration of Discipline* (1998).

[91] Dallas Willard. *The Divine Conspiracy: Rediscovering Our Hidden Life in God* (San Francisco: Harper Collins, 1998), 137.

[92] Mulholland, *Shaped by the Word*, 103.

[93] Ibid.

[94] Parker J. Palmer, *To Know as We Are Known* (San Francisco: Harper & Row, 1983); Charles Foster, *Educating Congregations: The Future of Christian Education* (Nashville: Abingdon, 1994).

[95] Foster, *Educating Congregations*, 76.

[96] Ibid., 78.

[97] Tony Jones, *The Sacred Way: Spiritual Practices for Everyday Life* (Grand Rapids: Zondervan, 2005), 87; Keith Drury, *Spiritual Disciplines for Ordinary People* (Indianapolis: Wesleyan Publishing House, 2004).

[98] Tony Jones, The Sacred Way: Spiritual Practices for Everyday Life (Grand Rapids: Zondervan, 2005), 175.

[99] Ted Ward, "Forward," *Nurture That Is Christian*, James Wilhoit and John Dettoni, eds., (Wheaton, Illinois: Victor Books, 1995), 16.

[100] Ibid., 14.

[101] Stephen Lowe and Mary Lowe, *Spiritual Formation in Theological Distance Education: An Ecosystems Model as Paradigm* (Unpublished paper for National Consultation on Spiritual Formation in Theological Distance Education, 2007), 13-5.

[102] Eugene Roehlkepartain, et.al., *The Handbook of Spiritual Development in Childhood and Adolescence* (Thousand Oaks, California: Sage, 2006), 9.

[103] Lowe and Lowe, *Spiritual Formation in Theological Distance Education*, 13-5.

[104] R. M. Lerner, ed., *Concepts and Theories of Human Development* (Mahwah, New Jersey: Lawrence Erblaum Associates, 2002), 176.

[105] Ibid., 178.

[106] Ibid.

[107] Ibid.

CHAPTER 9

CULTURAL DEVELOPMENT AND CHRISTIAN FORMATION

By Jonathan H. Kim

Does culture influence faith? Deeply woven into the fiber of Christian consciousness, culture, for average believers, is difficult to understand in the extent of its influence on spiritual life. While the average Christian's understanding of the relationship oftentimes can be nebulous or even erroneous, its impact is real and felt by many. How can the Church assist in the Christian's understanding of the relationship?

Despite the increasing influence of culture on Christian belief and practice, Evangelicals have done little to spell out how exactly culture influences spiritual development. There is a lack of adequate study on the issue. Perhaps such a shortcoming was contributed by the Church's negative stance toward culture in the past. In order to stay relevant as agents of change in the global era, Christians must deepen the understanding of culture. Church ministry increasingly requires the proper knowledge of its context.

The concern of this chapter is to study the interrelation of culture and Christian formation. In pursuing this investigation, the chapter explores the extent of cultural effect on *the fundamentals, i.e., essence of faith, and development, i.e., religiosity of faith.* Based on various sociocultural and anthropological theories, the complex association between the higher form of culture-regulated consciousness and Christian life will be explored. The basic assumption of this chapter is that Christian formation can no more be removed from its cultural context as from its theological underpinnings.

Since individuals appropriate and live out faith within the world, we can better understand the extent of culture's influence on the construction and maintenance of spiritual life by studying the effect of meaning-laden cultural consciousness on day-to-day Christian living. Having a proper understanding of culture will strengthen our understanding of Christian formation.

This chapter is divided into five sections. Following the introduction, the first section provides the definition of culture in relation to collectivism and individualism. The second section presents a theoretical overview of sociocultural development theory by Rothbaum and his colleague.[1] The third section discusses a biblical theology of Christian formation in culture and its place in Christian thought. The fourth section explains the interrelationship of culture and the two domains of faith: belief and religiosity. The fourth and the last sections provide ministry implications and concluding remarks. Having introduced the concern of the chapter, we now turn to the definition of culture.

What Is Culture?

When you hear the word "culture," of what do you think? Most likely, you may think of what people think, do, and eat. Is this truly what culture is? Or is culture much deeper and more intrinsic than that?

The term "culture" comes from the Latin word *colere* which means "to till, tend, or take care of" as in agriculture and horticulture. It implies an idea of what is pieced together and refined—as opposed to what is natural and inherent.[2] As a matter of fact, culture is whatever we fashion, cultivate, and pass onto others—whether intended or unintended—like knowledge, ideology, art, language, fashion, and even physical artifacts. Belonging to the subjective domain of human construct, culture represents—as will be argued later—a sum total of human ideas, experiences, and expressions situated in a particular set of worldviews that people hold.

Despite the widespread use of the word "culture," there is no single definition upon which scholars generally agree. Including Michael Moffitt[3] and Charles Nuckolls[4], many argue against limiting the concept of culture to a single definition. Why? They claim the intricacies and variety of meanings associated with the concept cannot be explained with a few words.

Despite differences of opinion surrounding culture, some have attempted the strenuous task of producing a less contentious definition to serve as a baseline. One such definition is Edward B. Tylor's.[5] An English Quaker, Tylor was a professor of anthropology at Oxford University, England. In his book *Primitive Culture: Researches into the Development of Mythology, Philosophy, Religion, Language, Art, and Custom*, he defined culture as the complex whole which includes knowledge, belief, art, morals, law, custom, and any other capabilities and habits acquired by man as a member of society. Tylor's publication on culture drew wide acclaim and influenced generations of researchers to subsequently dive into cultural studies. Following his seminal work, numerous definitions and theories weaved their way into scholarly literature, proposing various views and angles on the issue. One such view was proposed by Schmidt.[6]

Building on Tylor's and other influential work on culture, Schmidt proposed the following definition, which is a bit simpler than Tylor's. Schmidt defines culture as "society's institutionalized (established) values, beliefs, norms, knowledge, and practices that are learned through human interactions."[7] While this definition might sound oversimplified, it is neither too vague nor too constraining. Actually, it is rather right on target. He asserts how culture, as a whole, represents the metaphysical, epistemological, axiological, and physical derivatives of human existence in its entirety. In consolidating Tylor's and Schmidt's definitions, we can conceptualize culture into two spheres: the inner sphere, which consists of an ideological system of values and beliefs, and the outer sphere, which consists of sociocultural practices and expressions such as attitudes, actions, communication patterns, and even physical artifacts.

Collectivism

To gain a deeper understanding of culture, scholars sought to deconstruct it in relation to worldview—the integrated set of presuppositions which people hold about the basic makeup of their world. While different opinions still exist, scholars generally agree there are two worldviews on culture: collectivist and individualist (see figure 9.1).[8] The collective worldview views society as a homogenous whole that values the need for interrelatedness, while the individualistic worldview perceives society as a collection of individuals who value the need for self-autonomy. These orientations represent the relative emphasis a society places on meeting group needs over individuals' needs.[9] They reflect the degree to which the self positions himself/herself from others on a bipolar worldview continuum—either as connected to others (i.e., interrelatedness) or separate (i.e., autonomy) (see figure 9.1). In general, collectivism is best exemplified in Asia, Africa, and Latin America; whereas individualism is best exemplified in Western countries such as England, the United States, and Canada.

Generally speaking, the collectivism is a worldview that centralizes the We-consciousness and peripheralizes the I-consciousness (see figure 9.2). Collectivism values duty over personal rights, social responsibility over personal freedom, and group advancement over individual achievement. It assumes that culture is not an aggregate of individuals but rather a determinative metastructure in its own right. As a result, each individual is seen as a component of this metastructure. The very notion of the autonomous self as the key factor in society is rejected over the acceptance of interdependence and homogenization. Common goals, values, and norms are diffused into the social sphere through a complex hierarchical network. The result of having a We-consciousness is the development of a self-identity that is collective, sociocentric, holistic, connected, and relational (see figure 9.2).

Feature Compared	Collectivism	Individualism
Definition	Connected with social context	Separate from social context
Structure	Flexible, variable	Bounded, unitary, stable
Important Features	External, public (statutes, roles, relationships)	Internal, private (abilities, thoughts, feelings)
Tasks	Belong, fit-in	Be unique
	Occupy one's proper place	Express self
	Engage in appropriate action	Realize internal attributes
	Promote others' goals	Promote own goals
	Be indirect: "Read others' minds."	Be direct: "Say what's on your mind."

Feature Compared	Collectivism	Individualism
Role of others	Self-definition: relationships with others in specific contexts define the self	Self-evaluation: Others are important for social comparison, reflected appraisal.
Basis of self-esteem	Ability to adjust, restrain self, maintain harmony with social context	Ability to express self, validate internal attributes

Figure 9.1: Summary of Key Differences between
Collectivism and Individualism[10]

Interestingly, there are two variations of collectivism: vertical and horizontal.[11] Vertical collectivism is based on a hierarchy of power relations. This perspective identifies the self as an unequal part or an aspect of the collective whole; and the social network is reinforced by authoritarian hierarchies (e.g., Asians, Africans). Horizontal collectivism, on the other hand, is based on a heterarchy. This perspective is also known as a conformist structure which views the self as an equal part of the collective whole that shares the same position of power and authority (e.g., postmoderns). Social network is based on communal sharing and reward systems, and cultural traditions and beliefs play a major role of uniting its members. These differences within collectivism cause different patterns of social structure, behavior, and communication patterns.

Individualism

The antipode of collectivism is individualism, a worldview that centralizes the I-consciousness and peripheralizes the We-consciousness (see figure 9.2). Contrary to collectivism, individualism values personal rights above duties, personal freedom above social responsibility, and individual achievement above group advancement (see figure 9.1). The term "individualism" was first used during the French Revolution to describe a worldview that was antagonistic to collectivism. Such a worldview results in the development of self-identity that is individualistic, egocentric, separate, autonomous, and self-contained (see figure 9.2).

There are three principal roots of individualism: self-concept, self-expression, and relationality. First, concerning self-concept, individualism suggests the idea of an autonomous self and encourages each person to define identity according to his/her own degree of individuality. It values the development and preservation of a positive self-esteem—the preordained purpose to basic human existence and endeavor. Having personal success, satisfaction, and growth are critical to the positive concept of the self.

Second, concerning self-expression, individualism assumes that human nature seeks self-expression and encourages the attainment of individual goals and personal rights. Individualistic people often respond effectively to their pursuit of personal rights and goals since success or failure will generate either a positive or negative sense of well-being and satisfaction. Consequently, the development of the self is oriented toward the person rather than the social context.

Lastly, concerning relationality, individualism implies relationality. While relationships are highly valued, the primacy of self-interests and self-relevant goals will determine the type of relationship a person will have. Creating or terminating relationships will occur as personal interests and goals change. The plausible outcome of such an orientation in life is being in nonbinding and non-intensive relationships with others.

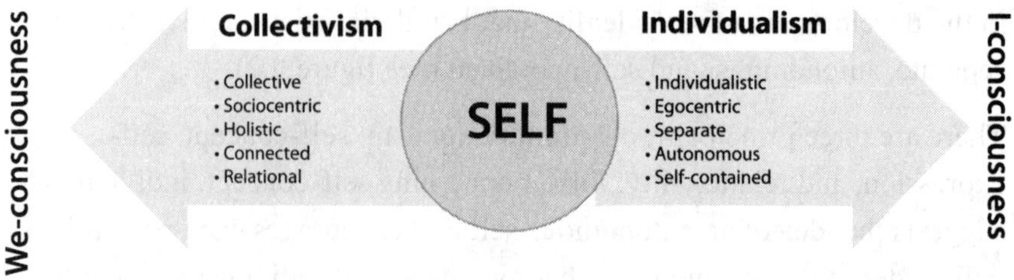

Figure 9.2: Collectivism vs. Individualism[12]

Having understood culture in relation to collectivist and individualistic orientations, we now turn to Rothbaum's sociocultural theory. The theoretical perspective presented in the subsequent section is not meant to be an exhaustive explanation on a new theory of cultural development; rather, it is limited to a conceptual overview on the function of sociocultural consciousness in the development of self. Such a theory is helpful to our study in that it will clarify how culture affects Christian formation. With the emphasis on how knowing and being are situated, we perhaps could better understand how Christians in collective cultures may have different spiritual expressions than those in individualistic cultures. A study of Rothbaum's theory will definitely further our understanding.

Sociocultural Development Theory

The conventional studies on the relation between culture and faith were limited to a set of determinants associated with the person's social environment; e.g., Erikson's psychosocial (1950) and Bowlby's attachment theories (1969). Although these theories served as a catalyst to augment our understanding of Christian formation, their analyses overlooked the legitimate functions of cultural consciousness influencing human development.

For the purpose of developing an enhanced framework of the relationship between culture and faith, this portion of the chapter focuses on the sociocultural theory developed by Rothbaum and his colleagues.[13] Although Rothbaum's study is not unique to sociocultural studies, his theory definitely augmented people's understanding of the relationship between culture and the formation of self. While Erikson and Bowlby's theories provided a crucial link between the self and psychosocial categories, Rothbaum's theory, on the other hand, provided a link between the self and psychocultural categories. Rothbaum understood self-identity as the output of one's sociocultural consciousness and further explored Erikson and Bowlby's theses in the cross-cultural settings of Japan and the United States. In particular, his investigation focused on the *meaning* and *function* of sociocultural consciousness in the development of We-self and I-self. As a result, he unequivocally challenged the universal claims of the Eriksonian and Bowlbian theories and explained the differences in human development between collective East and individualistic West. The following section will explain Rothbaum's sociocultural theory in detail.

Infancy: Union vs. Reunion

Cultural differences are seen quite early in life. Rothbaum found significant cultural differences in the modes of parent-child interactions, starting with infancy. He asserted that the differences stem from the infant's desire for dependence on and union with the mother in the collective culture versus separation from/reunion with the mother in individualistic cultures (see figure 9.3). He also noted that the difference is also noticeable in the use of language. Mothers in the collective East nurture more with affect-oriented language—such as lulling, onomatopoeia, and idioms—to orient infants to themselves; whereas mothers in the individualistic West use more information-oriented language that familiarizes infants with the outside world.[14]

The extent to which these varying maternal behaviors affect the development of self is quite visible. Infants in collective cultures tend to derive a sense of security from a near-constant union with the mother. By contrast, infants in individualistic cultures establish their sense of security in their exploration of the world and reunion with the mother. In each of these cases, these differences cause people to develop either heteronomous or autonomous orientation in life.

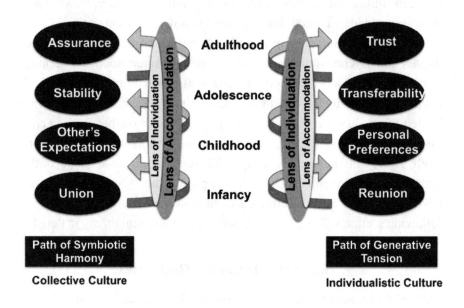

Figure 9.3: Cultural Development Theory[15]

Childhood: Other's Expectations vs. Personal Preference

Cultural differences during childhood are formed by a concern for obligation in collective cultures and a concern for personal preference in individualistic cultures (see figure 9.3). Rothbaum found that children in collective cultures are nurtured with the importance of obligation and honoring others' expectations. They are discouraged from expressing their personal will and preference out of the higher concern for others' expectations in the maintenance of group harmony and cohesion. Asserting one's preference and need is not generally regarded as a social value in collective cultures. Instead, children are encouraged to honor the interest of the group above their own—whether the interest belongs to a member of their family or not. The emphasis is placed on attending to others and being in congruent relationships with others. Personal identity, in this sense, is placed within a large social structure and defined in terms of whom they are associated with rather than who they are. With family and society being so closely intertwined, it is not surprising that children in collective cultures are more concerned about group harmony and turn often to close-others for decision help (e.g., choosing friends and a spouse) than those from individualistic cultures.

By contrast, a concern for personal preference and self-expression is important for children growing up in individualistic cultures. The major concern of parenting is on nurturing children with unique idiosyncratic qualities matched by self-assertiveness. Emotional expressiveness, self-assertion, and even noncompliance are seen as valuable indicators of healthy personality. Thus, children are taught to consider themselves in terms of internal qualities and assertiveness that will distinguish them from others. Although the emphasis is still placed on proper behavior, children of individualistic cultures are taught to negotiate and assert their personal preferences over others.

Adolescence: Stability vs. Transferability

Cultural differences during adolescence stem from the centrality of loyalty. Adolescents in collective cultures remain loyal to family. Thus, they maintain stability in family relationships, while adolescents in individualistic cultures transfer allegiance from family to friends (see figure 9.3). The primary difference is where adolescents exhibit the high level of loyalty.

Collective cultures value the harmony of parent-child relationships. The demand for the solidity and continuity of close family relationships is expected—no matter the age of the children. Even adults are expected to maintain strong social affiliations and to identify with the group. A socially valued task of adolescence is to develop a close relationship with parents and siblings—even with extended family members. In managing relational ties, adolescents in collective cultures generally invest a significant amount of time and energy in developing and maintaining harmonious relationships with close-others. To a large degree, the culture expects adolescents to strive for self-autonomy yet remain closely connected to family members. It is precisely these elements of tradition which lead parents and adolescents to view each other quite strongly in terms of their relational bond and expect such a relationship to last a lifetime—even beyond marriage.

Individualistic cultures, by contrast, value the synchronization of parent-peer relationships. Adolescents are not expected to remain under family influence; rather, they are expected to individuate themselves from parents by identifying more strongly with their peers. Rothbaum indicates how adolescents, who desire to secure new relationships outside the immediate family, create a perpetual, generative tension in adolescents[16]—the tension between togetherness and separation which corresponds to two distinct orientations of the self: interdependent or independent. Consequently, adolescents transfer their loyalty from parents to peers. This type of individualistic orientation is mirrored in many of the Western cultures.

Adulthood: Assurance vs. Trust

Differences of self-construal patterns in adulthood are contributed by two distinct sources: collective efficacy based on assurance (i.e., loyalty-based love) and self-efficacy based on trust (i.e., faith-based love) (see figure 9.3). The first calls for attending to the interdependent self, and the latter calls for attending to the individuated self. The variability of these orientations influences and, in many cases, determines the development of the adult self and influences the way adults unpretentiously think, behave, and relate to others. Having been nurtured under a particular set of beliefs and having attended to various demands of cultural groups, adults will have a distinctive construal of the self.

Adulthood in collective cultures is strongly influenced by a belief in collective efficacy—a group's shared belief in group-capabilities and on group-reliance to achieve a goal. While it is common for adults in collective cultures to express their unique inner attributes, they are more likely to redefine and reground their selfhood according to a larger cultural ethos which surrounds them. In most cases, assurance—the loyalty-based love which is commonly practiced by collectivists—functions as an adhesive to guarantee the continuity of social network and relationships.

Adulthood in individualistic cultures carries with it the most complete autonomy that a person can attain. A closely related concept to that of self-autonomy is self-efficacy: believing in the basic level of self-belief and self-reliance to achieve a goal. Adulthood means having complete self-efficacy in navigating the challenges of life, making right decisions and following through. The choice and control of life fall solely on the individual. Having the ability to project one's choice and control to the world becomes a clear sign of adulthood.

Summary

Rothbaum's sociocultural theory recognizes a dialectical relationship between self and culture, highlighting the interplay between worldview orientations and the development of We-self or I-self. The path of symbiotic harmony—the development path which collectivists are more inclined to take—predisposes people toward accommodation and interdependency, while the path of generative tension—the developmental path which individualists are more inclined to take—predisposes people toward individuation (see figure 9.3). We must note, however, that these predispositions are the general tendencies influenced by cultural frameworks; they are not predetermined or permanent. Either tendency may vary, depending on the degree to which individuals have internalized the values of the culture in which they were socialized.

As a functional significance, these developmental predispositions signify cultural differences in human development. While members of collective cultures are inclined to focus on the *We-self identity* in relation to interdependency, submission, and adherence to cultural norms, the members of individualistic cultures are more likely to focus on the *I-self identity* in relation to self-autonomy, personal right, and self-fulfillment.

Biblical Theology of Christian Formation in Culture[17]

Sumerian, Canaanite, Hebrew, Egyptian, Assyrian, Babylonian, Persian, Jewish, Greek, Roman—it is not as if the Bible does not acknowledge the presence of cultures in its historical narrative. While the Bible is not devoid of culture—even being written in the ancient languages—the Word of God, likewise, does not purport to argue the superiority of a particular culture over another. When Paul engaged in his missionary work, his intent was not to impose a Jewish culture upon a Gentile population but to engage them with Someone who transcends culture. However, Scripture does demonstrate a sensitivity toward each culture; e.g., when Paul's preaching accommodated the Christian message to a Jewish audience (Acts 17:1-3,16-17) and to the Greek intellectuals in Athens (Acts 17:18-34). However, this chapter is not on the Bible and culture. More specifically, *how does the Bible depict the influence of culture on Christian formation?* The following are four ways in which culture and Christian formation intersect in the New Testament.

First, faith in Jesus is consistent throughout the New Testament—*regardless of culture.* Whether he is regarded as Messiah (Hebrew) or Christ (Greek), He is still Jesus. Hence, Philip encounters the Ethiopian eunuch—probably a convert to Judaism: "So Philip proceeded [Isaiah 53:7-8 in LXX] to tell him the good news about Jesus, beginning from that Scripture" (Acts 8:35). Even in Paul's messages to Jewish and Greek audiences, while much of the content may alter and the method of argumentation change, he inevitably ends with a call to Jesus Christ (Acts 17:3,31).

Second, practices and disciplines designed to promote Christian formation often are culturally based but not universally practiced by the Christian community. For example, Romans 14 contains several paradoxical views of religious practices that facilitate one's Christian formation:

- Non-vegetarian vs. Vegetarian (v. 2)

- Special Days vs. All Days Alike (v. 5)

- Unclean Food vs. No Food Unclean (v. 14)

- Abstains from Wine vs. Imbibes (v. 21)

It is not that difficult to see, in part, some level of conflict between Jewish and Gentile elements within the church in Rome. But Paul moves them beyond these arguments by giving them the general principle: "Do you have faith? Keep it to yourself before God. Blessed is the man who does not condemn himself by what he approves. But whoever doubts stands condemned if he eats, because his eating is not from faith, and everything that is not from faith is sin" (Romans 14:22-23). *Faith* is the definitive mark of a Christian formation religious practice.

Third, Christian formation is done in-community—not just individually; and that community is an intercultural setting. As Moo comments, "Through the good news of Jesus Christ, God is both *transforming* individuals and *forming* a community."[18] The Christian community, the Church, is a *transcultural*, but not an *acultural*, community. The Church does recognize the diversity of cultures she serves. Even within the New Testament, congregations acknowledged the presence of different groups comprising them. Perhaps most evident would be Jews and Gentiles. Rather, Romans 15:7 says, "Therefore accept one another, just as the Messiah also accepted you, to the glory of God." It is not that we are a part of an acultural community of faith but one that transcends culture with acceptance—not mere tolerance. "There is no *Jew or Greek*, slave or free, male or female; for you are all one in Christ Jesus. And if you are Christ's, then you are Abraham's seed, heirs according to the promise" (Galatians 3:28-29; emphasis added). Again, "Here there is not *Greek and Jew*, circumcision and uncircumcision, *barbarian, Scythian, slave or free*; but Christ is all and in all" (Colossians 3:11; emphasis added). Yes, these elements of society and culture are present within the Church; but they are not primary for the Christian community. For the early Church, as for us today, Jesus is the common denominator who unites a culturally diverse faith community.

Finally, sometimes a particular aspect of cultures presents unique challenges for Christian formation. Would not the church in Corinth face a different cultural challenge to their Christian formation than the church in Jerusalem? The cultural milieu of the churches in the New Testament obviously impacted their Christian formation. Corinthian Christians faced the challenges to their faith that were indigenous to Corinth, e.g., eating meat offered to idols (1 Corinthians 8:10). Whereas the believers in Jerusalem were assailed by the Judaizers, Christian believers still were tied to the Mosaic Law (Acts 15:1ff). While some may say these issues are theological, they are likewise issues of cultural context.

Christian Formation and Niebuhr's *Christ and Culture*

What are the cultural expectations of a Christian? What relationship does the Christian have with the society at large? The response to such questions is contingent on one's understanding of what *culture* means. Most Christian scholars who engage culture maintain that culture is an extension of creation. As such, culture is good—as the creation is good; but it is also subject to the effects of the fall and capable of redemption.[19] Culture arises from the human interaction and interpretation with nature, which is God's creation and general revelation. As such, culture is regarded on a sliding scale between *fallen* at one end and *good* at the other end and *redeemed* in the middle (see figure 9.4).

Culture is FALLEN Corrupt	Culture is REDEEMED Refined	Culture is GOOD Pure

Figure 9.4: Christian View of Culture

Based on these various appreciations of culture within the Christian community, numerous responses can be made about the relationship of the Church, culture, and Christian formation. However, perhaps the most comprehensive response already has come from H. Richard Niebuhr. In his *Christ and Culture,* Niebuhr postulates five possible relationships— illustrated by church history from ancient to modern times—that the Church has shared with the community for good or for ill (see figure 9.5).

Approach	Proponents	Description	Approach to Christian Formation
Christ against Culture	1 John Tertullian Tolstoy	*Separatistic*: radical rejection of any inculturation or contextualiza-tion of faith.	Culture would be regarded as something incapable of redemption, requiring rejection. As such, Christian formation would seek to separate one from culture as facilitated by *separation* from society and posturing one's faith as anticultural.
Christ of Culture	Gnostics Abelard Kant A. Ritschl	*Accommoda-tion*: Culture is normative and faith subject to it, i.e., "Cultural Protestantism."	Culture would be considered innately good—something not requiring critique but only affirmation. Christian formation would seek to align itself with the culture as facilitated by *accommodating* one's faith and beliefs to the culture. Christian faith simply would be a part of the broader culture.

Approach	Proponents	Description	Approach to Christian Formation
Christ above Culture	Justin Martyr Clement of Alexandria Origen Aquinas	*Synthesis:* affirming the uncritical acceptance of culture and blending it with the Christian faith.	Culture would be regarded as neutral, simply needing "labeling" to be accepted as Christian. Christian formation would seek to see the presence of Christ in every aspect of culture. It would be facilitated by *synthesizing* all of culture with Christian terminology and rationale but without actually changing the substance of culture.
Christ and Culture in Paradox	Paul Martin Luther Marcion, the Heretic	*Dualistic:* Christians exist within the tension between sources of norms with no definitive direction given to the individual.	Culture would be seen as valuable but possessing a *dual* nature, i.e., in part fallen and in part good. Christian formation would seek to be faithful both to God and another authority (e.g., the State) and, thus, would be somewhat inconsistent, depending on one's allegiances and situations. It would not seek to integrate faith into culture but rather to live in the margin between the two.
Christ the Transformer of Culture	Gospel of John Augustine F. D. Maurice	*Conversion:* Culture is good as an expression of God's interaction with human history. Hence, the culture should reflect God's presence, e.g., Augustine's *City of God*.	Culture would be viewed as internally redeemable by Christ—just as an individual can.be redeemed. It is neither good nor fallen but transformed by Christ. Christian formation would be holistic, seeking the total transformation of both the individual and the cultural context in which he/she lives. Christian formation would be a process of continual engagement with the culture for the purpose of *conversion*.

Figure 9.5: Culture and Christian Formation[20]

Hence, the relationship shared by the Church and her culture—across the previously mentioned spectrum—does indeed influence one's notion of Christian formation. To a large extent, it provides the frame upon which the portrait of formation is drawn.

A Christian Approach to Culture and Its Implications for Christian Formation

Having discussed sociocultural theory and surveyed the biblical-theological insights to culture, we will shift our focus to conceptual integration. The remainder of the chapter provides an integrative reflection of the relation between culture and Christian formation. For the sake of clarity, the reflection will be divided according to two domains of faith: belief and religiosity (see figure 9.6).

Belief: Essential Domain of Faith

It is very important to distinguish the essential from the experiential domain of faith when studying Christian formation. The essential domain refers to the content dimension of faith where belief is gained based on intellectual assent to the revealed truth of Scripture, the Bible; the experiential domain, on the other hand, refers to the practical dimension where faith is appropriated and lived out. These domains also are known as the content and structure of faith, respectively (see figure 9.6).

Faith

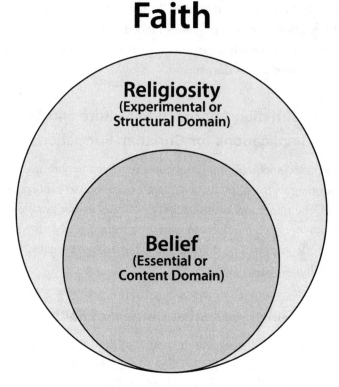

Figure 9.6: Essential and Experiential Domains of Faith

Although faith is appropriated within cultural confinements, its substance is independent of cultural influences. To an extent, culture shapes the experiential domain of faith, but the content domain is not subject to a contextual influence or interpretation. As noted earlier, culture is a human product; it is a mere part of human existence and expression. It, therefore, does not have a legitimate authority to judge nor validate the content of faith. The Bible is the sole basis and standard of faith (2 Timothy 3:16-17; Romans 10:17; Hebrews 11:6).

Despite this truism, postmodern theologians have been trying to subjugate faith to culture. While a host of ideological and hermeneutical variations exists, there is a loose confederation of movement towards indigenizing theology. The movement is called contextual theology, an umbrella term that includes numerous schools of thought—such as Feminist, Black, Liberation, Homosexual, Min-Jung (Korea), Dalit (India), Ecological, Deconstructive, and Reconstructive theologies.[21] Generally speaking, these theological persuasions are framed largely within a postmodern reading of self, text, and meaning. Although a terrain of contextual theology is vast and varied, the above theological perspectives uniformly reject the evangelical stance of *sola scriptura* (Lat., *by Scripture alone*) and seek to redefine the content of faith, according to poststructural hermeneutics.

Poststructural hermeneutics is the principal ideological ingredient of contextual theology. It asserts that a text is incomplete and contains infinite meanings which can be determined by the readers—regardless of the original authorial intention. At the root of this hermeneutics are the basic premises that knowledge is generated with the recognition of subjectivity and rejection of the possibility of any objective structure, constituting the ultimate reality. The depth and extent of this flawed hermeneutical method are wrapped in this postmodern presupposition: *All theology is contextual* which highlights the cultural context from which theology is transpired and the cultural context to which theology is communicated.

The end results of this type of ideological persuasion are embracing the multiplicity of knowledge, focusing on the existential and contextual meanings of Scripture, and redefining faith as the culturally conditioned human mind, experience, and tradition. Such a presupposition obviously will consider Scripture as a product of a culture—written in a culture, for a culture, from a culture's historical point of view—which, in my opinion, is *absolutely preposterous and absurd!* Faith is the metacultural belief in the objective facts and truth of Scripture that generate complete trust in the person and work of Jesus Christ. It stands beyond the confinements of culture. The content of faith describes what is real based on *the* story recorded in the Bible. Cultures, however, tell stories that may or may not be true to reality.

Subjugating the content of faith to culture is senseless and unbiblical. The content basis from which faith proceeds is quite precise and independent—solely based on the bibliocentricity that transcends the frameworks of culture, language, and tradition. For us Christians, this is one of the fundamentals that cannot be compromised on any grounds whatsoever. Culture *does not* influence the content of faith (i.e., belief). With this understanding in mind, let us turn to a next set of reflection on the interrelationship of culture and religiosity.

Religiosity: Experiential Domain of Faith

How are we to explain the lack of symmetry between Christians in collective East and individualistic West despite the common core of belief that profoundly shaped our faith? The conception of the spiritual life in collective East tends to be affect-behavior oriented while individualistic West tends to be cognitive-behavior oriented (see figure 9.6). If observed carefully, the affect-behavior conception of faith tends to articulate spirituality in the form of relational knowing (e.g., empiricism); whereas the cognitive-behavior oriented conception tends to articulate spirituality in the form of rational knowing (e.g., rationalism).

Most likely, the discrepancy was created by deep, underlying psychocultural categories influencing religious behaviors (i.e., religiosity). This is where the complex operations conditioned by a person's culture inform and shape the appropriation and application of faith. As the person lives out faith, culture—in particular, its worldview frameworks—acts as one of the embedded ideological forces influencing the individual's thoughts (not the foundational belief), emotions, and behaviors. Scholars call this experiential dimension of faith religiosity. The term "religiosity" comes from a Latin word *religio,* which means a "fear of God" and "way of life." Putting these two meanings together, religiosity basically means "faith in action or living a life that reveals a belief in God."

As contended, cultural differences carry over into spiritual life in the form of religiosity. While the essential domain of faith remains constant throughout the culture, the experiential domain, where faith is appropriated and lived out, is subject to cultural influences (see figure 9.7). As a matter of fact, the cultural elements affecting religiosity distinguish one group of Christians from another.

The religious expression of collectivist East differs distinctly from that of individualistic West. As indicated earlier, the predisposition of collective cultures towards the We-consciousness and the affect-orientated language/behavior is a worldview built into the very fiber of their being, obviously affecting how they appropriate and express faith. Evidenced in such a tendency are East Asian Presbyterians. In spite of their belief in reformed theology (i.e., belief), these Christians are highly charismatic in their religious orientations (i.e., religiosity).

Christians in the individualistic West are, however, more inclined to the I-consciousness and use of the cognitive-oriented language/behavior. Hence, their religious orientations tend to be cognitive-behavioral (see figure 9.7). For example, the modern evangelical stance on faith and spirituality is definitely confined more to head knowledge (i.e., cognition) than heart knowledge (i.e., affect).

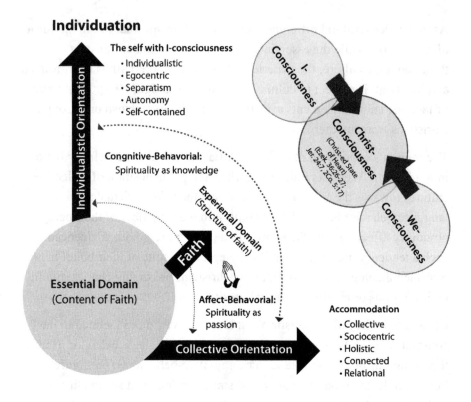

Figure 9.7: Integrative Reflection on Culture and Christian Formation

Before we move onto the conclusion, let me briefly summarize the main point of this section: The boundaries between the *spiritual-I* (i.e., self-focused spiritual identity) and the *spiritual-we* (i.e., other-focused spiritual identity) are clearly defined in individualistic cultures but not in collective cultures. As a result, the expression of religiosity in the collective East tends to be uniform, affective, and highly affiliative; while the expression of the individualistic West tends to be varied, cognitive, and highly personal (see figure 9.7). We must note, however, that not all Christians of the collectivist East express their faith relationally (i.e., affect-behavioral) and not all Christians of individualistic West express their faith rationally (i.e., cognitive-behavioral). To some extent, spiritual expressions may vary from person to person, depending on the degree to which individuals internalize their own cultural values and beliefs.

Pastoral and Educational Implications

This chapter explored the relation between culture and Christian formation. As asserted in the chapter, the difference exists in people's religiosity. This leads to the next obvious question: How should the Church respond to such an understanding? Is respecting or being tolerant of the differences in religiosity appropriate? The answer to this question will be critical to the future of church ministry since cultural diversity is becoming ever more apparent in God's Church. The broad aim of this conclusion is to examine the implications of the understanding regarding culture and faith. The conclusion will highlight areas of concern and derive recommendations for further reflection.

One of the crucial challenges facing Christians today is finding the proper balance in our response to culture and various challenges that come with it. Sadly, the quest for an appropriate response has polarized Christians along the line of a love-hate continuum (see figure 9.4). While some overly embrace culture, others remain hostile. Under modernity, Christians took a negative stance toward culture. They remained either hostile or indifferent toward culture; an exclusionary criterion was applied in defining culture. But there is a new voice in the twenty-first-century Church, calling Christians to take an optimistic stance toward culture. The voice is calling Christians to engage in Christ-centered cultural renewal with grace and truth (John 1:14,17).

To move towards a critical understanding of the relationship and to respond appropriately to the challenges that culture brings to ministry, we will consider Niebuhr's five-part typology which was introduced previously in this chapter: *faith against culture, faith of culture, faith above culture, faith and culture in paradox, and faith transforming culture.*[22] These motifs represent varied perspectives on the relationship that have emerged and undergone extensive discussions in the Christian community. In particular, we will rely on Niebuhr's fifth motif, the conversionist approach, to deepen our understanding of the relationship between faith and culture.

The first motif, *faith against culture*, reveals a strict separationist position regarding the relationship. Culture is considered an inevitable domain of the fallen world that competes against faith and, at times, acts as a destroyer of faith. Consequently, people with the first perspective seek to disengage and ignore culture.

The second motif, *faith of culture*, suggests harmony between the two. This perspective denies any antagonism between the two and seeks to fuse them—regardless of their ideological differences. Placing faith on the same footing as culture, people with the second perspective contend Christianity is a multifaceted cultural phenomenon and call believers to the uncritical embracement of culture.

Being weary of the first two perspectives, the people with the third perspective, *faith above culture*, promote a hierarchical synthesis of faith and culture. While affirming the legitimacy of culture as a by-product of God's act of grace toward humanity, people with the third view seek to create not an *either-or* but a *both-and* type of view. This view emphasizes an ascendancy of faith.

The fourth view is *faith and culture in paradox*. This view highlights tension between the two and rejects the possibility of solidifying them. It, thus, affirms a coexistence of the sacred and secular dualism. This dualistic view, which is erroneous in my opinion, differs from the previous three in that it maintains a two-realm mentality. Though it encourages the interaction between the two, the same perspective could lead to the compartmentalization of faith and culture, meaning we will have Christians with dual personalities—religious and secular. The concept of paradox would seem to naturally suggest a tension between faith and culture, but it insinuates the idea of duality.

Then the final motif, *faith transforming culture,* which is biblical and what Christians should support as a new paradigm for twenty-first-century ministry, maintains a high view of faith while accentuating the responsibility of Christians to amend culture. Although it expresses the parody of culture, the inner structure of this motif also affirms culture as the arena of God's transforming work. With belief in the divine possibility of a personal and cultural renewal, Niebuhr advocated people of faith as the primary agents of cultural renewal. However, to become agents of transformation, Christians must be radically transformed by Christ.

Through Christians, Christ is redeeming culture. Christ does so by transforming people with I- and We-consciousness and then imputing a *Christ-ed* state of heart—*Christ-consciousness*—which, in essence, is the new heart that the Bible promises to those who believe (Ezekiel 36:26-27; Jeremiah 24:7; 2 Corinthians 5:17) (see figure 9.7). The new heart allows individuals to have the spiritual consciousness to commune with God and with others, thus, experiencing the ultimate unity in Christ (John 6:56, 1 Corinthians 6:17; 12:27-28). However, receiving this spiritual consciousness is only possible on the sole ground of faith that focuses on Christ's redeeming love. As the Source of all things, Christ is the core of faith since He is the embodiment of eternal Truth (Deuteronomy 32:4; John 14:6; 1:14; 17:17; 8:32). With the *Christ-ed* state of heart (i.e., Christ-consciousness), we can form spiritual unity even with cultural differences. The Church is where this type of unity already is being formed. Cultural differences are respected, while spiritual unity in Christ unites everyone to oneness in God.

Conclusion

Does culture influence faith? With the chapter discussion, we are now better positioned to answer this question. As we explored throughout this chapter, the critical aspect of our chapter discussion was on understanding the constancy of belief (i.e., essential or content domain of faith) and the subjectivity of religiosity (i.e., experience or structure domain of faith).

Different cultures have different expressions of religiosity—despite the common belief that we all share in Christ. This understanding should allow people to respect those who are culturally different in the Church yet move toward the ultimate unity in God through the person of Jesus Christ and the transforming work of the Holy Spirit (John 3:16; 2 Corinthians 5:15). After all, that was the exact prayer offered by Jesus to God on behalf of all believers before His crucifixion. Listen to John 17:20-23:

> I pray not only for these, but also for those who believe in Me through their message. May they all be one, as You, Father, are in Me and I am in You. May they also be one in Us, so the world may believe You sent Me. I have given them the glory You have given Me. May they be one as We are one. I am in them and You are in Me. May they be made completely one, so the world may know You have sent Me and have loved them as You have loved Me.

Reflection Questions

1. What is culture? Formulate your own view of culture.

2. What is your critique of popular culture? How is it a benefit or detriment to Christian formation?

3. Compare and contrast individualism and collectivism. How do these cultural orientations influence human development? How about their influence on spiritual life?

4. Explain and criticize Rothbaum's theory of sociocultural development. How might it be useful in your ministry?

5. What is your view of the relationship between culture and spirituality? Where do you fall on Niebuhr's spectrum of Christ and Culture?

6. What are some of the emerging spiritual ideas that are becoming rather popular among young people these days? Give several examples from popular culture.

ENDNOTES

[1] Fred Rothbaum, Martha Pott, Hiroshi Azuma, Kazuo Miyake, and John Weisz, "The Development of Close Relationships in Japan and the United States," *Child Development,* 71(5): 1121-42.

[2] William Smith, *Dictionary of Greek and Roman Antiquities* (New York: Harper and Brothers, 2008), 315; Michael P. Gallagher, *Clashing Symbols: An Introduction to Faith and Culture* (New York: Paulist Press, 2003), 12.

[3] Michael L. Moffitt, *The Handbook of Dispute Resolution* (San Francisco: Jossey-Bass, 2005), 199.

[4] Charles W. Nuekolls, *Culture: A Problem That Cannot Be Solved* (Madison, Wisconsin: University of Wisconsin, 1998), 12.

[5] Edward B. Tylor, Primitive Culture: Researches into the Development of Mythology, Philosophy, Religion, Language, Art, and Custom (New York: G. P. Putnam's Sons, 1920), 1.

[6] Alvin Schmidt, *Veiled and Silenced: How Culture Shaped Sexist Theology* (Macon, Georgia: Mercer University Press, 2000).

[7] Ibid., 4.

[8] Gert H. Hofstede, *Cultures and Organizations: Software of the Mind* (New York: McGraw-Hill, 1991); *Culture's Consequences: Comparing Values, Behaviors, Institutions and Organizations across Nations* (Thousand Oaks, California: SAGE, 2003); Moffitt, *The Handbook of Dispute Resolution*; Hazel R. Markus and Shinobu Kitayama, "Culture and the Self: Implications for Cognition, Emotion, and Motivation," Psychological Review, 98(2): 224-53.

[9] Moffitt, *The Handbook of Dispute Resolution*, 121.

[10] Adapted from Markus and Kitayama, "Culture and the Self: Implications for Cognition, Emotion, and Motivation," 230.

[11] Theodore M. Singelis, Harry C. Triandis, Dharm P. Bhawuk, and Michele J. Gelfand. "Horizontal and Vertical Dimensions of Individualism and Collectivism: A Theoretical and Measurement Refinement," *Cross-Cultural Research*, 29(3): 240-75.

[12] Adapted from Markus and Kitayama, "Culture and the Self: Implications for Cognition, Emotion, and Motivation," 226-7.

[13] Rothbaum, et. al., "The Development of Close Relationships in Japan and the United States."

[14] Ibid., 1126.

[15] Ibid., 1125.

[16] Ibid., 1132.

[17] Adapted from James Riley Estep, Jr., CE605: Human Development and Ministry Course Notes, Lincoln Christian University (Lincoln, Illinois) and CE661: Theological Foundations of Education Course Notes, Lincoln Christian University (Lincoln, Illinois).

[18] Douglas J. Moo, "Romans," *The NIV Application Commentary* (Grand Rapids: Zondervan Publishing House, 2000), 482.

[19] Cf. Kevin J. Vanhoozer, Charles A. Anderson, and Michael J. Sleasman, *Everyday Theology: How to Read Cultural Texts and Interpret Trends* (Grand Rapids: BakerAcademic, 2007); David K. Naugle, *Worldview: The History of a Concept* (Grand Rapids: Eerdmans, 2002); Nancy Pearcey, *Total Truth: Liberating Christianity from Its Cultural Captivity* (Wheaton, Illinois: Crossway Books, 2004); H. Richard Niebuhr, *Christ and Culture* (New York: Harper and Row, 1951).

[20] Based on Niebuhr's *Christ and Culture*, produced by James Riley Estep, Jr.

[21] Stephen B. Bevans, *Models of Contextual Theology* (Marynoll, New York: Orbis Books, 2002); John Parratt, *An Introduction to Third World Theologies*, (Cambridge, England: Cambridge University Press, 2004).

[22] Niebuhr, *Christ and Culture*.

Name Index

Scripture Index